I0833989

“Beyond the Frame”

The Films and Film Theory of Andrei Tarkovsky

About the Author

Dr Terence McSweeney is a Senior Lecturer in Film and Television History at Southampton Solent University. He has written and published on a diverse range of topics connected to film, literature and history.

McSweeney, Terence. *The 'War on Terror' and American Film: 9/11 Frames per Second.* Edinburgh: Edinburgh University Press, 2014.

Sinha, Amresh, and Terence McSweeney, eds. *Millennial Cinema: Memory in Global Film.* London and New York: Wallflower Press, 2012.

"Beyond the Frame"

The Films and Film Theory of Andrei Tarkovsky

Terence McSweeney

αporetic press

This edition first published 2015 by

αporetic press
Registered Office: Samou 4, Konia, 8300, Paphos, Cyprus

http://aporeticpress.wordpress.com
Email: aporeticpress@gmail.com

Cover Design George Dickie

ISBN: 978-9963-2214-0-0
A copy of this book has been deposited at the Cyprus Library.

Dedicated to Dima, Nikolai, Valentina, Galina, Bill and Grandad Mac.
Those who are gone but live on forever in our memories.

Contents

Acknowledgements

This book would not have been possible without the help and support of a list of people too numerous to mention here. I would like to thank the staff and students at both the University of Essex and Southampton Solent University for their support and encouragement. A large part of the manuscript for this project was written at the dacha belonging to my parents-in-law, a small cottage in the middle of a forest in southern Russia. A better place to write about Andrei Tarkovsky would be hard to find.

I would like to thank the staff at Aporetic Press especially Aspasia Stephanou for their support in the preparation of the manuscript and their belief in the project.

Tarkovsky's films are very often about families and I cannot help but see my own reflected in them. I would like to thank my sister Catherine, a stronger and more independent woman than many give her credit for, and my nephews Jimmy, Lewis and Billy. But as always the one constant in my life is my wife Olga, who is the foundation for all that I am and everything that I do.

Finally, during the course of this journey my family experienced great grief and great joy. We lost too many loved ones: grandfathers Tom, Bill and Nikolai and grandmothers Valentina and Galina. Most painful of all, my brother-in-law Dima, a great lover of film, tragically died. Yet in the same time period my two beloved sons Harrison and Wyatt were born and in them we all live on.

List of Illustrations

Biographical Note

1932	Andrei Arsenevich Tarkovsky is born on 4 April in Zavrazhye, near Yurievets in Russia. His father is the poet Arseny Tarkovsky and his mother Maria Vishniakova. The family lives in Moscow.
1934	His sister Marina is born on 3 October.
1937	Arseny leaves the family and remarries, Maria never remarries.
1941	Is evacuated to Yurievets with his mother, grandmother and sister during the Second World War.
1947	Is taken ill with tuberculosis.
1951	Enrolls at the Oriental Institute in the Department of Arabic.
1953	Leaves the Institute and spends the summer on a geological expedition in Siberia.
1954	Is accepted at the State Institute of Cinematography (VGIK) and is supervised by Mikhail Romm.
1956	Directs the short film *The Killers* based on the Ernest Hemingway short story. Khrushchev delivers his famous "On the Personality Cult and Its Consequences" Speech at the 20th party Congress. The period known as the Thaw begins.
1957	Marries fellow VGIK student Irma Rausch. Directs the television film *There Will Be No Leave Today.*
1961	Completes his diploma short film *The Steamroller and the Violin* and completes his VGIK studies. Shortly after he begins work on his cinematic debut *Ivan's Childhood.*
1962	Is awarded the Golden Lion at the Venice Film Festival for *Ivan's Childhood.* His first son, Arseny is born.
1964	Begins work on *Andrei Rublyov.*
1966	Work on *Andrei Rublyov* is completed. Distribution and release is delayed.

1969	*Andrei Rublyov* wins the Jury Prize at Cannes.
1970	Begins filming *Solaris*. Divorces Irma Rausch and marries Larissa Yegorkina. His second son, Andrei, is born.
1971	*Andrei Rublyov* is finally released in the Soviet Union.
1972	*Solaris* is awarded the Special Jury Prize at Cannes. He lectures at Goskino.
1973	Production of *Mirror*.
1977	Production of *Stalker*. He directs *Hamlet* in Moscow. He suffers from a heart attack.
1979	*Stalker* is released and wins three major prizes at Cannes. His mother dies.
1980	Named "People's Artist of the Russian Soviet Federated Socialist Republic."
1982	In Italy makes the documentary *Voyage in Time*. Also films *Nostalghia*.
1983	*Nostalghia* wins the Best Director Prize at Cannes. He directs the opera *Boris Godunov* in London. Is sacked by Mosfilm for unauthorized absence.
1984	Announces his decision to not return to the Soviet Union at a press conference in Milan.
1985	Production of *The Sacrifice*. Is diagnosed with cancer.
1986	His son and mother-in-law are given permission to live with him in Paris. He receives treatment for his condition. *The Sacrifice* wins the Special Jury Prize at Cannes. He dies on December 29th.

Introduction

"Beyond the Frame"

How does time make itself felt in a shot? It becomes tangible when you sense something significant, truthful, going beyond the events on the screen; when you realise, quite consciously, that what you see in the frame is not limited to its visual depiction, but is a pointer to something stretching out beyond the frame and to infinity; a pointer to life.

~Andrei Tarkovsky

For me *Mirror* is not a film, it is something that goes beyond cinema.

~Olivier Assayas

Despite a body of work comprised of only seven completed feature films, Tarkovsky's legacy and his influence on the cinematic art have been profound. Contemporary directors as diverse as Nuri Bilge Ceylan, Michael Haneke, Lars von Trier, Andrei Zvyagintsev, Pawel Pawlikowski and even Christopher Nolan have all had their works, on occasion, described as "Tarkovskian," a term that has become shorthand for both a cinematic aesthetic (long, lingering takes and quasi-dreamlike imagery) and a thematic (concerned with the intimate relationship between memory, experience and time) approach to film.[1]

In the years since Tarkovsky's death in 1986 many books have attempted to "explain" his films "once and for all." "*Beyond the Frame": The Films and Film Theory of Andrei Tarkovsky* suggests that such an interpretative methodology, while endlessly fascinating, ultimately becomes redundant. Pre-meditated attempts to explain Tarkovsky's films are impossible and even largely superfluous given their deliberately polyphonic and multivalent design. In fact, one of the key aspects of his body of work is the overwhelming desire to keep his films open and irreducible in a similar way to what Shohini Chaudhuri and Howard Finn have called, in the context of Iranian Cinema, the "open image."[2]

Tarkovsky's discussions of his own film theory can be found in the book *Sculpting in Time*, a collection of his talks and writings completed over a number

1. Christopher Nolan himself refers to Tarkovsky and Nuri Bilge Ceylan as influences in the "Anatomy of a Scene" series in *The New York Times*, December 18, 2014, <http://thefilmstage.com/news/nolan-dissects-interstellar-scene-linking-tarkovsky-and-ceylan-top-10-shots-of-2014-and-more/>.
2. Shohini Chaudhuri and Howard Finn, "The Open Image: Poetic Realism and the New Iranian Cinema," *Screen* 44.1 (Spring 2003): 38-57.

of years in which he asserted quite distinctly that the fundamental reason he wrote about his work was not as a peremptory effort to explicate the "truth" behind them, rather he stated that "Reading and rereading books on the theory of cinema, I came to the conclusion that these did not satisfy me, but made me want to argue and put forward my own view of the problems and the objectives of film-making."[3] In this respect Tarkovsky's "problems and objectives" become the very purpose of this study.

This book is entitled "*Beyond the Frame": The Films and Film Theory of Andrei Tarkovsky* and its aim is both to examine and interrogate the connections between Tarkovsky's theory and his practice, while at the same time attempting to explore what this idea of "Tarkovskian" might actually mean and why Tarkovsky's works continue to resonate with audiences all around the globe so many years after they were originally made. What is it about his defining works like *Solaris* (*Solyaris*, 1972), *Mirror* (*Zerkalo*, 1975) and *Stalker* (1979) that spectators in the first decades of the new millennium still find vital, relevant and affective? Audiences who, on the surface at least, seem far removed from both the protagonists and the subject matter of Tarkovsky's films, but nevertheless find themselves returning to them again and again.

In the years since his death the archetypal academic approach to Tarkovsky has been to examine his oeuvre from an authorship perspective, attempting an analysis of recurring thematic and image patterns, most often related to his perceived interests and preoccupations.[4] These works have provided substantial insights into the understanding of Tarkovsky's methods, his relationship with the authorities and the palimpsest-like nature of his films. What they fail to do, on the whole, is to interrogate the significance of Tarkovsky's film theory to his canon and the impact of this methodology on the viewers. This project suggests that Tarkovsky's film theory and its relationship to his work has been significantly underestimated. Robert Bird, in his book *Andrei Rublyov*, defines the central role it played to Tarkovsky's films: "Andrei Tarkovsky was one of those relatively rare directors who develop their own cinematic aesthetic and apply it in an uncompromising fashion, making their body of work into a space of constant dialogue between theory and practice."[5] The relationship between theory and practice was one of the reasons Tarkovsky admired Robert Bresson, regarding him as, "the only man in the cinema to have achieved the perfect fusion of the finished work with a concept theoretically formulated beforehand."[6] However, the very same

---

3. Andrei Tarkovsky, *Sculpting in Time: Reflections on the Cinema*, trans. Kitty Hunter-Blair (London: Faber and Faber, 1986), 7.
4. See Bird's *Andrei Tarkovsky: Elements of Cinema*, Green's *The Winding Quest* and Johnson and Petrie's *The Films of Andrei Tarkovsky.*
5. Robert Bird, "Gazing into Time: Tarkovsky and Post-Modern Cinema Aesthetics," para 1, (A paper read at the 2003 meeting of the American Association for the Advancement of Slavic Studies in Toronto).
6. Tarkovsky, *Sculpting in Time*, 94.

assertion almost certainly applies to Tarkovsky himself.

While it is possible to see the diverse influence of Realism, Expressionism and Romanticism in his film making style, his strong sense of spirituality makes for a fragile balance in the debate between Realism and Formalism, especially given his predilection for expressionism and habitual moves away from naturalistic representations of temporality and space. Aspects of his cinematic aesthetic undoubtedly offer some parallels to Realism: from his protracted use of long take and depth of field and his opposition to the principles of montage, to the themes present in his work; plots often concerning so called "ordinary people," his narratives meander and digress as environment and mood take precedence over any conventional sense of narrative drive, frequently capturing what feels like spontaneous moments on the camera. However, his predisposition towards dream, ambiguity of perspective, overtly lyrical compositions and spatial and temporal ambiguities problematise such simplistic associations. This idiosyncrasy reveals him to be both a director and a film theorist *sui generis*.

At the heart of the Tarkovsky experience are a range of paradoxes. He is perhaps the foremost autobiographical filmmaker of the medium, not only in the obvious cinematic memoirs of *Mirror* and *Nostalghia* (1983), but also more obliquely in films which have no immediate autobiographical connection to their creator, such as the science fiction films *Solaris* and *Stalker*, and the historical biopic *Andrei Rublov* (*Andrei Rublyov*, 1965), films which evocatively map out Tarkovsky's world view, spiritually and artistically. Yet he frowned on self-expression: "I simply cannot believe that an artist can ever work for the sake of 'self-expression.' Self-expression is meaningless unless it meets with a response."[7] A self-avowed elitist film-maker, Tarkovsky believed that "The artist cannot, and has no right to, lower himself to some abstract, standardised level for the sake of a misconstrued notion of greater accessibility and understanding."[8] However, he is able to touch a broad range of viewers from disparate backgrounds in a distinctly personal fashion. One woman who wrote to Tarkovsky asked: "Thank you for *Mirror*. My childhood was like that…. Only how did you know about it?"[9] He is intimately connected to the past masters of cinema tradition, yet a profoundly experimental film-maker, even though he vigorously denied it: "Nothing can be more meaningless than the word 'search' applied to a work of art. It covers impotence, inner emptiness, lack of true creative consciousness, petty vainglory."[10] He is a collaborative artist, yet ultimately authorial; if there are auteurs in film, he is among them. As he stated, "What the director can be given by his colleagues in the course of their work together is inestimable; but all the same it is his conception alone

7. Ibid., 40.
8. Ibid., 166.
9. Ibid., 10.
10. Ibid., 95.

that finally gives the film its unity."[11]

Several questions have framed the approach of the book from its inception. What relevance does Tarkovsky still have for new millennial audiences? Why have such a diverse range of film-makers and spectators continued to return to him for inspiration? How does the preoccupation with temporality that resonates through his work connect him to other film theorists? What does that most nebulous of terms "poetic," which is almost always applied to Tarkovsky's cinema, actually mean in practice? What does his habitual use of long-take aesthetics share with André Bazin? How far does his depiction of memory deviate from classical narrative cinema? It seems to me that these are vital questions, and yet ones which have not yet been explored by Tarkovsky scholars at any sustained length.

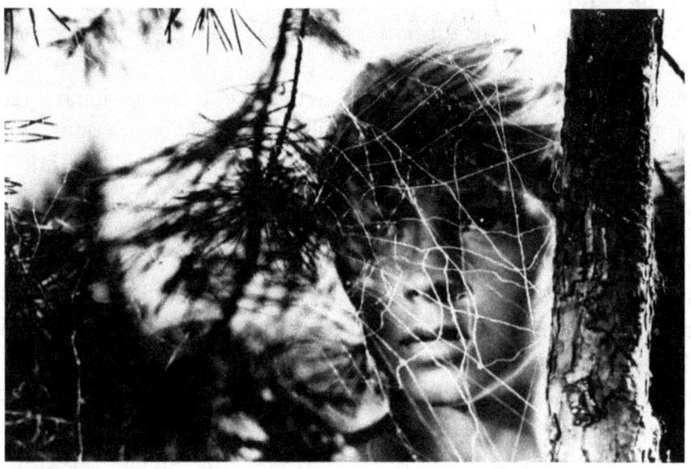

Figure 1 What is it about Tarkovsky's films that continues to resonate with modern audiences? His cinematic debut, *Ivan's Childhood*, was released in 1962 and is the first of only seven completed films in his body of work.

The most common interpretation of Tarkovsky's career, that he was some sort of martyred artist struggling to create masterpieces against all the odds, remains pervasive, even though it was effectively skewered by Johnson and Petrie in their *Andrei Tarkovsky: A Visual Fugue* in 1994. So, even though some continue to ask "Why was Tarkovsky only able to make seven films?," a more pertinent question might be, in fact, "How was he even able to make seven?"[12]

11. Ibid., 33.
12. "The American cinema is a classical art," André Bazin suggested in 1957, "why not then admire in it what is most admirable, i.e., not only the talent of this or that filmmaker, but the genius of the system." Few writers have considered the impact of the Soviet regime on the films produced in the Soviet film industry. Quoted in "André Bazin: 'On the *politique des auteurs*,'" trans. Peter Graham. Originally from "De la politique des auteurs," *Cahiers du Cinéma 70,* April 1957,

His work consistently deviated from the party line, and he was described just after his death by Vladimir Matusevich as, "One of the very few artists in the history of Soviet film whose creative world is in no way in conformity with the prevailing ideology."[13] Despite this, he remained able to produce films with significantly less challenge to his authorial vision than many of his contemporaries.

Robert Service in his *A History of Modern Russia* draws a valuable distinction between overt dissent and veiled criticism of the state which could be found across all aspects of art and culture in the Soviet Union. Service positions film directors like Tengiz Abuladze and Tarkovsky, writers like the Strugatsky Brothers (with whom Tarkovsky worked on *Stalker*), composers like Alfred Schnittke and performers like Vladimir Vysotski as those of the latter group. He states that "none of them belonged to the groups of overt dissent, but their works offered an alternative way of assessing Soviet reality."[14] This "alternative way of assessing Soviet reality" was, for many, filtering it through an allegorical prism without confronting party ideology directly. Those who challenged the regime and dared to speak and act freely suffered the consequences. Alexander Solzhenitsyn, the author of *The First Circle* (1968) and *Cancer Ward* (1968) served eight years in prison for anti-Soviet writings in 1945. Ossip Mandelstam died in the Gulag for a fourteen-line poem describing Stalin as a Kremlin mountain man with a cockroach whistler's leer.[15] Vasily Grossman, author of *Life and Fate* (1959), regarded by many as the twentieth century *War and Peace* (1869), had all his work confiscated and destroyed. These were just three artists among thousands who paid the price for their criticism of the regime under which they lived and worked.[16]

Tarkovsky's criticism of the state is apparent for those looking for it, yet it is undeniably veiled. It can be found in the tellingly vague misprint of Stalin's name, the allusions to Chekhov's *Ward Six* (1892) and the palpable sense of paranoia in *Mirror*, the portrayal of the ruthless and petty princes who persecute, harangue and even murder the artists who desire their creative independence in *Andrei Rublyov* (*Andrei Rublyov*, 1965), the myopic bureaucracy and mistrust of the individual which permeates *Solaris* (*Solyaris*, 1972) and

Cahiers du Cinéma: The 1950s – Neo-Realism, Hollywood, New Hollywood, ed. Jim Hillier (London: Routledge and Kegan Paul, 1985), 258.

13. Vladimir B. Matusevich, "Tarkovsky's Apocalypse," *Sight and Sound* 50.1 (Winter 1980/81): 8.

14. Robert Service, *A History of Modern Russia* (London: Penguin, 2003), 415. The Georgian director Tengiz Abuladze made *Confession* (1984) and *The Tree of Desire* (1978). Vladimir Vysotski was a popular singer, poet and actor.

15. See Ossip Mandelstam, "The Stalin Epigram" [1933], *The Moscow Notebooks*, trans. Elizabeth McKane (Tarset, Northumberland: Bloodaxe Books, 1991), 74.

16. Even those who wrote in allegory or were not explicit in their criticism of the regime were not safe; the science fiction writer Alexander Zinoviev was exiled in 1978, the cellist, Mstislav Rostropovich had his citizenship revoked in 1978, theatre director Vsevolod Meyerhold was executed by a firing squad in a gulag on trumped up charges of conspiring with Japanese Intelligence agencies.

Stalker. Yet it can be persuasively argued, that not once in his whole body of work is an explicit political point made, even in those films made while he was an exile. Likewise, in *Sculpting in Time* very few references are made to his exilic status or the political situation in the Soviet Union. Tarkovsky even quoted Tolstoy on why art must remain distinctly separate from politics: "The political is not compatible with the artistic, because the former, in order to prove, has to be one-sided."[17] These are the reasons above all, why Tarkovsky was able to make five films in the Soviet Union, while many of his colleagues found themselves denounced or even imprisoned. Compare Tarkovsky's fate to those of his contemporaries, like Alexander Askoldov, who was never allowed to direct again after his debut *Commissar* (*Komissar*, 1967) caused such consternation for its portrayal of Semitism in the Soviet Union and its anti-war message, that it was banned for twenty years. Tarkovsky never had his work forcefully taken away from him and recut like Marlen Khutsiev, whose *The Lenin Gate* (*Zastava Ilyicha*) was drastically edited and re-released as *I am Twenty* (*Mne dvadtsat let*, 1962). He never spent time in prison like his friend and colleague Sergei Paradzhanov, who served five years in a labour camp, ostensibly on charges of bribery and homosexuality, but in reality for the sentiments expressed in *The Colour of Pomegranates* (1969). Paradzhanov once called Tarkovsky, "a phenomenon…amazing, unrepeatable, inimitable and beautiful…He is a genius."[18] He also somewhat contentiously remarked: "You are my great friend but there might be something lacking in your art, and it's that you haven't spent at least a year in a Soviet prison. Being in total darkness, hungry and full of lice, man begins to think differently about the universe, to experience differently the sunlight, life."[19]

Even Tarkovsky's frequent periods of inactivity were not entirely unfruitful: he spent his time writing, speaking, teaching, he directed an opera in London, *Boris Godunov* (1983), and a play in Moscow, *Hamlet* (1977). In this light, Tarkovsky's plight does not seem so severe. Ian Christie asserts, "There can be no doubt that he was disliked and at times badly used by the Goskino bureaucracy, but equally he was granted privileges that most western film-makers could only dream of."[20] Vida Johnson and Graham Petrie ask a provocative yet valid question: "What would Orson Welles have given to have made 'only' five films in twenty years—*all of them* with adequate, if rarely generous, budgets, shot under conditions of complete creative freedom."[21]

---

17. Tarkovsky, *Sculpting in Time,* 54.
18. Herbert J. Marshall, "Andrei Tarkovsky's *The Mirror,*" *Sight and Sound* 45.2 (Spring 1976): 92.
19. Janusz Gazda, "Paradjanov's Collage," *Kwartalnik filmowy collection*, 9-10 (Spring-Summer, 1995): 265-7.
20. Quoted in Maya Turovskaya, *The Films of Andrei Tarkovsky: Cinema as Poetry*, trans. Natasha Ward (London: Faber and Faber, 1989), xxiv.
21. Vida Johnson and Graham Petrie, *The Films of Andrei Tarkovsky: A Visual Fugue* (Bloomington and Indianapolis: Indiana University Press, 1994), 13. Although one must qualify that Tarkovsky never made a film with complete creative freedom, such was the pressure he was

One must recognise that a comparative account of his woes is not entirely fair: just because Tarkovsky did not suffer as badly as some, this does not mean his suffering was insignificant. His heartfelt accounts of these trials and tribulations in his diary make very clear what impact they had on him emotionally and physically. In a letter to the chairman of Goskino Tarkovsky wrote:

> I would be so bold as to call myself an artist, and more than that, a Soviet artist. My two guiding beacons are what I can create, and life itself. When it comes to problems of form, I seek new ways forward. This is always arduous and can lead to conflict and unpleasantness, so that I cannot count on being able to live a cosy little life in a nice flat, untroubled by anything. What is demanded of me is courage, and in this respect, I will try not to betray the trust that you have shown me. [22]

There is considerable evidence that the Soviet authorities were often unsure of how to treat him. It can be taken for granted that they appreciated the continued international acclaim for Soviet cinema they received through his work and the foreign currency that was generated from selling his films abroad. About his critical stature Mark Cousins writes, "Tarkovsky's work alone would have been enough to establish the Soviet Union as a major force in the evolution of the 1960s film schema."[23] However, the price of this was high: a deliberately provocative challenging of established Soviet cinema through his films, interviews and writings, which must have made him at times almost unbearable.

In 1983 Tarkovsky shared the Best Director Prize at the Cannes Film Festival with Robert Bresson for their films *Nostalghia* and *L' Argent*. The French master, for whom Tarkovsky had frequently professed an admiration, was in his eighties and approaching the end of a long and distinguished career. During the making of *Nostalghia* Tarkovsky had just turned fifty, yet within three short years and just one further film he was dead. Many of Tarkovsky's contemporaries were still making films well into the first decade of the new millennium and beyond: he was born within a few years of Roman Polanski (1933), Woody Allen (1935),[24] Andrei Konchalovsky (1937, formerly

---

under. However, considering the fact that his exile films do not differ significantly in content or style from those made in the Soviet Union they raise a valid point.

22. Turovskaya, *The Films of Andrei Tarkovsky*, 48-9.

23. Mark Cousins, *The Story of Film* (London: Pavillion Books, 2004), 307. The two other directors Cousins regards as defining Soviet Cinema on the international stage are Sergei Paradzhanov and Kira Muratova.

24. Polanski's debut *Knife in the Water* (1962) was released in the same year as *Ivan's Childhood*. His most recent films were *Carnage* (2011) and *Venus in Fur* (2013). Woody Allen's official directorial debut was *What's Up, Tiger Lily?* (1966) but it is perhaps more accurate to call *Take the Money and Run* made in 1969 his true debut as a director. Andrei Konchalovsky and Otar Ioselliani both defected in the 1980s, to considerably less fanfare. Konchalovsky, who studied in the same class

Mikhalkov-Konchalovsky) and Otar Iosselliani (1934). Compared to many of these directors, Tarkovsky's seven completed films seem slight, but his impact on world cinema has been considerable.

Perhaps his most famous film, *Mirror*, has become a symbolic touchstone for Tarkovsky's legacy in the years since his death, to the extent that many film-makers influenced by Tarkovsky frequently return to it in a quasi-spiritual act of homage or inspiration. Michael Haneke, who has also had his work described as "Tarkovskian" on occasion, admitted to having watched *Mirror* "at least twenty-five times" and he added "each time I discover something new."[25] During the nineties it was commonly suggested that the Serbian Emir Kusturica was laying a "claim to the throne of European cinema, vacant since the death of Tarkovsky."[26] Yet Tarkovsky's own visual motifs and narrative tropes become subsumed in Kusturica's recreation of Tarkovsky's signature camera moves, locations and even characters to such an extent that, in his early films at least, he struggled to emerge with a cinematic identity of his own. In her compelling book length analysis of his work called simply *Emir Kusturica*, Dina Iordanova agrees, "scenes from almost all Tarkovsky's films have been replicated in Kusturica's. A listing of all examples would take more space than I can afford here."[27]

Since the release of his debut *The Return* (*Vozvrashcheniye*) in 2003, it has seemed almost impossible to discuss a film by the Russian director Andrei Zvyagintsev without mentioning the influence of Andrei Tarkovsky. *The Return* won numerous accolades on its release, most significantly the Golden Lion in Venice, forty-one years after Tarkovsky received the same prize for his own debut film *Ivan's Childhood*. Zvyagintsev's subsequent films *The Banishment* (*Izgnanie*, 2007) and *Leviathan* (2014) open up a dialogue with Tarkovsky's films and Tarkovsky the artist in a similar way to Tarkovsky's homages to his own influences. A cursory glance at *The Return* is enough to register the parallels: Zvyagintsev calls his two young protagonists Ivan and Andrei and centres the film around the return of a mysterious father figure played with a palpable intensity by Konstantin Lavronenko. Louis Menashe stated, "In its formal

---

with Tarkovsky at the State Film School (VGIK) and co-wrote Tarkovsky's earliest films, had great success in the U.S.A before returning to Russia. For his first Russian film in thirteen years, *House of Fools* (*Dom durakov*, 2002), he won the Special Jury Prize at the Venice Film Festival and made *The Postman's White Nights* in 2014. The Georgian Otar Iosselliani won the Silver Bear at the Berlin Film Festival for *Lundi Matin* (2002) and his *Chantrapas* was made in 2010.

25. Haneke's ideological approach to film was described as "Tarkovskian" by Charles Warren in "The Unknown Piano Teacher," in *A Companion to Michael Haneke*, ed. Roy Grundmann (Wiley-Blackwell: Chichester, 2010), 495-510, 498.

26. Adam Mars-Jones, "Vision improbable: Serbian film-maker Emir Kusturica's elephantine comedy lays claim to the high ground of European art cinema," *The Independent* (7 March 1996): 7.

27. Dina Iordanova, *Emir Kusturica* (London: British Film Institute, 2002), 139. The list of directors described to be "Tarkovskian" is almost too long to list here: Alexander Sokurov, Gus Van Sant, Kim Ki Duk, Béla Tarr, Bruno Dumont, Krzysztof Kieślowski to name but a few.

contours it will immediately bring to mind the work and film aesthetics of Andrei Tarkovsky. Zvyagintsev shares the late Russian master's hydrophilia; their films are waterlogged; rain is almost a member of the cast."[28] Julian Graffy concurred, "The placing of the story so firmly in the natural world is also evocative of Tarkovsky – the wind and the earth, and especially the rain and the water of Tarkovsky's films are prominent here. A number of scenes – a mother smoking a cigarette, coals burning in a fire – are direct quotations."[29] However, it is when Zvyagintsev discusses his directorial style that he comes closest to Tarkovsky. When asked to elaborate on the meanings contained within *The Return* he stated, "I wouldn't like to be a mediator between the screen and the viewer."[30] He echoes Tarkovsky's refusal to explain what, in their shared opinion, is unexplainable. They both contend that after the film is completed, it no longer belongs to them. For Tarkovsky, the "film then becomes something beyond its ostensible existence as exposed and edited roll of film, a story, a plot. Once in contact with the individual who sees it, it separates from its author, starts to live its own life, undergoes changes of form and meaning."[31]

Zvyagintsev's characterisation of the Tarkovsky experience as a profoundly erotetic one is fairly common. Tarkovsky's is a cinema which asks questions rather than answers them and for some audiences raised on the formulaic narratives of mainstream cinema this can be frustrating. "Beyond the Frame" refers to a central concept in Tarkovsky's film theory, to which he and writers on him return frequently, that of the ability of the cinema to transcend the medium itself and somehow move "beyond the frame" in its dialogical relationship with spectators. While "beyond the frame" sounds like a quasi-mystical and somewhat esoteric concept, it is actually the result of a considered, systematic and sustained process of cinematic techniques which are present both in his films and in *Sculpting in Time* and will be explored throughout the course of this book. The foundation of Tarkovsky's films and his film theory, as I will show, is time; and it is through time that everything flows: philosophy, imagery, theme, narrative and style.

For those like Olivier Assayas, the writer and director of the films *Late August, Early September* (1998), *Summer Hours* (2008), and *Clouds of Sils Maria* (2014), a quote from whom opens this book, Tarkovsky's films become a living entity, which changes incommensurably from encounter to encounter, and a filter through which experience is processed. When Assayas attempted to describe what he found most powerful about Tarkovsky's films he stated: "[W]hat moves me in *Mirror* is that it sends me back to my own childhood, to similar feelings I have experienced: this is why I see it as *beyond* the dramatic or

28. Louis Menashe, "*The Return*," *Cineaste*, 29.2 (Spring 2004): 27.
29. Julian Graffy, "*The Return*," *Sight and Sound*, 14.7 (July 2004): 64.
30. Quoted in "Return to Nature," *Film Ireland*, 99 (July/August 2004): 13.
31. Tarkovsky, *Sculpting in Time*, 118.

syntactic structure of cinema."[32] For Assayas, Tarkovsky's films move "beyond the frame" in the reverberations they are able to create within the spectator, who brings them to life and it is the associations and memories it evokes which are as important, if not more important, than the texts themselves. This symbiotic imbrication between film and spectator is echoed in the work of Astrid Widding who states, "Tarkovsky's films also seem to invite the spectator to cross several borders, both the border to the film image and the limits within the image, which seem to lead over to a dimension beyond."[33] This "dimension beyond" for many will be a spiritual one, because for Tarkovsky, film is a sacrilized art, primarily designed to be a transcendental experience, akin to holy icons of the medieval period, widely regarded as devotional aides. For a variety of reasons, as I intend to show, it is not exclusively spiritual. Such is the openness of the construction of the films, that this "beyond" is many things: it is as much about time, memory, image and art, as it is about the divine. When Tarkovsky remarked, "Anyone who wants can look at my films as into a mirror, in which he will see himself,"[34] he was referring to the apophenic qualities of his films, which are not just an afterthought, but central to their construction. Spectators will view Tarkovsky's work through the prism of their own experience and bring meaning to it like some sort of experiential, cinematic Rorschach inkblot test.

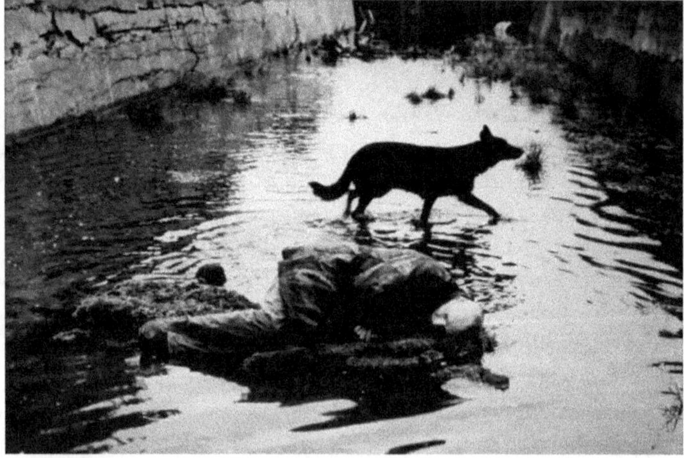

Figure 2 Tarkovsky's images are richly suggestive and profoundly open in their construction. One brings the totality of one's own experiences and memories to a screening of *Stalker*.

32. Olivier Assayas, "Tarkovsky: Seeing is Believing," *Sight and Sound*, 7.1 (January 1997): 24.
33. Astrid Widding, "Deus Absconditus – Between Invisible and Visible in the Films of Andrei Tarkovsky," *Through The Mirror: Reflections on Tarkovsky*, 160.
34. Tarkovsky, *Sculpting in Time*, 184.

This concept of a film being able to move "beyond the frame" is not a new one in film theory. Film-makers and theorists have speculated on the role of more active spectators throughout the history of film. When Neia Zorkaya described every Tarkovsky film as an "event" in 1989, she meant that their infrequency provoked great interest in Russia and outside, but the events generated by Tarkovsky are much more than this.[35] As early as 1916, Hugo Munsterberg in his *The Photoplay: A Psychological Study* saw the potential of film, here described as a photoplay, not just to represent, but generate sensations: "The photo play tells us a human story by overcoming the outer forms of the outer world, namely space, time and causality, and by adjusting the events to the forms of the inner world, namely attention, memory, imagination and emotion."[36] Already Munsterberg observes a distinction between mainstream films and those which embrace the specificity of the medium by instigating a succession of mental events in the mind of the viewer and in doing so anticipating the interpenetrational discourse between viewer and text which Tarkovsky strove all through his career to achieve.[37] Munsterberg's work is remarkable for a number of reasons, not least because it was written so early in the evolution of the cinematic language, just one year after *The Birth of a Nation* (Griffith, 1915) and a year before the October Revolution was to change the history of Russia in the twentieth century irrevocably.

Consider that other Formalist theorist, Béla Balázs, whose *Theory of the Film (Character and Growth of a New Art)* described a similar account of the interplay between film and spectator, which also proved to be significantly ahead of its time, when it was published in Russian in 1945.[38] For Balázs, as for Tarkovsky, it is the dialogical relationship between the film and the spectator which is central to the cinematic experience: "Just as the contact of electrically charged objects evokes a spark, so the contact between pictures in a film evokes a mutually interpreting associative process, whether the director wishes to or not."[39] This affectual cinema which Balázs is suggesting, sets off reverberations

35. Neia Zorkaya, *The Illustrated History of Soviet Cinema* (New York: Hippocrene Books, 1989), 270.

36. Hugo Munsterberg, [1916] *Hugo Munsterberg on Film: The Photoplay: A Psychological Study and Other Writings* (New York: Routledge, 2001), 129.

37. In fact Munsterberg described three stages of the evolution of film, from fairground novelty and toy, to the functional role of narrative cinema, and finally the cinema of the mind. He even went so far as to comment, "To picture emotions must be the central aim of the photoplay." (Ibid., 99). J. Dudley Andrew remarks that Munsterberg revealed an art form which "is the medium not of the world, but of the mind. Its basis lies not in the technology but in mental life." J. Dudley Andrew, *The Major Film Theories: An Introduction* (Oxford: Oxford University Press, 1976), 20.

38. Interestingly Balázs taught at VGIK from 1933-1945 where he was frequently criticised for his unconventional views.

39. Béla Balázs, [1945] *Theory of the Film (Character and Growth of a New Art)*, trans. Edith Bone (London: Dennis Dobson Ltd, 1952), 126. He also suggested that the future of the medium would be creating art from what already existed in the world and transforming it into cinema. His assertion that "Only by means of unaccustomed and unexpected methods produced by

that will become the sensations discussed by Tarkovsky and Gilles Deleuze decades later. Furthermore he implies these associations will be different from viewer to viewer and not inherently a part of the author's intentions or the material itself. Tarkovsky places such an open and associative aesthetic at the centre of his film theory, and his most compelling concepts: "time pressure," "imprinted time" and "time memory" will depend on such an approach. Tarkovsky suggested, "The only manner in which a creative idea should enter the awareness of the audience is via the trust the creator has in his audience. A dialogue in which audience and creator are equal partners has to be developed. There is no other approach."[40]

However, while for Tarkovsky there was no other method, for mainstream cinema there most decidedly was. In Tarkovsky's time in the Soviet Union it was characterised as Socialist Realism, defined in 1934 as "a truthful, historically concrete representation of reality in its revolutionary development. Moreover, the truthfulness and historical concreteness of the artistic depiction of reality ought to be combined with the task of ideological transformation and education of workers in the spirit of socialism."[41] Films produced were required to be accessible, relevant, understandable to the workers, realistic and, above all, support the ideological aims of the party. The basic tenets of Socialist Realism (and here we might also suggest classical film) are the very aspects of film form that Tarkovsky rejected; its clarity, its lack of ambiguity, its rigidity and homogeneity were for him an anathema to the creation of art.[42]

Tarkovsky like all film-makers, of course, is a product of his time: that is to say he emerged from the 1960s as part of the New Wave of Soviet Cinema, alongside several New Waves sweeping across Europe, Asia and then the Americas. Gilles Deleuze, one of the foremost chroniclers of temporality in the cinematic art, detected the materialisation of what he called "pulses" in the

---

striking set ups can old, familiar and therefore never before seen things hit our eye with new impressions" (Ibid., 93), might be considered a formalist maxim and one that becomes strikingly echoed in Tarkovsky's films.

40. Quoted in "Encounter with Andrei Tarkovsky," *Filmkritik* 12 (December 1962), trans. Tanya Ott and Saskia Wagner, *Andrei Tarkovsky Interviews*, ed. John Gianvito (Jackson: University of Mississippi Press, 2006), 10.

41. See Herman Ermolaev, *Soviet Literary Theories 1917-1934: The Genesis of Soviet Socialist Realism* (New York: Octagon Books, 1977), 197.

42. The most famous exponent and exemplar of this style of film-making during Tarkovsky's career was undoubtedly Sergei Bondarchuk, awarded the title "Hero of the Soviet Union," director of films like *Fate of a Man* (*Sudba Cheloveka*, 1959), *War and Peace* (*Voyna i mir,* 1968) and *They Fought for the Motherland* (*Oni srazhalis za rodinu,* 1975). It is perhaps not surprising given the prominent status of both men that their careers intriguingly interact with one and other over the years. Tarkovsky's diaries are full of references to Bondarchuk, most of them venomous. For Tarkovsky, Bondarchuk is representative of all that is wrong with mainstream cinema. He called Bondarchuk "envious and unaccomplished, no further comment required" (Tarkovsky, *Time within Time: The Diaries, 1970-1986,* 81). Like the Writer in *Stalker,* Bondarchuk was regarded as a hack who sold his "soul for thirty pieces of silver" (165) in order to obtain recognition by the state, but in doing so lost his artistic credentials.

evolution of the cinematic language: "The timing is something like: around 1948, Italy; about 1958, France; about 1968, Germany."[43] It is not a coincidence then, that in the Soviet Union in the years after Joseph Stalin's death and Khrushchev's secret session denouncing Stalin at the 20th Party Congress in February 1956, a period known as the Thaw emerged, defined by a brief loosening of censorship for writers, film-makers and artists.[44] During this time Alexander Solzhenitsyn saw his *One Day in the Life of Ivan Denisovich* (1962) published in the Soviet literary magazine *Novy Mir*, a novel about a single day in the Gulag, and Yevgeny Yevtushenko wrote the poem *Babi Yar* (1966) about anti-semitism in the Soviet Union and the massacre of over 30,000 Jews by Nazis and Ukrainian police in 1939. These are subjects that would have been inconceivable to depict in print just a few years before. A group of young film-makers began making films that were to challenge the accepted norms of Soviet Socialist Realism: directors like Grigori Chukhrai, Mikhail Kalatozov, Andrei Mikhalkov-Konchalovsky, Larissa Shepitko, Kira Muratova and Sergei Paradzhanov, among whom Tarkovsky's, arguably, became the most powerful voice.

For me, it is almost self-evident that Tarkovsky's seven completed films represent not just isolated texts, but a cohesive body of work, intimately and symbiotically connected with one another. While this might be considered a standard auteurist assumption, I do not use it in the conventional auteurist sense. His are films which are designed to echo and reflect each other in a profoundly dialogical nature as they turn on themselves repeating and reflecting like a Möbius strip, a fractal pattern or a poem. There is even an apt symmetry to his oeuvre; his aesthetic evolves from his cinematic debut, *Ivan's Childhood* (*Ivanovo detstvo*, 1962), reaching an artistic peak with *Mirror*, his fourth of seven films and the focal point of his career, with his two science fiction films *Solaris* and *Stalker* on either side, before going abroad in exile to complete his two final films *Nostalghia* in Italy and *The Sacrifice* (1986) in Sweden. These echoes have frequently led to Tarkovsky being criticised for what some regard as his restricted *topoi*, the images to which he returns again and again: water, trees, the dacha, animals and children. One finds it hard to deny the presence of such a repeating set of motifs, but his canvas could not be broader: it is life and the meaning of existence itself.

Tarkovsky's films are often about the physical journey of his characters, in what Peter Green called (and titled his book) "The Winding Quest;" but this outer voyage is a manifestation of their inner conflict, a metaphor, which can be directly applied to the films themselves. To appreciate Tarkovsky is to go on this journey oneself, and the demands Tarkovsky places on a spectator are not

43. Gilles Deleuze, *Cinema One: The Movement Image*, trans. Hugh Tomlinson and Barbara Habberjam (Minneapolis: University of Minnesota Press, 2001), 211.

44. The Thaw derives its name from the Ilya Ehrenburg novel *The Thaw* (1954), and it is widely considered to begin in around the mid to late-fifties until the mid-sixties.

to everyone's tastes. Hamid Naficy in his *An Accented Cinema: Exilic and Diasporic Film-making* points out that these "journeys, real or imaginary, form a major thematic thread in accented films."[45] One might suggest that these characteristics embodied Tarkovsky's work long before he became an exile. It is not new to suggest that during the Soviet period generations of citizens felt themselves as exiles within their own country, both figuratively and for many, literally. Tarkovsky's films are too poetic and too far removed from the codes and conventions of mainstream cinema to be conventionally "enjoyable;" many find them slow and abstruse. These reactions are not inappropriate, in fact, they are entirely understandable. His philosophy has been described as "turgid" and "woolly,"[46] his narratives the "flabbiest kind of sentimental humanism" and the overall experience "genuinely brain-freezing."[47] Reviews often state the fact that the films "must be viewed actively and with some effort,"[48] as if such a way of viewing films is inappropriate. Tarkovsky recognised that his films were not for everyone: "The person watching either falls into your rhythm (your world), and becomes your ally, or else he does not, in which case no contact is made. And some people become your 'own,' and others remain strangers."[49] Thus spectators of Tarkovsky's films either become allies, or what we will later see him term "fellow travellers," or they do not. While it sounds rather melodramatic to suggest, nevertheless it is true, Tarkovsky's films are for individuals who seek them out, who want them, even those who need them.

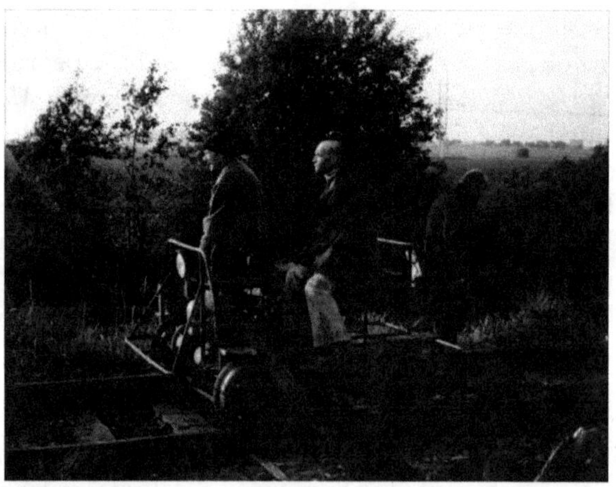

45. Hamid Naficy, *An Accented Cinema: Exilic and Diasporic Film-making* (Princeton: Princeton University Press, 2001), 33.
46. Geoff Andrew, *Film Directors A-Z: A Concise Guide to the Art of 250 Great Film-makers* (London: Carlton Books, London, 1999), 217.
47. Tony Rayns, *Time Out Film Guide 2007*, ed. John Pym (London: Time Out, 2007), 1070.
48. Richard Eder, *New York Times*, October 6th 1976 in *The New York Times Film Reviews 1975-1976* (New York: The New York Times & Arno Press, 1977), 268-9.
49. Tarkovsky, *Sculpting in Time*, 120.

Figure 3 Tarkovsky's films are an invitation to go on a journey: both for characters within the diegesis, like those shown here in *Stalker*, and for spectators gazing at the screen. (previous page)

It is clear to see that Tarkovsky's understanding of time also seems far removed from that of our own new millennial approaches to temporality, which seems increasingly defined by the demand for instantaneous experience. In his astute *Present Shock: When Everything Happens Now* (2012) Douglas Rushkoff argues that our compulsive reliance on new media technologies has led to the emergence of precarious states of digiphrenia (a dislocation caused by the attempt to live in the real and digital simultaneously) and fractalnoia (an attempt to understand everything only in the present tense). He writes, "Instead of finding a stable foothold in the here and now, we end up reacting to the ever-present assault of simultaneous impulses and commands."[50] Perhaps one of the reasons Tarkovsky's films have endured is because they offer a profoundly different experience to this; their narratives function as contemplative mediations on time and its complexities rather than an embrace of the fleeting visceralities of the present. This is not to say that the present moment is not deeply meaningful in the works of Tarkovsky, in fact, as it will be shown, it becomes even more significant in how it is held, examined and placed in relation to those moments that have gone before and those that are yet to come. In this way Tarkovsky's films seem to embody not the "presentist" society that Rushkoff describes, but that pervasive idea of "mindfulness" which has gained such cultural currency in the last decade and stresses "A kind of nonelaborative, nonjudgmental, present-centered awareness in which each thought, feeling, or sensation that arises in the attentional field is acknowledged and accepted as it is."[51]

The techniques used to achieve this decidedly poetic and affectual cinema are multifarious and will be studied in detail in the individual chapters, as the book progresses. With this intention the structure of the project emerges from its aims and is arranged thematically rather than chronologically. Chapter One focuses on time, the stylistic and thematic anchor of Tarkovsky's entire oeuvre. It interrogates how Tarkovskian time, what he describes as "time pressure," deviates from the construction and function of temporality in classical narrative cinema. It compares his "chronotopical signature" to the work of Andrei Bazin and Sergei Eisenstein. John Orr in his *Introduction to Post-War Cinema and Modernity* accurately surmised Tarkovsky's more fluid relationship with time, when he commented that Tarkovsky "endows film time with a positive moral value so that it resurrects not just the personal world of time

50. Douglas Rushkoff, *Present Shock: When Everything Happens Now* (New York: Penguin, 2012), 4.
51. S. R. Bishop, M. Lau, S. Shapiro, L. Carlson, N. D. Anderson, J. Carmody, et al., "Mindfulness: A proposed operational definition," *Clinical Psychology: Science and Practice* 11.3 (2004): 230–41, 5.

past but also the wider, public world of previous generations."[52] This provocative rendering of time is resolutely non-linear with decidedly historical, personal and ideological implications, one of the many factors, which would bring Tarkovsky into conflict with the authorities throughout his career. Tarkovsky quotes Gogol when he suggests that the true artistic image is able "to express life itself, not ideas or arguments about life. It does not signify life or symbolise it, but embodies it."[53] One might suggest that the experiencing of time is the key to his whole body of work; for Tarkovsky film does not just record life, it *is* life.

While Chapter One addresses broad patterns and structures throughout Tarkovsky's career, it primarily focuses on *Mirror*, which for many is Tarkovsky's most exigent and defining text. It features a close analysis of the film and in particular Tarkovsky's most identifiable aesthetic strategy, the long take. In the long take aesthetic we see what is at the heart of his confrontation with Sergei Eisenstein and the aspect of his film theory which connects him to André Bazin.

Following on from time but still intrinsically connected to it, Chapter Two proceeds to deconstruct the use of memory as a stylistic and narrative device while turning to the first of two films Tarkovsky made abroad, *Nostalghia*. Tarkovsky is a distinctly taxonomic film theorist and his concept of "time memory" is explored in detail. "Time memory" is designed to create a much more experiential cinema and an interactive relationship with the audience, who are tasked with drawing on their own memories, as the films progress. I suggest that a strong connection emerges between Tarkovsky and Gilles Deleuze, especially in Deleuze's work on memory in film contained in *Cinema Two: The Time Image*. Indeed, Deleuze's cinema of the time image is arguably the closest theoretical approximation of Tarkovsky's poetic cinema. Several writers over the years have made comments about the parallels between Tarkovsky and Deleuze, but they have only done so briefly. Robert Bird remarks that, "Deleuze's sparse comments on Tarkovsky mask the director's profound significance for the theorist,"[54] but he chooses not to pursue the imbrication between the two in his work. Fergus Daly and Katherine Waugh expand these associations even further, boldly pronouncing that, "*Sculpting in Time* greatly influenced Deleuze's formulations in *Cinema Two: The Time-Image*."[55] It is possible to discern several distinct parallels between Tarkovsky's film theory and the Deleuzian concepts of time image, irrational cutting, any-space-whatevers and the crystal image. In doing so, I also discern parallels between

52. John Orr, *Introduction to Post-war Cinema and Modernity*, eds. John Orr and Olga Taxidou (Edinburgh: Edinburgh University Press, 2000), 9.
53. Tarkovsky, *Sculpting in Time*, 111.
54. Bird, "Gazing into Time: Tarkovsky and Post-Modern Cinema Aesthetics," para 12.
55. Fergus Daly and Katherine Waugh, "*Ivan's Childhood*," *Senses of Cinema* 15.1 (July-August 2001): para 5, (n.d.). <http://www.sensesofcinema.com/contents/cteq/01/15/ivans_childhood.html> (8 May 2007).

Tarkovsky's presentation of imagery and what Shohini Chauduri and Howard Finn have called, in the context of Iranian Cinema, the "open image."[56]

Chapter Three explores Tarkovsky's two science fiction texts *Solaris* and *Stalker* from an imagesic perspective, registering how "time pressure" is altered by choices of image construction and how they are presented. It first discusses the implications of Tarkovsky's distinction between a symbol and a metaphor using his most familiar visual motif: water. While Tarkovsky's authorship status and his auteur signature have been covered before (there is a chapter on water imagery in every Tarkovsky book published!), I seek to distinguish this book from the others by considering how these images are self-consciously designed to function. This openness of interpretation places a greater emphasis on reflection and individual experience. I expand the chapter to take on Laura Marks's analysis of a haptic cinema in *The Skin of the Film* to further deconstruct the way Tarkovsky's images are formed and how they differ from mainstream cinematic techniques.

Chapter Four looks at Tarkovsky's two most overtly religious texts: *Andrei Rublyov* and *The Sacrifice*. It explores the paradox of making spiritual films under a totalitarian regime, where freedom of religious beliefs was effectively prohibited and how they differ from those he subsequently made in exile. As Paul Coates comments, "Andrei Tarkovsky had the courage and intransigence consistently to thematize the spiritual – thus inviting equally consistent state harassment."[57] How was he able to become perhaps the foremost spiritual film-maker of his generation despite such restrictions? The chapter looks at the concepts of a *Deus Absconditus*, or a Hidden God, and sees how close Tarkovsky is to Paul Schrader's influential *Transcendental Style in Film*. Schrader's definition of a transcendental style is one which draws obvious parallels with Tarkovsky; the transcendental style "chooses irrationalism over rationalism, repetition over variation, sacred over profane, the deific over the humanistic, intellectual realism over optical realism, two-dimensional vision over three-dimensional vision, tradition over experiment, anonymity over individualization."[58] This transcendental aesthetic is a key aspect of how Tarkovsky's films are able to move "beyond the frame," as they are deliberately designed to provoke an epiphany in the viewer.

One problem that has often arisen in Tarkovsky studies and, indeed, in explorations of much of poetic or European Art Cinema, is the frequently repeated aphorism that the films need to be felt or experienced rather than "read." A member of the Institute of Physics of the Academy of Sciences once said about *Mirror*, "You have to watch this film simply, and listen to the music of Bach and the poems of Arseny Tarkovsky; watch it as one watches the stars,

56. Shohini Chaudhuri and Howard Finn, "The Open Image: Poetic Realism and the New Iranian Cinema," *Screen* 44.1 (Spring 2003): 38-57.

57. Paul Coates, *Cinema, Religion and the Romantic Legacy* (London: Ashgate Publishing Ltd. 2003), 163.

58. Paul Schrader, *Transcendental Style in Film* (Berkeley: University of California Press, 1972), 11.

or the sea, as one admires a landscape. There is no mathematical logic here, for it cannot explain what man is or what is the meaning of his life."[59] This sense of inarticulation is multifaceted: how can one do justice in writing to some of Tarkovsky's haunting and beguiling images, widely regarded as some of the most remarkable ever put on film? Also Tarkovsky frequently strives to express what may be considered "the inexpressible." Yet I would argue this is integral to an understanding of Tarkovsky's cinema; for him film is an aesthetic object *and* an experience. As André Bazin poetically wrote,

> We can coldly isolate patterns in music or logic in dreams as does the psychoanalyst, but, more warmly, we can begin to live the rhythm of the music as an invitation to dance and to vibrate; and we can feel in it a sense, an unveiling of the world expressed in the epiphany of the sensible.[60]

Tarkovsky's works are an invitation to experience. Far from being a rational and objective view of the world, they are designed to instigate a symbiotic relationship between audience and object, which takes on a profoundly tangible and living form.

In a similar fashion Tarkovsky's characters frequently express the inadequacy of words to represent the human experience; many are alienated from those around them, they stutter or take a vow of silence. It is through the cinema that Tarkovsky believes that connections between individuals can be established. The cinema "like music, allows for an utterly direct, emotional, sensuous perception of the work."[61] Tarkovsky's focus on the inarticulatable has often been read as a commentary on the restraints placed upon artists under the Soviet regime. In this interpretation Tarkovsky's works become veiled in allegory and metaphor and meanings become elusive or hidden.

On a personal note, I find myself echoing many of the comments made about Tarkovsky's work that I have uncovered over the years of preparation for this project. I have been fortunate to undertake the writing of this book in what is undeniably a renaissance of Tarkovsky studies and this has presented me with not only the opportunity to disseminate some of my ideas at a variety of conferences, but also interact with those, for whom Tarkovsky has meant a great deal. The responses of many have been almost eerily familiar and have followed broadly two lines. Many discussed with me how it was as if Tarkovsky had somehow made the film especially for them, as if some part of the film connected to them in an intensely personal fashion. Secondly, what happened time and time again was how people told me they felt their experience of the films had changed over the years, like some sort of heraclitan flux. I can only

59. Tarkovsky, *Sculpting in Time*, 9.

60. André Bazin quoted in J. Dudley Andrew, *The Major Film Theories: An Introduction,* 245. Originally cited in Henri Agel, *Poétique du cinéma* (Editions du Signe, 1973), 9.

61. Tarkovsky, *Sculpting in Time*, 176.

echo that *Mirror* means something very different to me now, as a parent and as one who has suffered loss, than it did on first viewing, as an eighteen year old undergraduate student with his life stretched out in front of him. Tarkovsky expressed a similar opinion about *Persona* (Bergman, 1966): "I have seen Bergman's *Persona* a great many times, and on each occasion it has given me something new. As a true work of art it always allows one to relate personally with the world of the film, interpreting it differently every time."[62] The key to these responses, as I hope to reveal, lies in the ability of the films to reach "beyond the frame."

62. Ibid., 166.

Chapter One

Tarkovsky and Time

Time is necessary to man, so that, made flesh, he may be able to realise himself as a personality. But I am not thinking of linear time, meaning the possibility of getting something done, performing some action…

~Andrei Tarkovsky

Time is, without a doubt, the defining aspect of Andrei Tarkovsky's cinematic aesthetic. For Tarkovsky temporality is the *sine qua non* not only for the cinematic apparatus, but life itself; and it is this understanding of time which informs his attitude to film throughout his entire career. So central is time to Tarkovsky's approach, that his book on film theory was called *Sculpting in Time*, his published diaries *Time within Time* and the only documentary he ever made *Voyage in Time* (1983). Turovskaya agrees that "Time was the key concept for Tarkovsky's whole approach to cinema."[63]

The title for *Sculpting in Time* was derived from a metaphor he used to describe the film-making process:

> Just as a sculptor takes a lump of marble, and, inwardly conscious of the features of his finished piece, removes everything that is not part of it – so the film-maker, from a 'lump of time' made up of an enormous, solid cluster of living facts, cuts off and discards whatever he does not need, leaving only what is to be an element of the finished film.[64]

Tarkovsky's metaphor was, perhaps, inspired in part by Michelangelo Buonarroti, who famously described how he could visualise the finished sculpture within a block of marble before even lifting a chisel.[65] Michelangelo "saw" the "image to be sculpted in the mass, because in his imagination the marble is not inert matter but a living form, rich with three dimensional

---

63. Turovskaya, *The Films of Andrei Tarkovsky,* 85. Birgit Beumers also agreed. In her recent book *A History of Russian Cinema* (New York: Berg, 2008) she wrote, "Tarkovsky's approach to time is crucial to an understanding of his films" (166).

64. Tarkovsky, *Sculpting in Time*, 63-4.

65. Tarkovsky's metaphor could also have been influenced by Vachel Lindsay's description of film as "sculpture in motion" or Heinrich von Kleist referring to theatre as a "sculpture made of snow." Boris Eikhenbaum suggested that "In cinema time is not filled but built." "Problems of Cinema Stylistics," ed. Herbert Eagle, *Russian Formalist Film Theory* (Ann Arbor: Michigan Slavic Publications, 1981), 74.

possibilities."[66] Tarkovsky similarly believed that film was an organic, living material, pulsating with energy, simultaneously formed both in and from time. Much of the dramatic conflict in both Tarkovsky's and Michelangelo's work emerges from the juxtaposition of this very Aristotelian concept, that the completed work of art potentially already exists within before its realisation, with the Platonist belief that all forms of beauty in art come directly from the divine. Tarkovsky dramatised this philosophical conflict in many of his films: from the painter Andrei Rublyov's crisis of faith and artistic inspiration in *Andrei Rublyov* to the exiled poet Andrei Gorchakov's search for identity through the realms of his past in *Nostalghia.*

The time of which Tarkovsky spoke in *Sculpting in Time* and which he subsequently portrayed in his films is not a "linear time, meaning the possibility of getting something done, performing some action,"[67] rather it is a more provocative and experimental approach to the representation of temporality onscreen. It is predominantly in this way that Tarkovsky's films diverge from what is usually termed mainstream or classical narrative cinema, which itself has gone under a variety of names in the course of film theory: from Noel Burch's "Institutional Mode of Representation" (IMR) to Gilles Deleuze's movement image. This style of cinema has developed particular codes and conventions covering aspects of its construction of *mise en scène*, editing and performance to representations of space and temporality. Of course, over the decades and from culture to culture differences emerge, but, arguably, patterns are discernible. Deleuze, Burch and other writers of mainstream cinema aesthetics have emphasised how classical film narratives traditionally inculcate cause and effect, temporal and spatial coherence and prioritise space over time.

Tarkovsky described how mainstream cinema renders time in a highly spatialised sense, as a chronological process of "nows" along a fixed temporal line. For him this approach is a reflection of how we have culturally been conditioned to think of time uncritically and is both restrictive and artificial. He suggested, that the logic "of linear sequentiality, is uncomfortably like the proof of a geometrical theorem. As a method it is incomparably less fruitful artistically than the possibilities opened up by associative linking."[68] In its place Tarkovsky presented film with a less formally prescribed and causal structure, formed from patterns of associations, where the relationship between images and themes was not so easily apparent, consequently, demanding a fundamentally different relationship between spectator and text.

In stark contrast to the presentation of time in classical narrative cinema, the time that flows through the frames of Tarkovsky's films and beyond is an

66. Valerie Mariani, *Michelangelo* (Naples, 1964), quoted in Roberto Salvini, *The Hidden Michelangelo* (Verona: Book Club Associates, 1978), 109. Tarkovsky suggested that "It is a mistake to talk about the artist 'looking for' his subject. In fact the subject grows within him like a fruit, and begins to demand expression. It is like childbirth" (43).

67. Tarkovsky, *Sculpting in Time*, 57.

68. Ibid., 20.

explorative and ambiguous understanding of cinematic temporality. By creating an environment of temporal unity through oneiric narratives and the use of particular stylistic devices, Tarkovsky's films distance themselves from traditional dramaturgy, revealing a time with the power to transform and disrupt, a time which expresses the very dynamism and perceptual flow of life.

This conceptualisation of time was revealed when Tarkovsky considered his notion of an ideal film. Despite being a practical impossibility, it is a cogent philosophical exercise:

> This is how I conceive an ideal piece of filming: the author takes millions of metres of film, on which he systematically, second by second, day by day and year by year, a man's life, for instance, from birth to death, is followed and recorded, and out of all that come two and a half thousand metres, or an hour and a half of screen time.[69]

Thus the original material would span the entire length of the individual's life, recording every moment of their existence, every event that happens to them, no matter how mundane or trivial. Then in the hands of the filmmaker, like a sculptor freeing his previously hidden subject from the confines of the marble, a film is created. Tarkovsky went on to pose the question of how different the resulting film of the same man's life would look in the hands of an Alexander Dovzhenko, an Ingmar Bergman or a Federico Fellini?[70] As we as modern audiences might ask the same of a Wong Kar-wai, an Apichatpong Weerasethakul or a Richard Linklater.[71] By harnessing the properties of time within and based on their own unique understanding of time and cinema, different directors would create an entirely unique film from the exact same source. Tarkovsky's assertion that the identity of the film-maker will always remain clear is indefatigably auteurist: "You will always recognise the editing of Bergman, Bresson, Kurosawa or Antonioni; none of them could ever be confused with anyone else, because each one's perception of time, as expressed in the rhythm of his films, is always the same."[72]

---

69. Ibid., 65.
70. Tarkovsky's ideal film recalls Pier Paolo Pasolini's comment, "Cinema is identical to life, because each one of us has a virtual and invisible camera which follows us from when we're born to when we die. In reality cinema is an infinite film sequence-shot. Each individual film interrupts and rearranges this infinite sequence-shot and thus creates meaning, which is what happens to us when we die. It is only at our moment of death that our life, to that point undecipherable, ambiguous, suspended, acquires a meaning. Montage thus plays the same role in cinema as death does in life." Pier Paolo Pasolini, "Ora tutto è chiaro, voluto, non imposto dal destino," *Cineforum* 68 (October 1967): 609. In Fabio Vighi, *Traumatic Encounters in Italian Film: Locating the Cinematic Unconscious* (Bristol: Intellect Books, 2006), 44-5.
71. Richard Linklater's ambitious *Boyhood* (2014) was filmed over a twelve year period between 2002 and 2014 and saw the lead characters played by the same actors age onscreen including the protagonist Mason Evans Jr (Ellar Coltrane) going from a six year old to an eighteen year old.
72. Tarkovsky, *Sculpting in Time*, 121.

For Tarkovsky, it is the realisation of film's relationship with time and the spectator that gives it the potential to be the art form *par excellence*:

> For the first time in the history of the arts, in the history of culture, man has found the means *to take an impression of time*. And simultaneously the possibility of reproducing that time onscreen as often as he wanted, to repeat it and go back to it. He acquired a matrix for *actual time*.[73]

Yet, despite the priority afforded to time in his films, Tarkovsky has a decidedly ambivalent relationship with it, alternating between the bitter sweetness of a Proustian "time regained" and a much more mournful, threnodic lament for a time irretrievably lost. Family friend, collaborator and film critic Olga Surkova believes that this aspect of his character ultimately brought about his downfall: "The time that is sculpted in his films holds traces of his difficult and often unsuccessful struggles with himself, his inability to cope with the corrosion that gradually ate away his soul, treacherously crawling over the screen."[74] Tarkovsky's films are full of onscreen alter egos, thinly veiled surrogates for the author, but they are never purely narcissistic and flattering self portraits, rather heavily critical and painfully revealing dissections of his own character.

For Tarkovsky, the essential act of watching film is the creation of a relationship with time as an experiential force; it is this relationship which is at the core of the cinematic experience:

> I think that what a person normally goes to the cinema for is *time*: for time lost or spent or not yet had. He goes there for a living experience; for cinema, like no other art, widens, enhances and concentrates a person's experience—and not only enhances it but makes it longer, significantly longer.[75]

This more challenging approach to time places Tarkovsky among a group of emerging voices in the arts, particularly in cinema, in the aftermath of the Second World War; these were film-makers, writers and theorists who progressively confronted the representation and perception of ideas by exploring the way time is depicted onscreen, including directors like Michelangelo Antonioni, Alain Resnais, Marguerite Duras, writers like Alain Robbe-Grillet and theorists like André Bazin, Béla Balázs and Gilles Deleuze.

However, in *Sculpting in Time* Tarkovsky points out that this particular way of depicting time was not restricted to his contemporaries, but could be seen as

73. Ibid., 62.
74. Olga Surkova, "Tarkovsky vs. Tarkovsky," trans. Kirill Galetski, para 8, (n.d.), <http://www.ucalgary.ca/~tstronds/nostalghia.com/TheTopics/Surkova1.html> (30th May 2008).
75. Tarkovsky, *Sculpting in Time*, 63.

early as the birth of the medium. The Lumière brothers' shorts like *L' arrivée d' un train en gare de La Ciotat* (1895) and *Repas de bébé* (1895) astonished their spectators not just because of their verisimilitude and their presentation of movement, but due to the fact that they captured the duration of time and its living essence, rendering it viewable for audiences to witness and experience for the very first time. Their images were not manipulated, they opened up a window on the world for viewers to feel the rhythm of time coursing through. In this sense he suggests that the Lumière shorts "were the first to contain the seed of a new aesthetic principle."[76] The fact that this "new aesthetic principle" was, for the most part, dissipated, even by the Lumières themselves, in favour of an aesthetic that privileged comparatively fast editing technologies, which came to characterise the evolving language of film and would later be known as montage, is inherently part of Tarkovsky's lament which will reach a peak with his ferocious attacks on the methodologies of one of the forefathers of montage, Sergei Eisenstein.[77] For Tarkovsky, and those of a similar opinion, it is only when directors self-consciously choose to express themselves through the display of time in film that they embrace the qualities which make film a unique art form, distinct from literature, painting and the theatre.

This dedication to an exploration of the properties of time can already be seen in Tarkovsky's early works, even his diploma film *The Steamroller and the Violin* (*Katok i skripka*, 1960) but it became much more evident as his career progressed.[78] Despite aspects of the construction of his first two films, *Ivan's Childhood* and *Andrei Rublyov* adhering to the aforementioned codes and conventions of classical narrative cinema, both seem dissatisfied with linearity and simplistic naturalistic reproduction, as content to wallow in memory, fantasy, dream or reverie as to anchor themselves in any permanent, objective state of reality or time. As his career continued, Tarkovsky's films became more and more introspective and experimental, progressively favouring a discursive and ambiguous recreation of atmosphere and emotion over rigidly defined plot progression.

Like Tarkovsky, Michelangelo too experimented with the properties of his medium as his career progressed. After the formal perfection of early pieces like *Pietà* (1499) and *David* (1504) his later sculptures appear to very deliberately emerge from the marble. Valerie Mariani describes works like *Captive – The So Called Atlas* (1519-36) as follows:

---

76. Ibid., 62.

77. Tarkovsky's assertion, of course, is problematic: these earliest films favour the presentation of time in a continuous flow, what would later be termed "a long take," out of expediency rather than purely artistic choice. Even if it had occurred to the Lumière brothers and those forefathers of film so early in the evolution of cinema, that their films could be comprised of sequences of shots, it was not technically possible.

78. In *The Steamroller and the Violin* many of Tarkovsky's thematic and stylistic motifs can be found in an embryonic fashion, from his obsession with time, the relationship between parents and children and the role of art in society.

> Michelangelo arrives at formal expressions that seem to share something of the nature of the original block from which the images take life; instead of eliminating the rough appearance of the stone block's form, he makes it part of the artistic experience, in moments of supreme lyric tension creating the figure at the very heart of the mass that thus becomes for the artist an integral part of the work.[79]

For Tarkovsky it is as if in the later films time itself becomes more and more the object on display, as powerfully present onscreen as the protagonists themselves. Many of the post-war theorists and film-makers considered time as not just a stylistic property, but a key element in the entire fabric of film. Bela Balázs commented on the significance of time and its organic properties when he wrote, "Time is just as much a theme for a work of art as is action, characterisation, or psychological analysis. The reason for this is that time belongs to all of them as an organic component."[80] Tarkovsky's films emerge from time, and it is time which becomes their defining essence. Many regard *Mirror*, a sensual and experimental film, as his finest work. For Tarkovsky *Mirror* is not only about time, it *is* time.

1.1 "Time Pressure" and *Mirror*

The image becomes authentically cinematic when (amongst other things) not only does it live within time, but time also lives within it, even with each separate frame. ~Andrei Tarkovsky

There is a moment when every true creator makes such a leap forward that his audience is left behind. For Renoir, *La Règle du jeu* was the sign of maturity, a film so new that it looks confusingly as if it might be a failure; one of those failures that leaves you, the morning after, counting your friends on the fingers of one hand. ~François Truffaut

For many Tarkovsky's *Mirror* was a failure: the authorities considered the film overly personal, obfuscatory and found that it moved too far away from the

79. Valerie Mariani, *Michelangelo* (Naples, 1964), quoted in Roberto Salvini, *The Hidden Michelangelo*. (Verona: Book Club Associates, 1978), 109.
80. Béla Balázs, *Theory of the Film (Character and Growth of a New Art)*, 121. He also continued, "A stone on the hillside and Michelangelo's sculptures are both stone. As stones their material is more or less the same. It is not the substance but the form that constitutes the difference between them" (161).

prescribed conventions of Soviet Socialist Realism. Vladimir Naumov's words are indicative of most of the criticisms: "Many, including the most sophisticated viewers, could not make out what was happening onscreen."[81] Contemporary critics often still write that it is "almost unfathomable on a first viewing."[82] However, few are able to disagree with its originality and ambition: James Clarity wrote in 1974, "Nothing quite like *Mirror* has ever been made by a Soviet director before."[83] Even now there are few films to which it can be comfortably compared.[84]

Mirror occupies a privileged place in Tarkovsky's body of work, being central both chronologically and stylistically; the fourth of seven completed films, it marks a turning point in his career and a distinct evolution in his cinematic aesthetic. Many believe it to be the defining work of his canon; Turovskaya states that, "*Mirror* marked the fullest expression of Tarkovsky's personality as a director."[85] The film is a pronounced departure from conventional narrative film making and even from Tarkovsky's previous films, presenting Tarkovskian time at its most vividly realized. Despite his reluctance to use the word, it is more experimental in form: its achronological structure moves between dream, reality and recreated reality, relying on an artistic stream of consciousness, associative linking and a de-emphasis of conventional relationships between time and space.

It is Tarkovsky's sometimes abstruse concept of "time pressure," as detailed in *Sculpting in Time*, which embodies his presentation of temporality in the cinema. Tarkovsky recounted how each shot has time flowing through it, as if it were in possession of an authentic pulse, an internal and sensory rhythm, which can not only be seen, but more accurately felt or experienced. This "time pressure" largely dislocates itself from conventional techniques of editing, creating an aesthetic that replicates a tempo and cadence in film, combining shots together based on their inherent capacity for recording time's ebb and flow, what might be described as its living essence, not on rational development of plot or conventional demands of dramaturgy. Indeed, Tarkovsky often returned to organic metaphors, a practice he shared with Bazin, Deleuze and Balázs. While discussing film-making, he stated, "Just as from the quivering of a reed you can tell what sort of current, what pressure there is in a river, in the same way we know the movement of time from the

81. Herbert J. Marshall, "Andrei Tarkovsky's *The Mirror*," 95.

82. G. C. Macnab, "Andrei Tarkovsky," in *International Dictionary of Films and Filmmakers: Directors Vol. 2*, eds. Tom Pendergast and Sara Pendergast (Farmington Hills, MI: St James Press, 2000), 980.

83. James F. Clarity, *New York Times*, April 13th 1975, in *New York Times Film Reviews 1975-1976* (New York: The New York Times & Arno Press, 1977), 30.

84. The usual films which are compared to *Mirror* are *Wild Strawberries* (Bergman, 1957), *Amarcord* (Fellini, 1974). To this I might add *Tarnation* (Caouette, 2003), *Kasaba* (Ceylan, 1997), Zvyagintzev's *The Return* (*Vozvrashcheniye*, 2003), Sokurov's *Mother and Son* (*Mat i syn*, 1997), the Bill Douglas trilogy of *My Childhood* (1972), *My ain Folk* (1973), and *My Way Home* (1978).

85. Turovskaya, *The Films of Andrei Tarkovsky*, 61.

flow of the life-process reproduced in the shot."[86] This "time pressure" and how it is articulated become one of the dominant aspects of his film theory. Tarkovsky himself registered that "time pressure" was the "idea that allowed me to develop a principle, with points of reference that would hold my fantasy in check as I searched for form, for ways of handling images."[87]

While "time pressure" seems a somewhat abstract and intangible quality, in more practical terms it is able to generate a rhythm through careful consideration of cinematic properties like imagery, pictorial composition, textures, objects, length of shot, camera movement, performance, music and sound, all of which become integral factors in the creation of a sense of flow or "life-process." This unconventional approach to temporality is undoubtedly difficult for some viewers to process and engage with; for spectators raised on the Euclidian nature of the cinematic narrative who have had traditional representations of cause and effect inculcated into their relationship with film, it can be both distracting and confusing.

However, "time pressure" is only partly revealed in the presence of life recorded by the camera; just as, if not more, important is the affectual force created in its interaction with the viewer. It is in this way that Tarkovsky's films are able to move "beyond the frame":

> Just as life, constantly moving and changing, allows everyone to interpret and feel each separate moment in his own way, so too a real picture, faithfully recording on film the time which flows beyond the edges of the frame, lives within time if time lives within it; this two way process is a determining factor of cinema.[88]

This two way process is central to Tarkovsky's film theory and films. As I will show, the time that can be felt coursing through the screen and beyond only comes alive in its relationship with the spectator; without the spectator the film has no value, it is quite literally lifeless.

Prior to beginning *Mirror* Tarkovsky recorded his emotions after the completion of *Solaris,* a film he was profoundly disappointed by: "something has been happening to me recently… I have started to feel that the time has come when I am ready to make the most important film of my life."[89] In *Sculpting in Time* he continued this line of thought, describing how his next film was to be a significant departure from those that preceded it:

> As I began working on *Mirror* I found myself reflecting more and more that if you are serious about your work, then a film is not merely the next

86. Tarkovsky, *Sculpting in Time*, 120.
87. Ibid., 94.
88. Ibid., 118.
89. Natasha Synessios, *Mirror: The Film Companion* (London: I. B. Tauris, 2001), 3.

> item in your career, it is an action which will affect the whole of your life. For I had made up my mind that in this film, for the first time, I would use the means of cinema to talk of all that was most precious to me, and to do so directly, without playing any kind of tricks.[90]

What was "most precious" to Tarkovsky was inspired by a series of dreams that had recurred since his childhood. Based in part on these dreams and his childhood experiences, the resulting film proved to be a philosophical meditation on life and time through an achronological memoir of a dying man's thoughts and memories. Like a sensory tapestry of events and moments from a person's life, in many ways it resembles Tarkovsky's vision of what an ideal film should look like. *Mirror* is constructed from fragments of time, with no formal narrative in the traditional sense: it has little conventional character development or plot. Like the thought process *Mirror* drifts from moment to moment, image to image, it hesitates, reflects and contemplates.

It is the thoughts of the protagonist, Alexei, a clearly recognisable portrait of Tarkovsky himself, around which the film is loosely structured. Set primarily during three time periods—Alexei's childhood during a pre-Second World War idyll, his teenage years during the conflict, and his contemporary adult life with an estranged wife and recalcitrant teenage son—it is ostensibly an autobiographical recreation of Tarkovsky's childhood and a depiction of his familial relationships. However in realisation it is something much more: an experiential and sensory film of kinaesthetic intensity and cinematic affect. When Olivier Assayas stated in the quotation that opened this book, that *Mirror*, for many, is "something that goes beyond cinema," he meant that for viewers who are able to engage with the film in the way Tarkovsky intended, it is not designed to be read or analysed from a detached, objective manner, but felt and experienced, even lived. Watching *Mirror* is something akin to a cinematic Rorschach inkblot test: while the images and situations presented in the film are far from abstract, they have an enigmatic quality, which is richly suggestive. Through a variety of cinematic devices and stimuli Tarkovsky creates an open character to the images and themes, promoting a multi-sensory engagement between the spectator and the film.

Critics of Art cinema have long decried what we might term its apophenic quality, yet for Tarkovsky this is one of the key aspects which makes the cinematic medium unique. Tarkovsky's lingering close ups of faces and natural objects contribute little formal narrative or thematic development but provide the film with powerful, poetic and ambiguous aesthetic images. Dirk Leonard and Peter Brugger suggest that, "The propensity to see connections between seemingly unrelated objects or ideas most closely links psychosis to creativity ...

90. Tarkovsky, *Sculpting in Time*, 133.

apophenia and creativity may even be seen as two sides of the same coin."[91] This creativity is a central component of Tarkovsky's poetic aesthetic, the creativity involved when one experiences a film in a highly individual and personal fashion.[92] Jay Leyda goes on to suggest, in a somewhat pejorative manner, that this apophenic aspect is central to how *Mirror*, and by extension all of Tarkovsky's oeuvre, is constructed. According to Leyda, "each flattered spectator could take away his interpretation as the only possible one."[93]

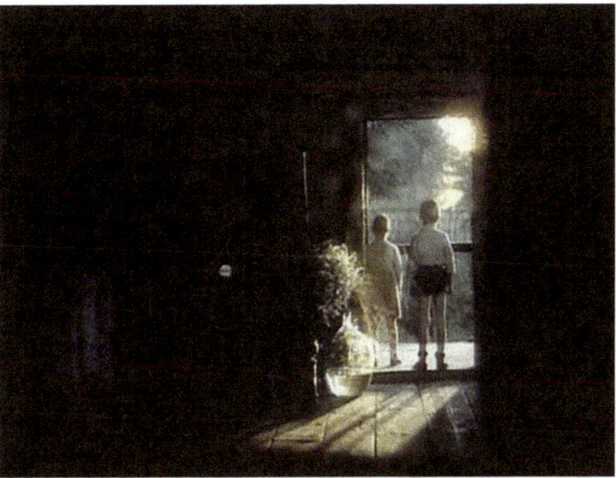

Figure 4 Time is the cornerstone of Tarkovsky's oeuvre from both aesthetic and thematic perspectives. Here it's presence is palpable in a scene from perhaps his defining film, *Mirror*.

---

91. Dirk Leonard and Peter Brugger, "Creative, Paranormal, and Delusional Thought: A Consequence of Right Hemisphere Semantic Activation?," *Neuropsychiatry, Neuropsychology, and Behavioral Neurology* 11.4 (1998): 177-183. Quoted in Robert Todd Carroll, *The Skeptic's Dictionary: A Collection of Strange Beliefs, Amusing Deceptions, and Dangerous Delusions* (London: John Wiley and Sons, 2003), 28. Brugger also suggested that the writer August Strindberg's diaries reveal him as one such creative apophenic, "He sees sticks on the bottom of a chest and is sure they form a pentagram. He sees tiny hands in prayer when he looks at a walnut under a microscope." Peter Brugger, "From Haunted Brain to Haunted Science: A Cognitive Neuroscience View of Paranormal and Pseudoscientific Thought," in *Hauntings and Poltergeists*, eds. James Houran and Rense Lange (North Carolina: McFarland & Company, Inc., 2001), 195-213. The term apophenia was first used by Klaus Conrad in 1958.

92. Regarding film as a potent apophenic object might not be as illogical as it first appears given that the whole cinematic experience is based on the imperfection of our senses and the illusion of seeing movement that isn't actually there, the phi phenomenon. The films *Blow-Up* (Antonioni, 1966) and *Pi* (Aronofsky, 1998) are both cinematic explorations of apophenia. *Blow-Up* concerns itself with a series of photographs which may or may not reveal a murder being committed and *Pi* is about the titular series of numbers which may hold the key to human existence and the true identity of God.

93. Jay Leyda, *Kino: A History of Russian and Soviet Cinema* (Princeton: Princeton University Press, 1983), 403.

There can be no doubt that this quality is both the root of many problems viewers have with Tarkovsky, and what makes his films so resonant for others. At times *Mirror* seems deliberately abstruse, moving backwards and forwards between temporalities without context or signification, using the same actors to play more than one role without making explicit the differences between the two. Fact and fiction are combined in an erotetic dramaturgical style that intersperses documentary footage with recreated autobiographical episodes; some feature actors performing roles, others feature "real" people. The ambitious visual structure, comprised of deceptively simple yet elaborately constructed sequences, is consolidated by a vibrant sound design, including a threnodic score composed by Tarkovsky's regular composer Eduard Artemyev (who had worked with him on *Solaris*) and an intensely multilayered use of sound effects. It might be argued that chronologically the film is reminiscent of a Möbius strip, in that it presents a sense of time with no beginning, middle or end but an endless flow. The film sends temporal echoes that are somehow able to be felt in different time zones. The result is a film, which takes place over the span of forty years, but is not much longer than an hour and a half. It is a site of extended ambiguity and contradiction compared to classical narrative cinema and even many examples of Art Cinema from the same period.[94]

The dreams that inspired Tarkovsky to create *Mirror* were primarily of his close relationship with his mother, the prolonged absence of his father and his early experiences at his grandparents' dacha where he spent many of his formative years, one of many Russian children evacuated from the largest cities during the Second World War. Of these dreams he recalled:

> I only know that I kept dreaming the same dream about the house where I was born. I dreamed… as if I was walking into it, or rather, not into it but around it all the time. These dreams were terribly real, although I knew even then that I was only dreaming.[95]

Indeed, Tarkovsky's description of what he here implies are lucid dreams can be regarded as a striking metaphor for his oneiric texts. In a Tarkovsky film the spectator frequently feels they are witnessing, or rather experiencing, a dream, which somehow remains harmonious despite its readily apparent incongruities.[96] Freud's description of lucid dreamers evokes the Tarkovsky protagonist and the Tarkovsky film experience. Freud suggested, that there are

---

94. On the subject of time in the cinema, Boris Eikhenbaum suggested that there were three particular types: "Actual Time" (that of perceiving the subject), "Fictional Time" (story in narrative), and "Narrative Time" (Differing temporal weight, tempo, pacing and rhythm etc.) See "Problems of Cinema Stylistics," ed. Herbert Eagle, *Russian Formalist Film Theory*, 55-80.

95. Quoted in Synessios, *Mirror,* 11.

96. Films like *Waking Life* (Linklater, 2001), *Science of Sleep* (Gondry, 2007) and the Spanish film *Abre Los Ochos* (Amenabar, 1997) have directly explored the lucid dream experience.

those who "possess the faculty of consciously directing their dreams. If, for instance, a dreamer of this kind is dissatisfied with the turn taken by the dream, he can break it off without waking up and start it again in another direction – just as a popular dramatist may under pressure give his play a happier ending."[97] Yet Tarkovsky departs from Freud's interpretation, in the sense that his characters rarely appear to have control of the world or dream in which they inhabit; in fact, this lack of narrative control, dynamic protagonists or urgency is a key aspect of his oeuvre. Tarkovsky's characters themselves are sometimes even unsure of their status in the world; they question their own sanity, whether they are dreaming or awake. Such lucid dreams are notable for their effervescent nature; they transgress physical "reality" and often the laws of physics, despite remaining overwhelmingly real to their dreamers.

The dreams stayed with Tarkovsky; he first explored them in a short story and then years later adapted them into a screenplay, which he originally called *Confession.* Somewhat ironically, this unused title anticipated two significant problems that Tarkovsky had throughout his career: the impact of his religious beliefs on his work and accusations of being too personal a film-maker in an environment where ideological values were always placed before individual artistic expression. The title and the material continued to change on numerous occasions, from *The Raging Stream* to *A Bright, Bright Day*, taken from one of his father's poems, a title with powerful connections to childhood and an ode to the vibrant properties of memory. It would have been an apt one for Tarkovsky's meta-recreation of his childhood:

> A stone lies by the jasmine.
> Under the stone, a treasure.
> Father stands on the road.
> A bright, bright day.[98]

The title was finally confirmed as *Zerkalo* in Russian or *Mirror*; the etymological roots of the word are extraordinarily apposite for such a text in both Russian and English, so fitting in fact, that in hindsight it would seem inappropriate to call the film anything else. The mirror, as both an object and a word, has a rich source of lexical, psychological and artistic associations: from William Shakespeare to Jacques Lacan, Lewis Carroll to Jorge Luis Borges, all use the fecundity of the mirror as metaphor for revealing essential truths about identity and perception. *Mirror* draws on its title both explicitly and implicitly throughout. Reviewers have tended to return to the name of the film as an appropriate metaphor for the text itself. Michael Dempsey comments that "*Mirror* is an extremely puzzling film. The looking glass that it offers us is not

97. Sigmund Freud, *The Standard Edition of the Complete Psychological Works of Sigmund Freud* (London: Hogarth Press, 1953), 571-72.
98. Arseny Tarkovsky, "The Bright Day," in Synnessios, *Mirror: The Film Companion,* 12.

just cracked but shattered, and we are seeing the jagged, jumbled reflections of its scattered shards."[99]

Dempsey's review evokes the perhaps apocryphal story, which Tarkovsky must have been aware of, by the Russian poet Alexander Blok, author of *The Twelve* (1918). When Blok returned to his ancestral mansion after the October Revolution, he found it in ruins. Amongst the devastation, the only recognisable things were the shards of an ornate family mirror, all that was left of generations of his family estate. He decided to take it with him as a suitably poetic memento, but on the road he was repeatedly stopped by victorious Bolshevik soldiers wishing to use his mirror to shave. Unimpressed by the soot blackened mirror, finding themselves unable to see their courageous visages clearly, one by one they sent him on his way.[100]

Blok's awareness of the powers of the mirror to debate concepts of subjectivity and identity is also key to Sabine Mechior-Bonnet's *The Mirror: A History*. In her analysis of the cultural role mirrors have played in history, she asserts, "To see oneself in the mirror, to identify oneself, requires a mental operation by which the subject is capable of objectivising himself, of separating what is outside from the inside."[101] Tarkovsky's films become one such mental operation, a dialogue between past and present, internal and external, individual and cultural.[102]

The opening sequence of the narrative of *Mirror* is a haunting and beguiling poetic image of almost transcendental natural beauty.[103] It is given no temporal or spatial context, we are not informed when, where or who the characters and the location are, although we will later infer that this is the dacha where Tarkovsky spent much of his youth. A more conventional film would situate itself in the present and then move into its protagonist's past with flashbacks, but there is no such exposition from Tarkovsky.[104] The moment is not even

---

99. Michael Dempsey, "Lost Harmony: Tarkovsky's *The Stalker* and *The Mirror*," *Film Quarterly* 35.1 (Autumn 1981): 14.

100. See Brian Moynahan, *The Russian Century: A History of the Last Hundred Years* (London: Random House, 1994), xii. In *Sculpting in Time* Tarkovsky reveals his admiration for Blok, a poet who he says was able to create "harmony out of chaos" (36).

101. Sabine Mechior-Bonnet, *The Mirror: A History*, trans. Katherine Jewett (London: Routledge, 2002), 5.

102. One of the greatest influences on Tarkovsky's films was his father, Arseny Tarkovsky. Arseny's poetry is abound with references to mirrors. Perhaps the most relevant poem as to how Tarkovsky's films move "beyond the frame" is "First Meetings," "Heady as vertigo you ran downstairs/Two steps at a time, and led me/Through damp lilac, into your domain/On the other side, beyond the mirror." Arseny Tarkovsky "First Meetings" in Andrei Tarkovsky, *Sculpting in Time: Reflections on the Cinema,* 101. The connections between the two are analysed by Natasha Synessios in her *Mirror: The Film Companion.*

103. This sequence follows a short documentary-style episode which will be analysed in greater depth in Chapter 2.3.

104. Alexei Germanov's *My Friend Lapshin* (*Moi drug Ivan Lapshin*, 1984) and Bondarchuk's *Fate of a Man* (1959) both begin with their protagonists in the present, flashbacks then move the action to before the Second World War began.

the film's "actual" present and the character is not the protagonist in any traditional sense of the word.

After the credits the image slowly fades into a woman sitting alone on the handmade fence of a dacha. Her head is facing away from the camera, off towards the horizon, but her body is turned towards the spectator. She is smoking a cigarette and simply sits. As the camera unhurriedly tracks behind her shoulder it moves away to the right, leaving her outside of the frame, directing our gaze towards the empty horizon. The shot continues for more than forty seconds, but in the slowness of the camera movements and the lack of an overt narrative function, the images take on a more meditative, dream-like quality, and, as a result, they seem to last much longer.

The audience remains unaware of what the young woman, who is perhaps in her late twenties or early thirties, is waiting for, and indeed we never truly know. The expression on her face is hard to read, but the implication is, like many young women of the period, she is waiting for her husband to return, perhaps, as we are on the eve of Stalin's Great Purge, from the gulag, where family members, friends or colleagues sometimes disappeared, never to be heard of again. In *Sculpting in Time* Tarkovsky revealed his technique for directing actors, which was never to tell them what was going to happen in the rest of the film:

> The story was kept secret from her [Margarita Terekhova] so that she would not react to it at some unconscious level of her mind, but would live through that moment exactly as my mother, her prototype, had once lived through it, with no foreknowledge of how her life would turn out.[105]

Tarkovsky, as he would frequently strive to do, sought to recreate not just how the moment looked from an external perspective, but also how it felt. The length of the shot allows time to flow deliberately through the image, pregnant with expectation. Indeed, as the fence swells beneath the woman's weight, there is even the possibility that she might be expecting a child; could this be what she is thinking of? Cuts to sleeping children, a boy and a girl, reveal her to be a mother and add to the dream-like nature of the images. She is a young woman in the prime of her beauty and sexuality, but she is alone. Off screen there is the sound of a train, but there is no train to be seen; the aural image in Tarkovsky's films frequently further intensifies the layers of ambiguity in a sequence. The sound that is disengaged from reality is unpredictable, forcing the viewer to engage with both the aural and visual image on not just an intellectual, but an intuitional level.

---

105. Tarkovsky, *Sculpting in Time*, 140-1. Tarkovsky continued, stating rather dictatorially, that actors are not allowed to ask "Why? What for? What is the key to the image? What is the underlying idea?" (145) This matter caused problems with several of Tarkovsky's classically trained actors, especially Donatas Banionis who played Kris Kelvin in *Solaris*.

A man emerges from the distance, at first just a speck on the horizon, the camera makes no move to reveal or recognise him. Perhaps it is the man that she is waiting for? Yet she remains impassive, as he makes his way slowly towards her. The voice over, from a poem written by Tarkovsky's father, Arseny, contradicts the image, "If he turned from the bush towards our house then it's father. If not, it meant that it was not father and that father would never come." The figure does indeed turn towards the house, but it is not the father, rather a doctor from a neighbouring village.[106]

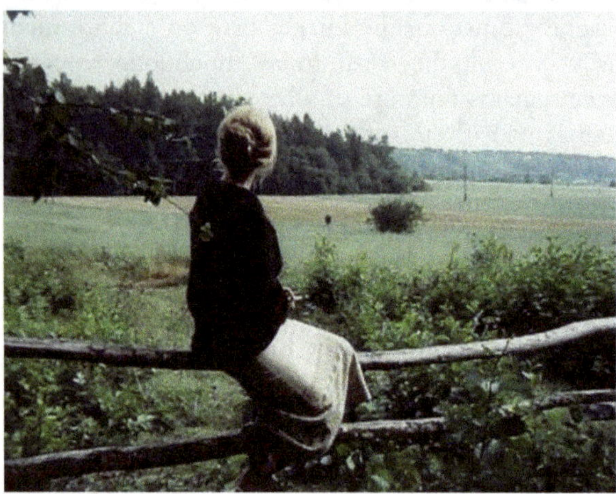

Figure 5 One of the most often reproduced images from Tarkovsky's *Mirror* sees the young mother wait on the fence as the spectator is forced to wait with her.

Another shot lasts one minute and twenty-eight seconds; by not cutting Tarkovsky allows the "time pressure" to be felt as it passes slowly in front of our eyes. What is insignificant becomes significant; the wind blows through the fields in an almost supernatural fashion; perhaps, in another film we would not have noticed this, yet here there is a weight and a sensuous texture to the images.

When the man finally introduces himself, he asks the young woman for directions. By his body language it is clear that he desires her. Despite her protestations he reaches for her wrist and takes her pulse, assuring her not to worry about impropriety, "Give me your hand, I'm a doctor." As they touch the audience can almost feel the reverberations of their bodily contact, the touch of their flesh is almost too sensual for the doctor and he seems profoundly moved by it. He sits next to her on the homemade fence, and it suddenly breaks under their combined weight. Lying on the floor he laughs, exclaiming, "What a pleasure it is to fall with a pretty woman," with both the

106. Tarkovsky may have been influenced by a haiku he quoted in *Sculpting in Time*. 'No, not to my house/ That one, pattering umbrella/ Went to my neighbour" (112).

sexual and the spiritual associations of the phrase "to fall" lingering long after the words have been spoken. On the ground he sees the world from a strange angle, "You know I fell down and found strange things here – roots, bushes. Has it ever occurred to you that plants can feel, know, even comprehend...Like us who are rushing, fussing, uttering banalities? That's because we don't trust nature that is inside us."

Tarkovsky's films frequently look at the normal, everyday world from an unfamiliar perspective, in essence to defamiliarise that which has become too familiar to us. Much of the poetic construction of "time pressure," in this respect, connects Tarkovsky to the Russian Formalists of the 1920s, who had such a significant impact on film theory. In *Sculpting in Time* we find evidence, which suggests knowledge of the writings of Viktor Shklovsky, Yury Tynyanov and Boris Eikhenbaum et al. He appears to draw on many formalist ideas, while creating his own film poetics. In the broadly taxonomic approach of the Russian Formalists, titles such as V. B. Kazanski's "cinematology," Piotrovsky's "Cinepoetics" and Boris Eikhenbaum's "Cine-stylistics," all now appear to be terms which have a distinctly Tarkovskian air to them.

Victor Skhlovsky argued that the primary function of art *was* to enable us to view previously routine and stable objects from different perspectives. He wrote:

> In order to return sensation to our limbs, to make the stone feel stony, man has been given the tool of art. The purpose of art, then, is to lead us to a knowledge of a thing through the organ of sight instead of recognition. By "enstranging" and complicating form, the device of art makes perception long and "laborious."[107]

"Long and laborious" is how some critics have categorised Tarkovsky's work, but it can be persuasively argued that this was his way of revealing the stoniness of the stone.[108]

The conclusions Tarkovsky draws about the affectual power of the cinema appear on occasion quite deliberately Formalist, as he frequently appears more concerned with the affectual properties of the text, rather than its representational qualities. Viktor Shklovsky's concepts of *ostranenie*, which has been broadly translated and defined as defamiliarisation, and *zatrudnenie*, i.e. making difficult, find their corollaries in Tarkovsky's theory and in his practice. Tarkovsky challenged the conventions of classical cinema language in order to provoke a different relationship between text and spectator. His aesthetics decry the cinema as a passive experience, where films are consumed "like

107. Viktor Shklovsky, *Theory of Prose*, [from second edition, 1929] trans. Benjamin Sher (Elmwood Park Illinois: Dalkey Archive Press, 1990), 6. He continued, "Art is a way of experiencing the artfulness of an object; the object itself is not important" (12).

108. Richard Rond, *Nostalghia* in *The Guardian*, 19th May 1983 called *Nostalghia* "excruciatingly pretentious and unremittingly boring" (11).

bottles of coca-cola,"[109] just as many of the Russian Formalists did before him. Piotrovski identified the conventions of mainstream film in a similar fashion, "the cinema needs.... transparent motivation which can be quickly grasped; these requirements often result in an easily predictable intrigue. It is also necessary to mark the turning points in the story in a precise and very noticeable manner."[110]

Standing at a stark contrast to this, Tarkovsky offers a medium which distinguishes itself from the static arts, in that it is able to instigate a dialogical relationship with the viewer. Far from being a passive reflector of life, it is a transformative device like no other. The film which embraces the uniqueness of the medium, will be a dialogue with the spectator. Yet as we will see time and time again, links between Tarkovsky and other film theorists become problematic due to his idiosyncratic and distinctly personal approach to the medium. Despite the significant consideration of how far aesthetic choices impact on spectators, Tarkovsky's ties, both figurative and literal, to representational approaches prove too strong to label him a Formalist without qualification. Such a scientific approach to art may have been too functional and rational for Tarkovsky's liking. Where the Formalists tried to isolate art, Tarkovsky embraced form and context, culture and heritage to bring together all these aspects in harmony. The echoes of his father's work and the works of Dostoyevsky and Tolstoy which permeate his texts are simply too resonant.

The events in *Mirror*, as in all Tarkovsky's films, are far from the defining moments of a person's life as one might expect from a more conventional film, they are much more inconsequential, yet they seem key to the fabric of an individual's existence. This small incident, the meeting between the mother and the doctor, is of no real significance to either of their lives, perhaps as easily forgotten as remembered, a meaningless interchange between two strangers, who will, in all likelihood, never meet again. The moment they and we are experiencing is a fragment of time, paradoxically both like any other, but unique, a moment that will remain eternal in its past.[111] However, it has been

---

109. Tarkovsky, *Sculpting in Time*, 179.

110. See Herbert Eagle, *Russian Formalist Film Theory*, 23.

111. This moment has always reminded me of Bernstein's (Everett Sloane) monologue from *Citizen Kane* (Welles, 1941). Welles's expansive paean to the life of Charles Foster Kane is reminiscent of one of Tarkovsky's ideal films, where the fragments of a person's life are selected by the director. In Welles's hands Kane emerges as an enigma whose personality is revealed only through the conflicting anecdotes of his friends, colleagues and enemies. Bernstein reveals one such fragment of time, an insignificant moment that has stayed with him through the years: "A fellow will remember things you wouldn't think he'd remember. You take me. One day back in 1896, I was crossing over to Jersey on the ferry, and as we pulled out, there was another ferry pulling in, and on it was a girl waiting to get off. A white dress she had on. She was carrying a white parasol. I only saw her for one second. She didn't see me at all, but I'll bet a month hasn't gone by since that I haven't thought of that girl." *Citizen Kane* and *Mirror* were later linked by Kieślowski, when he wrote that only a few times in the history of the cinematic medium has a director moved "beyond the literal, into true art," he stated, "Welles achieved that miracle once [in *Citizen Kane*]. Only one director in the world has managed to achieve that miracle in the last

captured in memory and replicated through the medium of film by Tarkovsky in "imprinted time." But whose memory? *Mirror* continuously problematizes notions of subjectivity. The film, while it takes itself generally from the perspective of Alexei and presents his memories, is not exclusively from his point of view. In this opening sequence he is just a small sleeping boy, who could not possibly recall or understand these events in their entirety. Later, in the film's present, a phone conversation between the adult Alexei and his mother will trigger a memory of an episode set at his mother's workplace, the printing press, where he is not present at all. Are these events Tarkovsky's memories from his childhood, fictional events or are they memories of a dream?

As *Mirror* continues, it moves backwards and forwards through time and space with little visual or narrative coding for the viewer. Tarkovsky's expressive and unconventional visualization of space and time is a provocative one, reminiscent of another pre-eminent narrative theorist, Mikhail Bakhtin. Bakhtin's work explored the representation of the interrelations between time and space in literature through his concept of the "chronotope," which Bakhtin himself defined as "the intrinsic connectedness of temporal and spatial relationships that are artistically expressed in literature."[112] The chronotope is an embodiment of how time and space are materialised in art, which, for Bakhtin is a crucial factor in experiencing narratives. A pattern of closed chronotopes would lead to a limitation of narrative possibilities and adherence to convention (as in mainstream cinema) but a more open chronologic pattern would lead to an opening of opportunities, an increased sense of ambiguity and potential. The opening sequence of *Mirror*, with its lack of temporal or narrative context, extended takes, stillness of image, lack of exposition and no emphatic characterisation identifies it as one such open text.

It is no coincidence that a great deal of Bakhtin's work focuses on Dostoyevsky, who is, in turn, one of the greatest influences on Tarkovsky's approach to art. Much of Tarkovsky's work has self-conscious echoes of Dostoyevsky, whom he regarded as one of the foremost voices in Russian literature. Many of Tarkovsky's long cherished projects, which remained unfilmed, were based on Dostoyevsky's novels, especially *The Idiot* (1869) and *Crime and Punishment* (1866).[113] Tarkovsky also wished to make a film of Dostoyevsky's eventful life and went as far as to say that "*Dostoyevsky* [the proposed film of Dostoyevsky's life] could become the whole point of what I want to do in cinema."[114] One of the many qualities Bakhtin admired about

---

few years and that's Tarkovsky." Quoted in *Kieślowski on Kieślowski*, ed. Danusia Stok (London: Faber and Faber, 1995), 195.

112. Mikhail Bakhtin, *The Dialogic Imagination: Four Essays,* [1930s] ed. Michael Holquist, trans. Caryl Emerson and Michael Holquist (Austin and London: University of Texas Press, 1981), 84.

113. Two notable versions of Dostoyevsky's *The Idiot* were filmed in the 1950s, one by Ivan Pyrev in 1958 and also by Tarkovsky's friend Akira Kurosawa in 1951.

114. Tarkovsky, *Time Within Time, The Diaries 1970-1986,* 3.

Dostoyevsky's work, a feature which can also be found in Tarkovsky's films, was its "unfinished quality," its dialogical nature in the sense that it can only be completed in the act of reading and creating a relationship with the reader.

Tarkovsky's chronotopic signature then, is a dream-like and fluid narrative, disconnected from conventional representations of time and space, freed from rigidity and the confines of temporal "coherence." By using actors in multiple roles, time and space collapses even further in on itself: the mother, Maria, who is a portrait of Tarkovsky's own mother, is played by the actress Margarita Terekhova in the "past" sequences, then, in the film's "present" the role of the mother is played by Maria Tarkovskyaya (Tarkovsky's real mother) and Terekhova plays the protagonist Alexei's wife, Natalya. The use of dual roles is not entirely uncommon in film, though in the mainstream it is tended to be used for comic effect: *Kind Hearts and Coronets* (Hamer, 1949), *The Great Dictator* (Chaplin, 1939). In more "serious" films the implications are more philosophical or psychological; in Angelopoulos's *Ulysses' Gaze* (1996) the actress Mai Morgenstern plays three separate women in Harvey Keitel's life, in *Fahrenheit 451* (Truffaut, 1966) Julie Christie plays the role of the wife of Guy Montag *and* his love interest. Some films use dual roles for both comedic and philosophical purposes as in *Dr. Strangelove or: How I learned to Stop Worrying and Love the Bomb* (Kubrick, 1964) and *Adaptation* (Jonze, 2002).[115]

The cumulative effect of these strategies in *Mirror* is the implication that time cannot be satisfactorily considered purely chronological. Events echo over time and space within the film, and in Tarkovsky's entire oeuvre. In a sequence in the present of *Mirror* Alexei's wife Natalya drops her purse on the floor, and Ignat helps her pick it up, remarking, "I felt an electric shock, as if it had happened before." In fact, it has happened before: in the past the two actors, this time playing Alexei and the mother, interact in a sequence which is almost exactly the same. Temporal echoes like these permeate the films like ripples in a pond: from the use of a poster from his previous film *Andrei Rublyov* hanging on a wall, to lines of dialogue and images from previous films being repeated almost exactly, and to the casting of many of the actors from his previous films in roles which act as a meta-commentary on the films themselves.[116]

115. In *Mirror* the roles of Alexei as a child and his son Ignat are played by the same actor Ignat Daniltsev. A recent development has been to effectively reverse this doubling process by having different actors play the same role with equally interesting implications for the nature of identity; *Palindromes* (Solondz, 2004) saw multiple performers playing the same teenage girl and *I'm Not There* (Haynes, 2007) saw several actors playing Bob Dylan. They may have been inspired by *That Obscure Object of Desire* (Buñuel, 1977) where Carole Bouquet and Angela Molina play two sides of Conchita's personality.

116. The role of the doctor who appears in the opening sequence of the film is played by Anatoly Solonitsyn, the actor who played Andrei Rublyov in Tarkovsky's previous film and appeared in every one of Tarkovsky's films until his death in 1982. Each of Tarkovsky's films refer to those that have come before it and even those which will follow. *Mirror* replays the obsession with the mother that is dramatised in *Solaris* and *Ivan's Childhood* and when Alexei says "I think it's good to keep silent for a while. Words can't express everything a person feels," he

One could ponder the Freudian associations of having the wife and the mother played by the same actress, especially as the film is largely about a son's close relationship with his mother.[117] Tarkovsky himself seems aware of this: the adult Alexei remarks, with para-textual irony, "Whenever I recall my mother in the past she looks like you." The point being, superficially, that she is played by the same actress, but beneath lies a more compelling observation, about the nature of memory and its ability to colour events through perception, a perpetual theme of Tarkovsky's. This interchanging of personalities enhances the already fluid sense of time presented in the film and further connects Tarkovsky to Bakhtin. Bakhtin's suggestion that "idyllic life and its events are inseparable from this concrete, spatial corner of the world where the fathers and grandfathers lived and where one's children will live"[118] is paralleled in a poem recited in *Mirror* written by Tarkovsky's father, Arseny Tarkovsky, appropriately called *Life, Life,*

> If you live in a house – the house will not fall.
> I'll summon any of the centuries,
> Then enter one and build a house in it.
> That's why your children and your wives
> Sit with me at one table, –
> The same for ancestor and grandson.[119]

Both Bakhtin and Tarkovsky, father and son, reject the presentation of linear time based on logic and rationality. Such interpretations are reductive and do not appreciate the whole organic nature of experience and memory. The dacha in *Mirror* becomes the very house that Arseny Tarkovsky wrote about, one which defies the traditional conceptions of time and space. In *Mirror*, as in all Tarkovsky's films, the past is as important as the present, and one is not privileged over the other. Just as T.S. Eliot asserted that "the past should be altered by the present as much as the present is altered by the past."[120] Tarkovsky himself asks,

> But what exactly is this 'past?' Is it what has passed? And what does 'passed' mean for a person when for each of us the past is the bearer of all

---

not only refers to Andrei Rublyov's vow of silence but also anticipates the vow of silence to come in *The Sacrifice*. As well as this he provides a commentary on one of the film's most palpable themes and Tarkovsky's own film theory.

117. For an intriguing Freudian interpretation of dreams in films see Charles Rycroft, *The Innocence of Dreams* (London: Hogarth Press, 1979). Slavoj Žižek makes some interesting connections between Freud and Tarkovsky in "The Thing from Inner Space," *Sexuation*, ed. Renata Salecl (Durham, NC, and London: 2000), 216-59.

118. Mikhail Bakhtin, *The Dialogic Imagination, Four Essays by M. M. Bakhtin,* 225.

119. Arseny Tarkovsky, "Life, Life," in Tarkovsky, *Sculpting in Time,* 143.

120. T.S Eliot, *The Sacred Wood: Essays on Poetry and Criticism* (London: Methuen, 1920), 38-9.

> that is constant in the reality of the present, of each current moment? In a certain sense the past is far more real, or at any rate more stable, more resilient than the present. The present slips and vanishes like sand between the fingers, acquiring material weight only in its recollection.[121]

Tarkovsky is aware of the dichotomy inherent in the medium itself, one which combines both the present and the past. It is the immediacy of film which gives its efficacy, one of the singular capabilities of the medium, which it shares with no other art form, the ability to make the past a tangible present. [122]

The sequence which follows Alexei's mother waiting on the fence and her meeting with the doctor takes an even further expressionist turn, and, consequently, the "time pressure" is structured very differently. As the child Alexei sleeps peacefully in his bed inside the dacha, the wind once again prowls almost supernaturally through the trees and bushes. The boy appears to wake up twice and call for his absent father. Filmed in black and white, the sequence could be a dream, but Tarkovsky moves so effortlessly between colour, sepia and black and white, that such an assertion is problematic. Tarkovsky continuously experimented in changing colours of film; and while some have looked for a formal methodology in his approach, they have been unsuccessful.[123] Tarkovsky's changes in colour and film stock do not always reflect conventional use of the technique, where black and white and sepia have come to reflect dream or memory; they are much more of an aleatoric and sensual nature.

When the father appears, he washes the mother's hair in an exaggerated, sexualised fashion, in almost monstrous slow motion, perhaps in a recreation of the Freudian primal scene. The mother's face is obscured, not by the camera, but by the hair itself. Water drips on the soundtrack, as rain falls inside the house, an image which frequents many of Tarkovsky's films; plaster falls from the ceiling in large lumps. Is the house falling to pieces linked to the destruction of the family? When the mother's face is revealed she is almost impossibly beautiful, a beauty only possible in dream or memory. She turns towards a misted mirror, the first of many mirrors in the film, only to reveal

121. Tarkovsky, *Sculpting in Time*, 58.

122. The film that *Mirror* has most frequently been compared to is Bergman's *Wild Strawberries* (1957), and such comparisons are entirely justified. Both films concern an intellectual reminiscing about his past, prompted by his surroundings into experiencing vivid memories. In the case of *Wild Strawberries* an elderly doctor Professor Isak Borg (played by Victor Sjostrom) embarks on a road trip to receive an award for his long and distinguished career. The title of the film is drawn from a patch of wild strawberries that prompt a Proustian sensory memory for Berg transporting him back to his youth. It is in parts both more and less challenging to the codes of mainstream cinema than *Mirror*. While Berg becomes an active participant in his memories as an old man in his younger self's place the memories are themselves structured in deliberate and separate episodes and the film follows a broadly chronological structure outside of them.

123. See Johnson and Petrie, *The Films of Andrei Tarkovsky*, 189-91.

not her "own" reflection, but the reflection of the old woman she will become in the future. For Tarkovsky the mirror does not just render and comment on the psychological dimensions of a character, it is also used as a metaphorical and literal bridge to not only the memory of the past, but also the future.[124] Tarkovsky's audacious image combines an almost dizzying amount of temporal ambiguity within a single shot; for the mother it is her present and her future, for Alexei it is his past and his present and for the viewer two moments from the past conjoined. This is the ultimate Bakhtinian chronotope, almost outside of time and space and one to which Tarkovsky will often return.

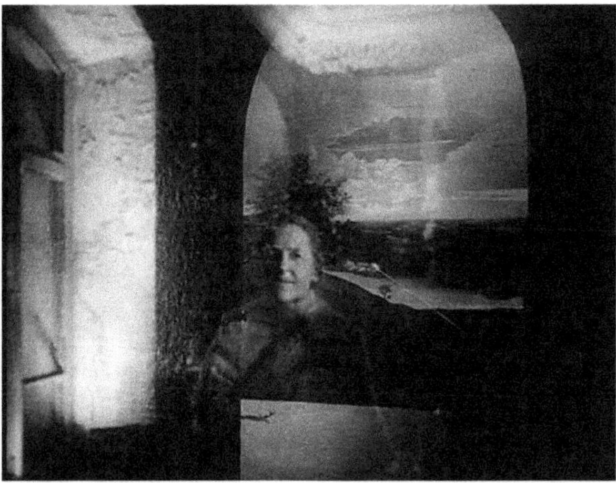

Figure 6 The young mother sees a reflection of her aged self in the future (played by Tarkovsky's own mother) in one of many scenes in *Mirror* to challenge how time has traditionally been represented in mainstream cinema.

Much has been written about the production of *Mirror* and the archetypal "dynamic milieu" that is the dacha in which the film is set; how Tarkovsky meticulously recreated his childhood home in minute detail.[125] The childhood home becomes a temporal and spatial nexus for Tarkovsky's films and the location of desire and nostalgia as he explores the inability to return home and

124. This is reminiscent of Kurt Vonnegut's reference to mirrors as leaks to other dimensions throughout his work and especially in *Breakfast of Champions* (1973). Vonnegut's work fluidly represents the connections between time and space. *Breakfast of Champions* ends with Kilgore Trout wishing to return to his youth: he exclaims "make me young!" In *Slaughterhouse Five,* aliens known as the Tralfamadorians are able to see in four dimensions, the fourth of which is time. The protagonist, Billy Pilgrim, becomes "unstuck in time" and the novel concludes with Pilgrim about to be killed, an event he is aware and not afraid of; he declares "everyone we know is alive and death is not a tragic event." Both were made into films, *Breakfast of Champions* (Rudolph, 1999) and *Slaughterhouse-Five* (Hill, 1972).

125. See Synessios, *Mirror,* 29.

the impossibility of returning to the past.[126] We see it extensively explored not just in *Mirror* but in *Ivan's Childhood*, *Solaris*, *Nostalghia*, *Stalker* and *The Sacrifice.* Bird aptly calls the dacha in *Mirror* a place "in which time itself lived."[127] The original dacha from the period, which had belonged to his grandparents, no longer existed, so he had to rebuild it as a perfect replica, relying on personal memories and hundreds of photographs. The photographs themselves had played a large role in Tarkovsky's life and his memories of that time; he "grew up with these photographs, with a tangible sense of the child he once was and the world he once inhabited; a tactile immediate visual reality,"[128] and this is what he wished to recreate on film. Under his instruction the production team carefully sowed the buckwheat seeds he remembered growing there as a child; the locals laughed at him, stating that buckwheat had not grown there for years and that the soil was not suitable for that type of plant. When it bloomed, he took it as an omen that the film would be the one he had long wished to make.

This idea of a location being much more than simply a place for the film to be shot stayed with Tarkovsky for the rest of his career. It had to create the right atmosphere that would permeate the entire production and set off a chain of sensual associations in Tarkovsky, the cast and the viewer. The recreation of the dacha and its surroundings proved even more effective than Tarkovsky had hoped for: when he took his mother to see it for the first time, what she experienced was what Tarkovsky wished for his viewers, "her reaction to seeing it surpassed my boldest expectations. What she experienced was a return to her past; and then I knew we were moving in the right direction."[129]

1.2 Tarkovsky and the Long Take

An artist may achieve an outward illusion, a life-like effect, but that is not at all the same as examining life beneath the surface.

~Andrei Tarkovsky

The quarrel over realism in fact stems from a misunderstanding from a confusion between the aesthetic and the psychological; between true realism, the need that is to give significant expression to the world both concretely and its essence, and the pseudo realism of a deception aimed at fooling the eye.

~André Bazin

126. See Peter King, *The Common Place: The Ordinary Experience of Housing* (Aldershot: Ashgate Publishing, 2005) for more on the home in not only Tarkovsky's films but also Ingmar Bergman, Carl Theodore Dreyer, Jacques Tati and others.
127. Bird, *Andrei Tarkovsky: Elements of Cinema,* 171.
128. Synessios, *Mirror,* 42.
129. Tarkovsky, *Sculpting in Time*, 132.

Tarkovsky's descriptions of "time pressure," and his assertion that film is some sort of living essence, evoke Henri Bergson's challenging interrogations of temporality in *Creative Evolution* and *Matter and Memory*. Like Tarkovsky, Bergson was dissatisfied with how society had increasingly withdrawn time from the realm of the abstract by spatialising it and measuring it through clocks and calendars. Bergson argued this was not "real" time: "real" time is incommensurable and cannot be recorded in such a strictly mathematical fashion. For both Bergson and Tarkovsky, "real" time is the inner life of man, it cannot be measured, but only felt through one's consciousness. It is a continuously changing, pulsing flow of singular events and, above all, entirely subjective. Tarkovsky's quasi-mystical assertion that time "cannot vanish without trace for it is a subjective, spiritual category; and that the time we have lived settles in our soul as an experience placed within time"[130] is evocative of Bergson's intuitive approach. Bergson suggested that "We do not think Real Time – but we live it because life transcends intellect."[131] Bergson termed this "real" time duration or *la durée*. Their shared examination of time led Donato Totaro to compare them:

> Beyond the role of time, they shared an epistemological dualism of intuition (or aesthetics) and intellect (or science), and greatly valued the former....They both looked to the inner world of consciousness and memory for answers to philosophical and moral questions. [132]

This sense of intuition is at the heart of Tarkovsky's cinema. Time for both men is much more than a measurement of how many moments or years have passed; it is profoundly a part of how we experience the world. Tarkovsky's entire career then could be seen as an attempt to present his interpretation of this *la durée* on screen. Such is the affective power of cinema, Tarkovsky goes on to suggest, that not only does cinema live within time, but time actually lives within it. Continuing his organic metaphor, he explained, how shots are "filled with time, and [editing] organises the unified, living structure inherent in the film; and the time that pulsates through the blood vessels of the film, making it alive, is of varying rhythmic pressure."[133] A film is not a solid, inanimate material, rather it is a thriving, pulsating being. This life force, or Bergsonian *élan vitale* views film as an organism, a pure force of becoming.[134] Tarkovsky's affinity with Bergson is very evident in his rather Bergsonian contention:

---

130. Tarkovsky, *Sculpting in Time*, 58.

131. Henri Bergson, *Creative Evolution*, [1910] trans. Arthur Mitchell (New York: Dover Publications, 1998), 46.

132. Donato Totaro, "Art For All 'Time,'" *Film-Philosophy* 4.4, para 15, (n.d.), <http://www.film-philosophy.com/vol4-2000/n4totaro> (7th May 2007).

133. Tarkovsky, *Sculpting in Time*, 114.

134. This organic nature is emphasised by the Russian formalist Boris Eikhenbaum in a telling metaphor, "the invention of the movie camera, properly speaking, breathed new life into the

> I am convinced that 'time' in itself is no objective category, as 'time' cannot exist apart from man's perception of it. Certain scientific discoveries tend to draw the same conclusion. We do not live in the 'now.' The 'now' is so transient, as close to zero as you can get without it being zero, that we simply have no way of grasping it. The moment in time we call 'now' immediately becomes the 'past,' and what we call the 'future' becomes the 'now' and then it immediately becomes 'past.' The only way to experience the now is if we let ourselves fall into the abyss which exists between the now and the future.[135]

Tarkovsky is far from alone in considering that time is the defining aspect of the cinematic art and the ingredient, which elevates its status as a medium, comparable in integrity with what can be achieved in literature, music and painting. This belief connects him to, among others, one of the defining film theorists of the post-war years, André Bazin. Bazin wrote that with film, "for the first time, the image of things is likewise the image of their duration"[136] and that because of this, and other factors, "the film-maker is no longer the competitor of the painter and the playwright, he is, at last, the equal of the novelist."[137]

For both it is the long take which is the preferred method of recording time onscreen. Both men felt that it allowed time to manifest itself with the minimum of authorial interference and was able to create a wholeness in time and space absent in other methods of cinematography. For Tarkovsky "time in a shot has to flow independently and with dignity, then ideas will find their place in it without fuss, bustle, and haste."[138] Bazin argued that when combined with depth of field the long take was able to give rise to a democracy of perception and a "freedom of attention"[139] demanding "a more active mental attitude on the part of the spectator and a more positive contribution on his part to the action in progress."[140] This more active mental attitude is integral to the success of Tarkovsky's "time pressure." The long takes which make up and even define his films have a significantly different impact on the viewer than classical techniques of montage. Films which veered from the long

---

realm of photography itself." "Problems of Cinema Stylistics," ed. Herbert Eagle, *Russian Formalist Film Theory*, 56.

135. Quoted in "To Journey Within," *Chaplin* 193 (September 1984), the answer to the question "Do you not believe in the concept of time as a gauge for the purpose of depicting the experience of existence?," trans. Trond S. Trondson (n.d.), <http://www.ucalgary.ca/~tstronds/nostalghia.com/TheTopics/Gideon_Bachmann.html.> (1st September 2008).

136. André Bazin, *What is Cinema? Volume 1*, trans. Hugh Gray (Berkeley: University of California Press, 1971), 15.

137. Ibid., 40.

138. Tarkovsky, *Sculpting in Time*, 120.

139. André Bazin, *Orson Welles* (Paris: Les Editions du Cerf, 1972), 58. Quoted in J. Dudley Andrew, *The Major Film Theories: An Introduction* (Oxford: Oxford University Press, 1976), 163.

140. André Bazin, *What is Cinema?*, 36.

take were problematic for them both. Bazin asserted "montage only calls for him [the viewer] to follow his guide, to let his attention follow along smoothly with that of the director who will choose what he should see."[141] As a distinct contrast to this, the long take aesthetic enables the viewer to play a more active role in the generation of meanings. While watching the long take, "he [the viewer] is called upon to exercise at least a modicum of personal choice. It is from his attention and his will that the meaning of the image in part derives."[142]

The aesthetic choices that Tarkovsky takes and Bazin endorses invite participation and present film as a poetic event and an experience rather than purely a narrative. Tarkovsky recorded, "The method whereby the artist obliges the audience to build separate parts into a whole, and to think on, further than has been stated, is the only one that puts the audience on a par with the artist in their perception of the film. And indeed from the point of view of mutual respect only that kind of reciprocity is worthy of artistic practice."[143] What explicit meanings are present, for example, in the opening sequence of *Mirror* and in the "dream" sequence which follows it? Over the course of several minutes very little actually happens from a conventional dramatic perspective, but on the part of the viewer it is a site of extended potentialities, due to the ambiguity of its presentation, which practically demands interaction and association through memory and experience.

Sustained use of the long take moves away from the codes and conventions of mainstream film, which has increasingly sought, since the days of D.W. Griffith, to spatialise cinema. In Tarkovsky and other film makers of the poetic aesthetic time is prioritised and rendered overwhelmingly present; *la durée* becomes palpable, as the image is processed on a conscious and unconscious level. This long take allows life to be viewed onscreen, hence the preponderance of images of nature, water and animals not only in the films of Tarkovsky, but in much of European Art Cinema, where the flux of life is most on display. In his later films like *Nostalghia* and *The Sacrifice* the long take reveals Tarkovsky's ambition and his desire for cinema to achieve both a philosophical and a spiritual goal. The famous candle sequence at the end of *Nostalghia* is the longest take in the film, and one of Tarkovsky's longest, lasting a remarkable unbroken eight minutes. The protagonist, Andrei Gorchakov (played by Oleg Yankovsky, who also played the father in *Mirror*), has been asked, as a gesture of faith, to walk across a drained swimming pool holding a lighted candle, making sure it does not go out. Krzysztof Kieślowski famously described the sequence as a miracle.[144] Yankovsky recalls Tarkovsky as saying to him:

---

141. Ibid. Bazin even suggested that the long take aesthetic was a "step forward in the history of film language" (Ibid., 35).
142. Ibid., 36.
143. Tarkovsky, *Sculpting in Time*, 20-1.
144. Quoted in *Kieślowski on Kieślowski*, ed. Danusia Stok (London: Faber and Faber, 1995), 195.

> Okay, I'll put it a different way. The thing is, could you — yes! yes! — you, Oleg! — display an entire human life in one shot, without any editing, from beginning to end, from birth to the very moment of death?[145]

Tarkovsky's ambition is remarkable, some might say quixotic, but one cannot deny his integrity and commitment to the art of film as achieving what he believes is its goal – to ask life's eternal questions. He believed that not only did every single shot display life, it *was* life.

Ivan's Childhood	**17.2**
Andrei Rublyov	**26**
Solaris	**28**
Mirror	**23.2**
Stalker	**63.2**
Nostalghia	**58.2**
The Sacrifice	**74.1**

Table 1. The average shot lengths of Tarkovsky's films in seconds calculated by using Cinemetrics Software.[146]

Table 1 displays the average length of shots (ASL) across Tarkovsky's seven feature length films. As previously suggested, the data reveals that *Mirror* does mark a turning point in Tarkovsky's career. After *Mirror* each of his films will have ASLs of around one minute. *Mirror* anticipates this: shots frequently go over a minute, seven times over two minutes and three shots last longer than three minutes. The ASL of *Mirror* is significantly lessened by the addition of the documentary footage which Tarkovsky cuts into the film in a series of very short edits, which frequently last just one or two seconds. With these sequences removed the ASL would also be around one minute. If we compare

145. Oleg Yankovsky, "How we shot the inextinguishable candle episode," para 4, (n.d.), WWW documents, <http://www.ucalgary.ca/~tstronds/nostalghia.com/TheTopics/Yankovsky.html> (19th October 2007).

146. Film theorists have frequently studied shot lengths in an effort to reveal patterns in editing practices over the decades, across periods of time, different cultures or even over a single director's career: from David Bordwell and Kristin Thompson to Barry Salt. In recent years the process has become much more accurate, utilising contemporary technology; Yuri Tsivian's computer programme Cinemetrics provides film scholars with a valuable method to record and study shot lengths in film. The process is very precise, detailed and scientific; it enables theorists to move away from the vagaries which used to inhabit arguments regarding editing patterns in selected directors' works. Of course one must be careful when employing average shot lengths but they are indicative of broad tendencies in an artist's work.

Mirror to Tarkovsky's final film *The Sacrifice*, we can see that Tarkovsky's predilection for the long take becomes even more pronounced as his career progressed. The ASL for *The Sacrifice* is seventy-four seconds, and contains twelve shots which go over three minutes. The film also features the longest shot in his whole body of work, the opening shot of the film, which is longer than nine minutes. With a running time of 139 minutes and 45 seconds there are a total of just one hundred and twenty-two shots.[147]

Considering Bazin praised both Michelangelo Antonioni and Orson Welles, among others, for their continued utilisation of the long take at its most masterful, it is somewhat ironic that Welles criticised Antonioni for the very same thing in *This is Orson Welles*. He said,

> I don't like to dwell on things. It's one of the reasons I'm so bored with Antonioni — that belief that, because a shot is good, it's going to get better if you keep looking at it. He gives you a full shot of somebody walking down a road. And you think, 'Well, he's not going to carry that woman all the way up that road.' But he *does*. And then she leaves and you go on looking at the road after she's gone.[148]

What Welles appears to be criticising is the non-narrative function of the image, a criticism that could be equally applied to Tarkovsky as much as, if not more, than to Antonioni. One might suggest that the long take in Welles is still predominantly narrative based, as in the distinctive long take in *Touch of Evil* (Welles, 1958), as it is in much of Hollywood cinema. In European Art Cinema and films which embody the poetic aesthetic, narrative is not the primary concern, as there are other, perhaps even more compelling factors involved. Nevertheless many, including Welles, it seems, consider this as a cinematic deficiency. As a contrast to Welles's dislike of the long take, in *A History of Film* Wexman suggests (as I have done about Tarkovsky), that "In Antonioni's work we must regard his images at length; he forces our full attention by continuing the shot long after others would cut away."[149]

Tarkovsky praised the French film-maker Pascal Aubier's works *Tenebrae factae sunt* (1965) and *L' Apparition* (1986), especially his short films, which

---

147. By way of comparison David Bordwell in *The Way Hollywood Tells It* (Berkeley: The University of California Press, 2006), 121-23, suggests that the ASL of an average Hollywood film has been declining since the 1930s from an average of between 8-11 seconds in the period between 1930-1960, through the 1970s where the average was between 4 and 5 seconds, to the 2000s where he has recorded the average at 5 seconds.

148. Quoted in Peter Bogdanovich, *This is Orson Welles* (London: Harper-Perennial, 1992), 102-3. Eisenstein suggests something similar, accusing those who favour the long take of having a lack of artistic intelligence. He saw its ambiguity of meaning as a weakness and questioned the necessity of recording the same image after it had already made its impression. See Ilisa Barbash and Lucien Taylor, *Cross Cultural Film-making* (Berkeley: University of California Press, 1997), 374.

149. Virginia Wright Wexman, *A History of Film* (Cambridge: Pearson Publishing, 2006), 312.

sometimes consist of single shots, stating that they show "the life of nature, majestic and unhurried, indifferent to human bustle and passions."[150] Tarkovsky expressed a similar desire to Bertolucci a number of times: about *Stalker* he commented, "I wanted it to be as if the whole film had been made in a single shot."[151]

The challenge of a single shot film was not taken up until thirty years after *Mirror* by the man many regard as being Tarkovsky's heir, Alexander Sokurov, in his *Russian Ark* (*Russkiy kovcheg*, 2002).[152] Even though it is comprised of a single shot, *Russian Ark* manages to move fluidly between past and present, creating a grand tapestry of Russia's history, entirely filmed in the Hermitage in St. Petersburg. The title comes from the closing shot, which poetically reveals the Hermitage as a distinctly Tarkovskian floating time capsule, in which Russia's past is preserved, yet constantly alive. On temporality in film Sokurov is distinctly Tarkovskian in his suggestion that,

> The greatest directors of our time were able to discover only one feature of cinematic art which they could develop to a certain degree: time. The passage of time was the main object of investigation for their profession….in Tarkovsky and Bresson a specifically cinematographic concept of time appears, born of genuinely visual methods and so able to exist as a true cinematographic reality – one which cannot be reproduced by any other medium. Tarkovsky is unquestionably engaged in the struggle for the birth of a real cinema.[153]

It has been easy for many critics to describe Bazin's assertions about the apoliticalism of the long take as naïve, a "style without style," especially in the light of Godard's famous maxim "tracking shots are a question of morality"[154] just two years later. Yet descriptions of Bazin as ideologue are themselves equally problematic: Bazin is fundamentally aware of the differences between, in his words, "true realism" and the superficial. Yet it is their definitions of Realism, so similar on the surface, which show a distinction between the two

---

150. Tarkovsky, *Sculpting in Time*, 114.

151. Ibid. 194.

152. The lengths of shots can be manipulated quite persuasively now through the use of modern technology. *Birdman or (the Unexpected Virtue of Ignorance)* (2014) appears to be filmed in one long take, but of course consists of several long takes spliced together which are skillfully hidden through the use of digital imaging techniques.

153. Aleksandr Sokurov, "Death, the Banal Leveller (on Tarkovsky)," *Film Studies: An International Review* 1 (Spring 1999): 67. Sokurov has also emerged from Tarkovsky's shadow to prove himself as one of the most talented film-makers working in cinema today.

154. Jean-Luc Godard, in *Cahiers du Cinéma: 1950s: Neo-Realism, Hollywood, New Wave*, ed. Jim Hillier, trans. Liz Heron (London: Routledge and Kegan Paul, 1985), 62. "Jean Somarchi, Jacques Doniol Valcroze, Jean-Luc Godard, Pierre Kast, Jacques Rivette, Eric Rohmer: 'Hiroshima, notre amour.'" Originally "Hiroshima, notre amour," *Cahiers du Cinéma* 97, July 1959 (extracts).

men.

Bazin compares the long take to a suspect under police interrogation. If held long enough, he will reveal the truth. He suggested "For the first time, between the originating object and its reproduction there intervenes only the instrumentality of a nonliving agent. For the first time an image of the world is formed automatically, without the creative invention of man."[155] But for Tarkovsky the assumption that the medium is formed through a non-living agent is problematic. Even though Tarkovsky stated "The basic element of cinema, running through it from its tiniest cell, is observation," he also suggested that "To be faithful to life, intrinsically truthful, a work has for me to be at once an exact factual account and a true communication of feelings."[156] Film could never be "objectivity in time," [157] as this form of a recreation of reality fails to take into account the relationship between director and text and text and spectator. Donato Totaro highlights this fact, which is at the centre of Tarkovsky's and Bazin's different approaches to reality: "Tarkovsky's notion of cinema image is a combination of what the camera records mechanically and the filmmaker's vision that shapes it."[158] For Tarkovsky the camera is not "just" a recorder of reality placed in front of it, it is "dependent upon our consciousness and on the real world it seeks to embody."[159] Perception plays as large a role as observation: "The image in cinema is based on the ability to present as an observation one's own perception of an object."[160] For Tarkovsky, embracing the organic nature of the medium, the camera is not just a static object, it is much more than that, rather a facilitator or a transformer, a device which enables an entrance into the subjective world of the director, a bridge or a door to a truthful reality.

What Tarkovsky's truth actually is, though, is hard to discern; his writings abound with enigmatic references to "the truth." For Tarkovsky it is intrinsically connected to the organic property of the shot, not an objective and stable truth, but one of many equally truthful interpretations. But he also calls for a spiritual truth,[161] truth through personal experience "endorsed by life,"[162] something which emerges from a "true communication of feelings"[163] and even a truth as "hope."[164] Those with a dislike of the abstruse nature of Tarkovsky's work use his predilection for extended takes as fuel for criticism. Fredric Jameson is quick to criticise Tarkovsky, not without some humour, for

---

155. Bazin, *What is Cinema?*, 13.
156. Tarkovsky, *Sculpting in Time*, 66; 23.
157. Bazin, *What is Cinema?*, 14-5.
158. Donato Totaro, "Art For All 'Time,'" *Film-Philosophy* 4.4 (2000): para 5.
159. Tarkovsky, *Sculpting in Time*, 106.
160. Ibid, 107.
161. Ibid., 37.
162. Ibid., 16.
163. Ibid., 23.
164. Ibid., 43.

his ability to "capture the truth of mosses."[165] Peter Wollen's more pragmatic approach to so-called cinematic truth is also shifting, fluctuating and above all subjective: "the truth is not out there in the real world, waiting to be photographed. What the cinema can do is produce meanings and meanings can only be plotted, not in relation to some abstract yardstick or criterion of truth, but in relation to other meanings."[166] Such multivalency is at the heart of Tarkovsky's film as dynamic experience, but for many such pronounced ambiguity is distinctly alienating.

On its release many criticised *Mirror* for being impenetrable. The influential Nikolai Sizov, director of the Moscow Film Studios, asserted that Tarkovsky "chose too complex a form to express his thoughts and feelings and this made the film inaccessible to the perception of the viewers."[167] Marlen Khutsiev, the director of *I am Twenty*, argued "in this film no dialogue takes place, only a monologue, in which the author, not caring about an interlocutor, talks only to himself."[168] While the fact that *Mirror* is an autobiographical film naturally provokes comments of this nature, there is much more to the film than a one sided monologue. Tarkovsky's friend and contemporary, Akira Kurosawa, disagreed with Sizov and Khutsiev,

> Many people grumble that Tarkovsky's films are difficult, but I don't think so. His films just show how extraordinarily sensitive Tarkovsky is. He made a film titled *Mirror* after *Solaris. Mirror* deals with his cherished memories in his childhood, and many people say again it is disturbingly difficult. Yes, at a glance, it seems to have no rational development in its storytelling. But we have to remember: it is impossible that in our soul our childhood memories should arrange themselves in a static, logical sequence. A strange train of fragments of early memory images shattered and broken can bring about the poetry in our infancy. Once you are convinced of its truthfulness, you may find *Mirror* the easiest film to understand.[169]

Tarkovsky was greatly inspired by letters sent to him by members of the public, especially during times when he felt he was being persecuted by the state. One

---

165. Fredric Jameson, *The Geopolitical Aesthetic: Cinema and Space in the World System* (Bloomington and Indianapolis: Indiana University Press, 1992), 99.
166. Peter Wollen, "Semiotic counter-strategies," *Readings and Writings* (London: Verso, 1982), 91.
167. Herbert J. Marshall, "Andrei Tarkovsky's *The Mirror*," 94.
168. Ibid., 95. One must consider Khutsiev's position in the light of these comments. The director of *I am Twenty,* originally called *Lenin Gate,* a film which caused such controversy it was recut and edited and not released for several years. How much pressure would he have been under in the seventies to adhere to party protocol?
169. Akira Kurosawa, "Tarkovsky and Solaris," trans. Sato Kimososhi, para 14, (n.d.), <http://www.ucalgary.ca/~tstronds/nostalghia.com/TheTopics/Kurosawa_on_Solaris.html> (1st September 2008).

person wrote to Tarkovsky with the comment, "My reason for writing is *Mirror*, a film I can't even talk about because I am living it."[170] Unknowingly the woman reproduces the ideas at the centre of Tarkovsky's film theory. It was not just the public that commented on Tarkovsky's ability to be simultaneously personal and universal. Some critics in the Soviet Union were able to appreciate the film. For V.I Solovyov the film's heroes "were not film images but my thoughts, my memories."[171]

Mirror in many ways begins the second stage of Tarkovsky's career; his films continue to use and develop techniques which allow the observer to engage with the material in their own manner. The film is not just an intellectual exercise, but rather a profoundly emotional experience for those willing to become Tarkovsky's allies. When, in 1997, more than ten years after Tarkovsky's death, the Russian cinema journal *Notes in Cinema Analysis* (*Kinovedcheskie Zapiski*) asked twenty film critics from all over the world to vote for the film which had achieved a profoundly personal effect on them, *Mirror* won more votes than any other.[172]

After seeing *Mirror*, Andrei Tarkovsky's sister Marina was heard to comment, that she did not recognise the character of her mother, that *her* mother was very different to the person she saw on the screen. From a perceptual perspective this makes perfect sense, as the person she saw onscreen was not *her* mother, but Andrei Tarkovsky's.[173]

1.3 Tarkovsky and Montage

Montage has become the indisputable axiom on which the worldwide culture of the cinema has been built. ~Sergei Eisenstein

The idea of 'montage cinema'—that editing brings together two concepts and thus engenders a new, third one—again seems to me to be incompatible with the nature of cinema. ~Andrei Tarkovsky

The post-production phase of *Mirror* continued far longer than Tarkovsky

170. Tarkovsky, *Sculpting in Time*, 10. These reactions to Tarkovsky's work were also frequently leveled at Kieślowski. One person remarked, "You've plagiarized my life. Where do you know me from?," in Krzysztof Kieślowski quoted in *Kieślowski on Kieślowski*, 193.
171. Johnson and Petrie, *The Films of Andrei Tarkovsky*, 133.
172. Julian Graffy, "Tarkovsky: The Weight of the World," *Sight and Sound* 7.1 (January 1997): 18.
173. In a 1997 interview Marina Tarkovskaya spoke about her brother and mother extensively. She commented that "their (sic) was nothing soft or blurred about her. She was very clear cut and strong. She made the decisions in her life. Andrei was unfair towards mother." She continued, "She sacrificed her life for us, she was one of those Russian characters who always choose the most difficult way." In "Mirror images of sad genius," *Independent Eye* interview conducted by Vitaly Yerenkov (12th December 1997), 11.

expected, as he became unable to find an ideal assemblage for the film. Such a large number of variations of form are unsurprising due to the film's poetic nature: the large amount of material he had shot, its elaborate temporal structure and the fact that a finalised script never existed (scenes were rewritten on a day to day basis and many were largely improvised). Such creative freedom during institutionalised film production is extremely rare. The film's sustained deviation from the conventions of Soviet Socialist Realism in its more experimental, associative editing patterns, the foregrounding of mood and atmosphere over plot and superficial "incoherence," proved difficult for many then as it does now. So central is "time pressure" to the way meanings are created in the film, that editing, for Tarkovsky, is even something of an afterthought. Synessios asserts that the phenomenological focus of Tarkovsky's editing could "without exaggeration, be characterized as mystical."[174]

From a theoretical perspective the prioritization of time passing in the shot over the juxtaposition of the shots themselves has particularly ideological implications. In some ways it must be read as a rejection of Tarkovsky's Soviet heritage, embodied by Sergei Eisenstein. There is even something oedipal in Tarkovsky's sustained attacks on one of the founding fathers of Soviet film. It is in his vehement rejection of Eisenstein's dialectical approach to editing that Tarkovsky's almost preternatural editing style is revealed.[175] For Tarkovsky, Eisenstein's techniques are manipulative and border on homiletic. Tarkovsky found it impossible "to accept the notion that editing is the main formative element of a film, as the protagonists of "montage cinema," following Kuleshov and Eisenstein, maintained in the "twenties, as if a film was made on the editing table."[176] Tarkovsky went on to attack the canonical *Alexander Nevsky* (*Aleksandr Nevskiy*, 1938):

> Take for example the battle on the ice in *Alexander Nevsky*. Ignoring the need to fill the frames with the appropriate time-pressure, he tries to achieve the inner dynamic of the battle with an edited sequence of short – sometimes excessively short – shots…what is happening on the screen is sluggish and unnatural. This is because no time-truth exists in the separate frames.[177]

---

174. Synessios, *Mirror,* 52.
175. Siegfried Kracauer disagrees with Tarkovsky "Of all the technical properties of film the most general and indispensable is editing." *Theory of Film: The Redemption of Physical Reality* [1965] (Princeton University Press: 1997), 29. Pudovkin disagrees with Tarkovsky in even more vehement terms. The first sentence of his book *Film Technique and Film Acting: The Cinema Writings Of V.I. Pudovkin,* [1929] trans. Ivor Montagu (London: Unwin Brothers Limited, 1968) is "The foundation of film art is *editing*" (23). He continues "The expression that the film is 'shot' is entirely false, and should disappear from the language. The film is not *shot*, but *built,* built up from the separate strips of celluloid that are its raw material" (24).
176. Tarkovsky, *Sculpting in Time*, 114.
177. Ibid., 119-20.

His criticism reached a peak with his critique of *Ivan the Terrible* (*Ivan Grozny*, 1944), "it almost ceases—in my own purely theoretical view—to be a cinematic work."[178] Not only criticising the subject matter and the style, but deeming it unworthy of even being called a film.[179]

For Tarkovsky the reliance on the juxtaposition of units to create a singular predefined meaning is dictatorial. Refusing to allow the audience any diversity of interpretation or experience betrays the organic nature of the medium, an aspect, which for Tarkovsky's experiential film-making style, is key. The audience needs to share "with the author the misery and joy of bringing an image into being."[180] For Tarkovsky, this experience of viewing film is akin to Bakhtin's example of a thousand different individual reactions to a single book, creating a thousand different individual books. Tarkovsky uses Tolstoy for his example:

> In the literal, superficial sense, *War and Peace* is read and envisioned by thousands of readers; this makes it a thousand different books as a result of the differences in experience between the writer and the reader.... In this is the guarantee of the reader's co-creation. A writer depends subconsciously on an imaginative reader to see more and to see more clearly than the presented, laconic description....This is in literature. But what about cinema? Where in the cinema does the viewer have this freedom of choice? Each and every frame, every scene and episode, outwardly doesn't even describe, but literally records actions, landscapes, characters' faces.... I've noticed, from my own experience, if the external, emotional construction of images in a film are based on the filmmaker's own memory, on the kinship of one's personal experience with the fabric of the film, then the film will have the power to affect those who see it.[181]

The rejection of Eisensteinian approaches to cinema for Tarkovsky is a reaffirmation of the life inherent in the cinematic process and the knowledge that film can move "beyond the frame." Balázs agreed with Tarkovsky, and he came very close to actually using the term "beyond the frame," when he suggested,

> Very deep subconscious idea-associations can emerge or be touched off by such editing. Sometimes the picture of the landscape is enough to conjure

178. Ibid., 68.

179. In *Sculpting in Time* Tarkovsky criticises a wide range of artists from Eisenstein to da Vinci. He is also unafraid to criticize himself, especially when he believes that he has inaccurately rendered "time pressure" on screen. He goes as far to effectively remove *Solaris* from his body of work, criticises sequences from *Ivan's Childhood* (32-3) and *Mirror* itself (109).

180. Ibid., 20.

181. Quoted in "Dialogue with Andrei Tarkovsky about Science-Fiction on the Screen," *Ekran*, 1970-1971, trans. Jake Mahaffy and Yulia Mahaffy, in *Andrei Tarkovsky Interviews*, 34-5.

> up the memory of a face or to characterize a situation. Such effects are certainly not 'literary,' for no words can convey this non-rational correlation of shapes and images which takes place in our conscious mind.[182]

For Tarkovsky, a film which utilises the unique strengths of the medium communicates with its spectator on a variety of levels. Eisenstein represents a cinematic language configured as some sort of intellectual and psychological puzzle, for which there is only one possible response. Tarkovsky rejects "the principles of 'montage cinema' because they do not allow the film to continue beyond the edges of the screen: they do not allow the audience to bring personal experience to bear on what is in front of them."[183] In this understanding of cinema a film has more meaning created in its interaction with the viewer than is inherent in it.[184]

To place this in perspective, considering what has come before, it is natural to compare Tarkovsky's editing patterns to Sergei Eisenstein's. Comparison of this sort is fraught with complications, but it is possible to select any work of Eisenstein's and receive similar results. Eisenstein's defining work *Battleship Potemkin* (*Bronenosets Potyomkin*, 1925) contains a remarkable 1500 shots in its seventy-two minutes running time, an ASL of 2.9 seconds. In Tarkovsky's seven completed films there are substantially fewer shots than in *Battleship Potemkin* alone. *Strike* (*Stachka*, 1925) has an even greater number of shots, 1846 in its 93 minute duration, giving an ASL of 3 seconds. In Eisenstein's later films the pace of editing slowed down, but still remained comparatively fast. In *Alexander Nevsky* (1938), the film Tarkovsky regarded as almost a "non-film," the ASL is 6.8 seconds.

Despite this animosity, there *are* intriguing similarities between Tarkovsky and Eisenstein, which Tarkovsky failed or refused to recognise. If nothing else, their shared belief in film's status as the pre-eminent art form unites them. They use an intriguingly similar, suitably Russian metaphor for the impact

182. Béla Balázs, *Theory of the Film* (*Character and Growth of a New Art*), 126. He also continued with a criticism of Eisenstein himself, "These are picture puzzles, not artistic effects... Eisenstein, who was perhaps the greatest master of sensuous picture effects that transcended the sphere of reason, unfortunately often fell victim to the mistaken idea that the world of purely conceptual thinking could also be conquered by film art" (128-9).

183. Tarkovsky, *Sculpting in Time*, 118.

184. The distinction between Tarkovsky and Eisenstein is revealed in their shared affinity for the haiku though for very different reasons, each emblematic of their approach to film. So in Matsuo Basho's famous haiku, "old pond/a frog jumps/the sound of water" (1686) what attracts Tarkovsky might be "the refusal even to hint at the kind of final image meaning that can be deciphered like a charade. Haiku cultivates its images in such a way that they mean nothing beyond themselves, and at the same time express so much that it is not possible to catch their final meaning" (106). Eisenstein admired the fact that three separate elements were able to create something new as a result of their combination, seeing in them an analogy for montage itself; each line creates a precise impression and their combination is what creates meaning.

cinema has on the spectator. Eisenstein's is couched in the Soviet rhetoric of the times and evocative of his Marxist politics: "A work of art… is first and foremost a tractor ploughing over the audience's psyche."[185] Tarkovsky's version is much more spiritual: "The allotted function of art is not, as is often assumed, to put across ideas, to propagate thoughts, to serve as example. The aim of art is to prepare a person for death, to plough and harrow his soul, rendering it capable of turning to good."[186]

However, Eisenstein's theories on editing encompass the audience in a more participatory way than Tarkovsky is prepared to acknowledge. Eisenstein's descriptions of overtonal montage and asynchronous sound take into account the experience of the cinema going process, as does his belief in pathos and sensual thinking, the emotional pull of the combination of a variety of factors within the spectator. These combinations of factors produce a multi-sensory cinema, which shares some of the construction of "time pressure." Eisenstein talked of sensations in his consideration of overtones: "visual as well as aural overtones are a totally physiological sensation."[187] Yet when metric, rhythmic and tonal montages are combined together, they do, in Eisenstein's words, "induce the desired effect." Undoubtedly, Tarkovsky would take offence at such a Pavlovian attitude to the sensory nature of the cinema. The only possible response upon viewing the Odessa Steps sequence from *Battleship Potemkin* is outrage, the single emotion Eisenstein has expertly designed the sequence to create. If we contrast this to the documentary extracts used in *Mirror*, what do they provoke in a viewer? It is almost impossible to suggest how an individual will react to the material, such is the openness and ambiguity of its construction. Ultimately their careers were to follow a similar pattern, they both fell from favour when their work was regarded as too experimental and deviated too far from party lines and they both died leaving seven films behind.

The interpolation of seemingly unconnected documentary footage into *Mirror* is one of Tarkovsky's most ambitious formal techniques. In *Sculpting in Time* Tarkovsky repeatedly stressed the importance of documentary film to him. In some ways Tarkovsky believed that what he had created with *Mirror* was a documentary of sorts. The film may have moved even closer to documentary, had Tarkovsky gone ahead with original plans to include secretly film interviews with his mother using a hidden camera. He repeatedly asserted that *Mirror* contained not one fictitious episode, regarding the film as some sort of progressive proto-documentary, in which he replicated not only the surface reality of the events, but, using the primacy of the cinematic medium he sought to provide the audience with the sense of what it actually felt like to be there.

185. Sergei Eisenstein, *S.M. Eisenstein Selected Writings 1922-1934*, ed. Richard Taylor, trans. Richard Taylor and William Powell (London: British Film Institute, 1998), 61.
186. Tarkovsky, *Sculpting in Time*, 43.
187. Sergei Eisenstein, *Essays in Film Theory*, ed. Jay Leyda (New York: Meridian Books, 1957), 70.

Paradoxically, this unremitting search for truthfulness, out of necessity, requires a certain amount of artistic license in the cause of the creation of the real.

Mirror begins with one such extract, which blurs the boundary between fiction and non-fiction. The television is turned on and the documentary begins, even before the sequence of the protagonist's mother waiting on the fence; it is one of many interludes interspersed throughout the film. What follows has no explicit narrative significance, it is never referred to again, the characters are unidentified and do not return to the film. The footage shows a speech therapist attempting to cure a young stutterer of his speech defect. It is comprised of two shots: one of twenty seconds followed by the second, an unbroken shot lasting three minutes and thirty eight seconds, which is the longest shot in the film. None of the documentary footage used has any direct narrative purpose in traditional terms and in some ways can be regarded as irrationally cut into the film, but they are an integral part of the way meanings are created and the concentration of "time pressure" that registers throughout.

An interesting distinction about the presentation of the documentary footage is that, while the film revels in its achronological structure, the extracts are presented largely chronologically as they proceed through the film. The material is quite startling and contrasts greatly with much of the officially approved, explicitly patriotic and familiar Soviet newsreels of the period. They simultaneously act as a counterpoint to the fluidity of the central narrative and serve as a mirror to the themes the film engages with as it progresses.

While there can be no doubt that *Mirror* has special significance to Russians who lived in this period, the documentary footage interwoven into the narrative is not exclusively Russian but human; it broadens the experience of the film by transcending the boundaries of the narrative and the medium functioning to historicize a profoundly personal film. The footage of the Spanish Civil War, the Hiroshima bomb and reminiscences of the child refugees add to the sense of nostalgia, which the film evokes among not only Russians but anyone, regardless of their nationality. For Russians the associations with the smallest details like clothes, lamp posts or even cigarettes might be enough to trigger Proustian levels of involuntary memory. Turovskaya poignantly concludes that the film is something akin to a living personal and cultural artifact, alluding to Tarkovsky's problematising of notions of subjectivity: "For my generation, the film also holds the elusive charm of recognition; since we share many of the protagonist's childhood memories, it could just as well been called 'We Remember.'"[188] *Mirror* presents an approach to national consciousness that is very different to the idealised patriotism of films like *Chapayev* (1934, Georgi and Sergei Vasilyev), perhaps, more truthful in a variety of ways, but ultimately just as mythical.

As with almost every aspect of Tarkovsky's films, the images and objects

188. Turovskaya, *The Films of Andrei Tarkovsky,* 65.

take on a uniquely temporal dimension in their construction:

> In *Mirror* I wanted to make people feel that Bach and Pergolesi and Pushkin's letter and the soldiers forcing the Sivash crossing, and also the intimate, domestic events — that all these things are in a sense equally important as human experience. In terms of a person's spiritual experience, what happened to him yesterday may have exactly the same degree of significance as what happened to humanity a hundred years ago.[189]

This dislocation from convention leads Synessios to comment that "There is a tremendous freedom at the heart of *Mirror*: an ease of associations....More than anything, it resembles a musical composition; it is polyphonic in its use of its disparate parts, but the sense of wholeness and harmony it creates makes it akin to a symphony."[190] The musical analogy is as apposite an analogy as an organic one for Tarkovsky's presentation of cinematic time. Just as in music, individual notes reveal little about a melody in isolation, it is only when they are connected to others in a flow that a melody is created; an individual moment in time only becomes an experience when related to others.[191]

As the Stutterer sequence progresses, the boy is heard speaking in a fragmented and pained fashion, he struggles to pronounce a simple sentence. The woman proceeds to hypnotise him and gives him a set of instructions. Moments later, when she brings him out of his hypnotic state, she orders him to "speak loudly and clearly, freely and easily, unafraid of your voice and your speech." Remarkably, the boy is transformed: he speaks once more, this time free of the stutter. The metaphorical associations with this sequence are clear for anyone with even a cursory acquaintance with Russian history of the twentieth century. Is this Tarkovsky's way of implying that Russia was restricted artistically, spiritually and emotionally by the shackles of Soviet censorship and the repression of a totalitarian regime? Could he be registering the relationship between film and dream, film and hypnotism, or film as therapy? How much of the film is an excavation of the subconscious, for Tarkovsky himself? When the young sufferer replies, "I can speak," it seems to be a gesture of hope for the future. Such is the multivalency of this sequence, commentators have had different reactions to it. For Johnson and Petrie it "unmistakeably voices an artist's and a society's need for unfettered expression."[192] For Le Fanu it explores "the necessary connection between

---

189. Tarkovsky, *Sculpting in Time*, 193.
190. Synessios, *Mirror,* 48.
191. Balázs observed this too: "The single notes have duration in time, their relation to each other, which gives meaning to the individual notes, is outside time." *Theory of the Film* (*Character and Growth of a New Art*), 62.
192. Johnson and Petrie *The Films of Andrei Tarkovsky*, 116. The stutterer sequence is paid homage to in Apichatpong Weerasethakul's film *Syndromes and a Century* (2006). Tarkovsky's stutterer is replaced by a patient suffering from carbon monoxide poisoning. The hypnotist, who

language and truth,"[193] and for Green it is "an autobiographical process of gaining articulacy."[194] David Gillespie, I feel, is quite correct, when he suggests that Tarkovsky "is offering his own life as a 'mirror' of the age, a reflection of national experience."[195]

While Tarkovsky disapproved of the unwarranted juxtaposition of shots through editing to create purely intellectual associations, he is not above utilising the contrast of shots for effect, but only if its use is in harmony with the corresponding atmosphere of the sequence. The narrative of a film, like the events of someone's life, does not always flow smoothly and continuously from moment to moment. The chaos and sudden change that exist in one's life would be reflected in a striking and disruptively edited sequence, but Tarkovsky advised careful use of this approach: "Joining segments of unequal time-value necessarily breaks the rhythm. However, if this break is promoted by forces at work within the assembled frames, then it may be an essential factor in the carving out of the right rhythmic design."[196] Tarkovsky is once again describing his move away from classical narrative cinema with its rapid cutting and reliance on movement and space over time. If the narrative requires disruption, this can be achieved stylistically as well as thematically by the breaking of rhythm, then two shots with varying "time pressure" can be joined effectively. However, if it is inharmonious, the shot will feel contrived or shallow: "If time is slowed down or speeded up artificially, and not in response to an endogenous development, if the change of rhythm is wrong, the result will be false and strident."[197]

What characterises Tarkovsky's "endogenous development" is, of course, entirely subjective: who can choose when slow motion is required and not required in a sequence, other than a director? Slow motion has characteristically been used in cinema either to accentuate a dream-like atmosphere, as in *Los Olvidados* (Buñuel, 1950), or to heighten emotion of moments of tension, in Pudovkin's *Storm over Asia* (*Potomok Chingis-Khan*, 1928) as the rifles of the firing squad raise slowly as the moment stretches on.

In *Mirror* Tarkovsky uses slow motion sparingly, but in a similar fashion. In the famous printing press sequence, the mother hurries back to her job as a copy editor, afraid she has made a spelling mistake in an important document. The slow motion is almost imperceptible, yet it adds an air of dream and tension to the sequence, "a vague feeling of something strange."[198] One might argue that in his most poetic scenes the stillness of the action itself, combined

---

even resembles Tarkovsky's, fails utterly, with the implication that Weerasethakul's characters will not be able to articulate themselves freely.

193. Mark Le Fanu, *The Cinema of Andrei Tarkovsky,* 82.

194. Peter Green, *Andrei Tarkovsky: The Winding Quest*, 87.

195. David Gillespie, *Russian Cinema* (Harlow, Essex: Pearson Education Limited, 2003), 176.

196. Tarkovsky, *Sculpting in Time*, 121.

197. Ibid.

198. Ibid., 110.

with the long take, often seems like slow motion. While we never learn what the spelling mistake she feared was, the sequence may refer to a widely reported and, perhaps, apocryphal episode also related in Vasily Grossman's novel *Life and Fate*, where it is Joseph Stalin's name, which is accidentally misspelt. The editor responsible is sentenced to seven years in prison. Grossman also does not reveal the nature of the misprint, but many have speculated that the editor used an "r" instead of a "t," making the word "Sralin" (a form of the verb "srat" which means "to defecate" in Russian) not "Stalin." Tarkovsky's scene reveals the paranoid atmosphere in the mid-thirties, where something as inconsequential as a spelling mistake could cost your job and perhaps even your life.[199]

Tarkovsky's frustration with the editing process in *Mirror* grew, as his filmed material would not fit together, and he could not understand why: "At moments it looked as if the film could not be edited, which would have meant that inadmissible lapses had occurred during shooting. The film didn't hold together, it wouldn't stand up, it fell apart as one watched, it had no unity, no necessary inner connection, no logic."[200] These lapses, according to Tarkovsky, would have been the failure to capture the truthful "time pressure" of the story itself as it developed during production. They could have come about through mistakes in conception, directing, acting or other aspects of the creative process, one of a myriad different factors that create the overall harmony of a film. He noted:

> It is not always easy to sense the pattern of relationships, the articulations between the shots, particularly if the scene has been shot inexactly, in which case you will have not merely to join the pieces logically and naturally at the editing table, but laboriously to seek out the basic principle of the articulations.[201]

So he went back to the original daily rushes, screened all the footage he had

---

199. See Vasily Grossman, *Life and Fate*, trans. Robert Chandler (London: Harvill Press, 1985), 364. While *Life and Fate* was written in 1959 it was not published in Russia until 1988 but it is distinctly possible that Tarkovsky read the book prior to filming *Mirror*. The novel was smuggled out of Russia on microfilm in 1974 but Grossman never got to see it in print in Russian or English as he died in 1964. The episode in the film is situated in 1935; just two years before the height of the Great Purge, the year of the first trials of Zinoviev and Kamenev, one time rivals of Stalin to be heirs of Lenin, who were sentenced to five and ten years in jail respectively and then retried and shot the year later. In Soviet cinema history 1935 was the year *Chapayev* won the Moscow Film Festival Award and the year before Mikhalkov's *Burnt by the Sun* (*Utomlyonnye solntsem*, 1994) is set. In November 1935 Stalin told a conference of Stakhanovite workers "Life has become better, Life has become merrier." The phrase was repeated all throughout the Soviet Union. See Helen Rappaport, *Joseph Stalin: A Biographical Companion* (Santa Barbara: ABC-CLIO, 1999), 171.

200. Tarkovsky, *Sculpting in Time*, 116.

201. Ibid.

shot for the entire film, including the documentary footage he had acquired. He pinpointed one of the documentary sequences, the footage of the Russian soldiers taken at Lake Sivash, as having some kind of problem; yet he still was not sure why. He recalled all of the footage shot from the Lake Sivash sequence from the archives and discovered the problem: what he had thought was documentary capturing natural reactions of those within the frame, was revealed to have been orchestrated for the camera. He found three takes of the same shot; this is why the sequence had felt false and unnatural and had not fitted appropriately with the rhythm of the sequence he was preparing. When he excised the offending shot and found something more suitable, he discovered that *Mirror* had once again regained its rhythm and stated "Time itself, running through the shots, had met and linked together."[202]

The film concludes with its most temporally and spatially ambitious sequence, another Bakhtinian "idyllic chronotope." In it a young Maria (before she has even conceived her child, therefore several years before the opening shot on the fence) lies in the grass near the dacha embracing her husband, the enigmatic father. He asks her whether she would prefer a girl or a boy, and she looks perturbed. Her expression, as it has been at numerous moments throughout the film, is extremely hard to gauge: she is momentarily happy, then sad, wise and fearful, almost all at the same time. She glances directly at the camera for a brief moment, as if she knows the future, then turns her head away in a replica of the pose with which the film opened. The camera slowly tracks across the field revealing the dacha to be simultaneously inhabited and abandoned, as it was then and as it is "now," in the same sequence, impossibly unified in time and space. In the field she sees her older self hand in hand with the young Alexei and his sister, as the children were/will be at the opening of the film. Three planes of temporality co-exist in a single harmonious shot: the woman she is now, the children she will have in the future and the grandmother she will become. Is she a young woman seeing the future or an old woman remembering the past? Tarkovskian time is fluid and has no boundaries; it is alive as the present. As the old woman and her children walk across the field, she can be seen in the background; silently observing them. Perhaps Tarkovsky had in mind the famous line of poetry by Boris Pasternak, "To live your life is not as simple as to cross a field."[203] The camera retreats into the forest, deeper and deeper. As darkness floods into the frame, the film fades to black.[204]

---

202. Ibid., 117.

203. Boris Pasternak, "Hamlet," in *Dr Zhivago,* [1957] "Poems of Yurii Zhivago," trans. Manya Harari and Max Hayward (London: Vintage, 2002), 467.

204. This shot is exactly reproduced in *The Return* and the shot of the mother and father discussing the future was paid homage to at the end/beginning of *Irréversible* (Noé, 2002), a film which is presented in reverse chronological order. The final sequence of *Mirror* has proved difficult for even contemporary writers to gauge. Beumers mistakenly asserts that it is Alexei's wife in the background watching the grandmother and her two children. See Beumers, *A History*

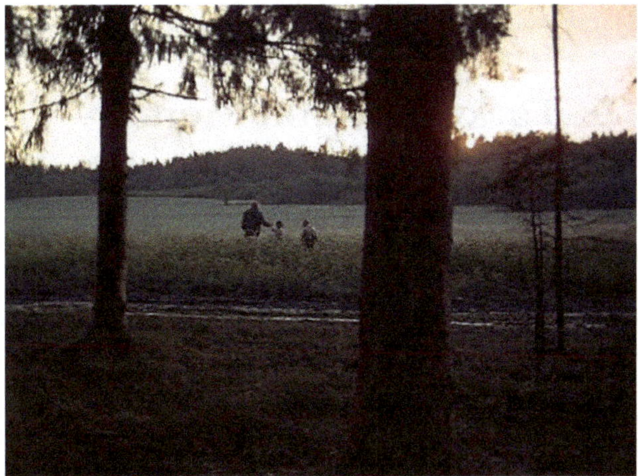

Figure 7 Pasternak's assertion that "To live your life is not as simple as to cross a field" is revealed to be true as multiple temporalities collide at the "end" of *Mirror*.

Finally, Tarkovsky has achieved what he set out to do. He frequently stated that *Mirror* was a love song to his mother and a denial of her mortality: "I cannot come to terms with the fact that my mother will die. I cannot agree with this. I will protest and show that she is immortal."[205] Through the film he *has* made his mother immortal; even though she is long gone, she lives forever in the material encounters which occur each time someone watches the film.

Viewing the film more than forty years after it was made is, perhaps, even more moving, given the range of paratextual associations on display. From Tarkovsky's own death at a relatively young age to the fact that his father outlived him and they were never reconciled. Although Tarkovsky himself said that *Mirror* was "closest to his concept of cinema,"[206] he remained profoundly ambivalent about its effect on his psyche. The dreams on which he had based the film, those that had come to him every night for years, full of the sights and sounds and even smells from his childhood, suddenly disappeared. Rather than feeling the sense of release that he expected, he was left with an overwhelming sense of emptiness, which led him to poignantly conclude: "So I have lost one more illusion, perhaps the most important one for the preservation of peace and quiet in my soul. I have buried my childhood home within my film."[207]

---

of Russian Cinema, 166.

205. Andrei Tarkovsky in Natasha Synessios, *Mirror,* 17.

206. Synessios, *Mirror,* 47.

207. Andrei Tarkovsky, from an unpublished transcript of Tarkovsky's Russian diary, quoted in Synessios, *Mirror,* 110.

Chapter Two

Tarkovsky and Memory

> Time and memory merge into each other… It is obvious enough that without time, memory cannot exist either. But memory is something so complex that no list of all its attributes could define the totality of the impressions through which it affects us.
>
> ~Andrei Tarkovsky

In *Sculpting in Time* Tarkovsky frequently described how time was intrinsically connected to memory, so much so that "they are like the two sides of a medal."[208] The time recorded in his films, as I have shown, often takes the form of recreated memories, dreams or reveries. For Tarkovsky memory is one of the fundamental aspects of identity and a pillar of his film theory; he commented that memory is "something so complex that no list of all its attributes could define the totality of the impressions through which it affects us."[209]

When he left the Soviet Union in March 1982, he was unaware that he would never return. Agonising about his future he called a press conference in Milan and announced his reluctant decision to defect, leaving his beloved homeland and much of his family behind. Journalists questioned him about his motives and plans, to which he angrily responded with a characteristically intense response, "You cannot ask me bureaucratic questions. Which country? I don't know. It's like asking me in which cemetery I wish to bury my children."[210] To Tarkovsky making films was much more than a vocation: his art, quite simply, *was* his life.

As early as January 1977 in his letter to Shauro he had made a threat to leave the Soviet Union, demanding justification for the way he had been treated: "I shall take the liberty of deciding that Soviet culture, Soviet society and its masters consider me to either be redundant or actually a harmful influence."[211] With so much of his work being distinctly influenced by his connection both physically and spiritually to Russia, audiences wondered what kind of films he would make in this new period of his career as an exile.

---

208. Tarkovsky, *Sculpting in Time*, 57.
209. Ibid.
210. Andrei Tarkovsky, at a conference in Milan July 1984 in John Gianvitto, *Andrei Tarkovsky Interviews* (University of Mississippi, 2006), xviii.
211. Tarkovsky, *Time Within Time, The Diaries 1970-1986,* 141.

It could be persuasively argued that Tarkovsky's works are as connected, if not more, to the culture, history and geography of the lands in which they are produced, as those of any European Art Cinema director of his generation. Are Bergman's films so inherently Swedish? Are Antonioni's so Italian? In the first of his exile films, *Nostalghia*, as Turovskaya remarked, he managed to "De-italianize Italy"[212] and then he did the same for Sweden in his second film, *The Sacrifice*; in the process creating two films that are as deeply "Russian" as the five films that preceded them without filming a single frame in his native land. As an exile he joined the ranks of other Russian artists who had left their country, voluntarily or otherwise, like Joseph Brodsky, Alexander Solzhenitsyn, Wassily Kandinsky and one of the subjects of *Nostalghia*, the fictional composer Pavel Sosnovsky.

Hamid Naficy in his *An Accented Cinema: Exilic and Diasporic Film-making* suggests that a sense of longing and nostalgia is a characteristic trope of exile cinema, which has a propensity to focus on properties of recollection and remembrance, characterised by a style described by him as "fragmented, multilingual, epistolary, self-reflective."[213] Naficy continues: "Accented films are personal and unique, like fingerprints because they are both authorial and autobiographical."[214] The two films Tarkovsky made in exile, *Nostalghia* and *The Sacrifice*, are perhaps the most personal, alongside *Mirror*, of all Tarkovsky's films, as in exile he turned even further towards the realms of memory, perception and dream. *Nostalghia* replicates aspects of Tarkovsky's life with poignant and at times disturbing honesty. Delving deep into his own psyche for inspiration he was forced to conclude, "The protagonist [of *Nostalghia*] is a mirror image of me. I have never made a film which mirrors my own state of mind with so much violence, and liberates my inner world with so much depth."[215]

This chapter explores how Tarkovsky reconstructs and recreates memories, either real, imaginary or inhabiting an ethereal area somewhere in between. These memories become an undergirding trope of Tarkovsky's cinema and can be found in each of his texts; whether it is an adult recalling the long passed, formative period of his youth in *Mirror*, a teenager's reminiscences of the pre-lapsarian, maternal idyll of lost childhood in *Ivan's Childhood*, or a scientist's memories of earth while in orbit in *Solaris*. Not only is memory central to the films thematically, it is a key component of the way they are stylistically constructed and of how "time pressure" is rendered within and beyond the frame. Film becomes a device through which memory is filtered, created and then projected, and in so doing becomes an articulation of not just memory, but the memory process itself.

---

212. Turovskaya, *The Films of Andrei Tarkovsky*, 120.

213. Hamid Naficy, *An Accented cinema: Exilic and Diasporic Film-making*, 1.

214. Ibid, 34.

215. Andrei Tarkovsky, Tony Mitchell, *Film Criticism* 8.8 (1984): 5. Originally from *La Repubblica*, May 17, 1983.

2.1 An Impression of Time: From *Ivan's Childhood* to *Nostalghia*

A film is bigger than it is – at least, if it is a real film. And it always turns out to have more thought, more ideas, than were consciously put there by its author. [...] Once in contact with the individual who sees it, it separates from its author, starts to live its own life, undergoes changes of form and meaning.

~Andrei Tarkovsky

Since its invention film has had an almost symbiotic relationship with memory. In her book *Dionysus Writes: The Invention of Theatre in Ancient Greece*, Jennifer Wise contends that, "The existence of writing changed memory."[216] It is equally the case that the invention of the photographic medium and then cinema also changed memory, perhaps in even as powerful and compelling ways. Tarkovsky asserted that it was with the invention of the cinema in the last decade of the nineteenth century that man had created the means to effectively capture and replicate time: "And simultaneously the possibility of reproducing that time on screen as often as he wanted, to repeat it and go back to it. He acquired a matrix for *actual time.*"[217] This "impression of time" that Tarkovsky described shares the functions of memory in its ability to create a replica of a moment from the past and store it for later "use." For film this moment is captured and projected onto a screen; in the realm of the mind a memory is recreated through thought; for what more is memory other than an "impression of time?" D. N. Rodowick in *Deleuze's Time Machine* takes this imbrication between cinema and the mind even further, by describing how they are both analogous to a time machine, in that both are able to recreate the past and then express it as a tangible present.[218]

The properties of memory, its functions, reliability, malleability and fallibility, have always been the subject of art. In the twentieth century alone writers like Marcel Proust, Georges Perec and Alain Robbe-Grillet all explored the properties of memory using the distinctive capabilities of their medium. The European Art Cinema of the late fifties, sixties and beyond was fascinated by the memory process. Tarkovsky was just one of many film-makers interrogating the properties of time and memory onscreen; from *Amarcord* (Fellini, 1974), *Hiroshima Mon Amour* (Resnais, 1959), to *Wild Strawberries* (Bergman, 1957) and *La Jetée* (Marker, 1962) this fascination has returned in the new millennium in films like *Memento* (Nolan, 2000), *Oldboy* (Park, 2003),

216. Jennifer Wise, *Dionysus Writes: The Invention of Theatre in Ancient Greece* (Ithaca and London: Cornell University Press, 1998), 25.

217. Tarkovsky, *Sculpting in Time*, 62.

218. Rodowick is not the only one to have explored this metaphor. Endel Tulving suggested that "remembering, for the rememberer is mental time travel." Quoted in Floyd Skloot, *In the Shadow of Memory* (Lincoln: University of Nebraska Press, 2003), 227.

Eternal Sunshine of the Spotless Mind (Gondry, 2004) and *Caché* (Haneke, 2005). Tarkovsky maintained that film has an ability to recreate the affective power of memory even more intensely than literature by using its unique properties. For him, "No other art can compare with cinema in the force, precision and starkness with which it conveys awareness of facts and aesthetic structures existing and changing within time."[219]

A brief analysis of Henri Bergson's understanding of memory provides a valuable context for Tarkovsky's memory imbued texts. In *Matter and Memory* Bergson identified three theoretical types of memory, which inform our day to day existence: habit formed memory, pure recollection and involuntary memory. It is the third type of memory which is explored most frequently, not only in Tarkovsky's films, but in many of the films of his contemporaries. Habitual memory (often called factual or propositional memory by psychologists) is the dominant practical form of memory. It has a pragmatic, functional value and its power comes from the fact that it requires no conscious recall; in fact, it is more like a reflex. Activities like riding a bike, reading or remembering historical dates are actions which at one time were learned to such an extent that they can be reproduced with little effort. When one remembers that Tolstoy wrote *War and Peace*, it is because we learned it some time in the past and the information has become stored. This memory requires no experience of the event or even a perception of it to serve its purpose.

The second type of memory is pure recollection, which differs from habit formed memory in that it is filtered by perception. Less functional, it is a latent form of memory, which lies dormant and is only activated when called upon by the thinker. As the mind actively pursues a memory, it consciously moves from one logical association to another, perhaps linked by a question or a cluster of events.

The third type of memory, which is even less tangible than pure recollection, is called involuntary memory. It is a transitive memory characterised by an involuntary reaction to outward stimuli. These involuntary memories are artfully illustrated in Marcel Proust's concept of "Sensuous Signs." For Proust an event, an image or even a smell could conjure up a concomitant association in the mind. In *Remembrance of Things Past. Volume 1: Swann's Way* the narrator is overcome by memories upon tasting a rather unattractive looking madeleine:

> No sooner had the warm liquid mixed with the crumbs touched my palate than a shudder ran through me and I stopped, intent upon the extraordinary thing that was happening to me. An exquisite pleasure had invaded my senses, something isolated, detached, with no suggestion of its origin.... And suddenly the memory revealed itself. The taste was that of

219. Tarkovsky, *Sculpting in Time*, 69.

> the little piece of madeleine which on Sunday mornings at Combray (because on those mornings I did not go out before mass), when I went to say good morning to her in her bedroom, my aunt Léonie used to give me, dipping it first in her own cup of tea or tisane.[220]

In Tarkovsky's films equally insignificant moments will inspire such vivid, affectual memories. Unlike with other forms of memory, with involuntary memories the thinker has no control over when and how these memories emerge. They are not just located in the mind, but are even given actuality in the body, and as a result the act of memory is a visceral, synesthetic experience, which recreates not only the visual image of that past event, but also the sensual impression of the occurrence in its entirety, even able, like a quasi-time machine, to transport a person back to that original moment of experience.

This concept of memory is a challenge to conventional memory interpretation, in that involuntary memories presuppose a world of memory that exists and runs concurrently alongside our day to day experience. For Proust, as for Tarkovsky, the past is always alive, hidden somewhere within us and may be discovered and recreated through mediating sensory perceptions at any given moment. Tarkovsky read and admired Proust, seeing in his use of memory a connection to his own work "Proust also spoke of raising a 'vast edifice of memories,' and that seems to me to be what cinema is called to do."[221] Like Proust's novels, Tarkovsky's films are both a representation of memory and an inducement to remember.[222] *Mirror* is about Alexei remembering his life (the memories are frequently involuntary), but it also calls on the viewer to recall their own experiences. Such a dual layered approach takes on the experience of his characters' involuntary memories and the involuntary memories of the reader/viewer inspired by the work of art itself. The visual medium of film, especially in its poetic guise, with the broad range of properties at its disposal, encompassing imagery, sound (both music and

---

220. Marcel Proust, *Remembrance of Things Past. Volume 1: Swann's Way,* [1922-31] trans. C.K. Scott Moncrieff (New York: Dover Publications Inc, 2003), 37-9. Proust's novel has been adapted into film three times: *Swann in Love* (Schlondorff, 1984), *Time Regained* (Ruiz, 1999) and *La Captive* (Akerman, 2000).

221. Tarkovsky, *Sculpting in Time*, 59.

222. Alexei Solonitsyn, Anatoly Solonitsyn's brother, recounted the following pertinent anecdote about the importance of Proust to Tarkovsky. He described a conversation between Tarkovsky and Anatoly Solonitsyn, "You see Anatoly, art is interesting when it deals with mystery. For instance, Marcel Proust. He began describing a scene from Proust's novel *Swann's Way*. A boy travelling at night sees the spires of three bell towers in the valley. As he rides along the road the spires seem to turn around, first separating and then merging into one. The boy feels a strange sense of anxiety that weighs heavy on his soul. Why? What's troubling him?...Do you understand Anatoly? said the director engrossed in his tale. Here we're dealing with something that cannot be conveyed in words. And in our film we'll go this route too." "Film as Magic," *About Andrei Tarkovsky, Memoirs and Biographies,* ed. Marina Tarkovskaya (Moscow: Progress Publishers, 1990), 96-105.

otherwise), theme and characterisation, can perform this associative function compellingly.

Films which portray thought in such a fashion deviate substantially from traditional cinematic representations of memory. In classical narrative cinema anamnesis is primarily represented through the mode of the flashback, where it is clearly indicated with dramatic visual and aural signifiers and located as distinct from the contemporary action of the film. Even narratives with relatively complex temporal structures are harmonized by the flashback, designed as "a precisely closed circuit which goes from the present to the past, then leads us back to the present."[223] The rigidly prescribed formation of the flashback defines strict boundaries between the past and the present, affirming the primacy of the present over the past and placing time in its strictly chronological and logical structure.

Despite being often formally and philosophically challenging, especially considering the environment in which they were produced, Tarkovsky's early films *Ivan's Childhood* and *Andrei Rublyov* are mostly conventional in their depiction of temporality and memory. Tarkovsky's debut, *Ivan's Childhood*, has long been marginalised in Tarkovsky studies, perhaps unfairly, deemed too un-Tarkovskian in its construction. While it does have more of a plot than the films which follow, it is much more than a realistic portrayal of events. Adapted from Vladimir Bogomolov's story *Ivan* (1957), the narrative follows the actions of a young Soviet scout during the Second World War and has four highly affective dream sequences interspersed throughout, which simultaneously function as memories.

It opens with the iconic Mosfilm logo, over which the mournful cries of a cuckoo can be heard. A young boy, the eponymous Ivan, clutches a tree; his face is framed and bifurcated by a spider's web anticipating the schism which envelops his character. His eyes are wide with amazement at his natural surroundings. Soft and lilting orchestral music sounds, as we are presented with the idyllic, natural images Ivan sees. A slow lateral tracking shot glides across the roots of a tree and the earth in which they reside, a camera move which will later be considered Tarkovsky's trademark and will be present in his every film without exception. The bright lighting gives the image a dream-like and poetic dimension, evocative of the nostalgic allure of memory, to which he will return in *Solaris* and *Mirror*. Unexpectedly, the boy begins to levitate; he is as surprised as the audience, as he rises above the tops of the trees and begins to fly through the sky.

223. Gilles Deleuze, *Cinema Two: The Time Image*, trans. Hugh Tomlinson and Robert Galeta (London, The Athlone Press, 1989), 48.

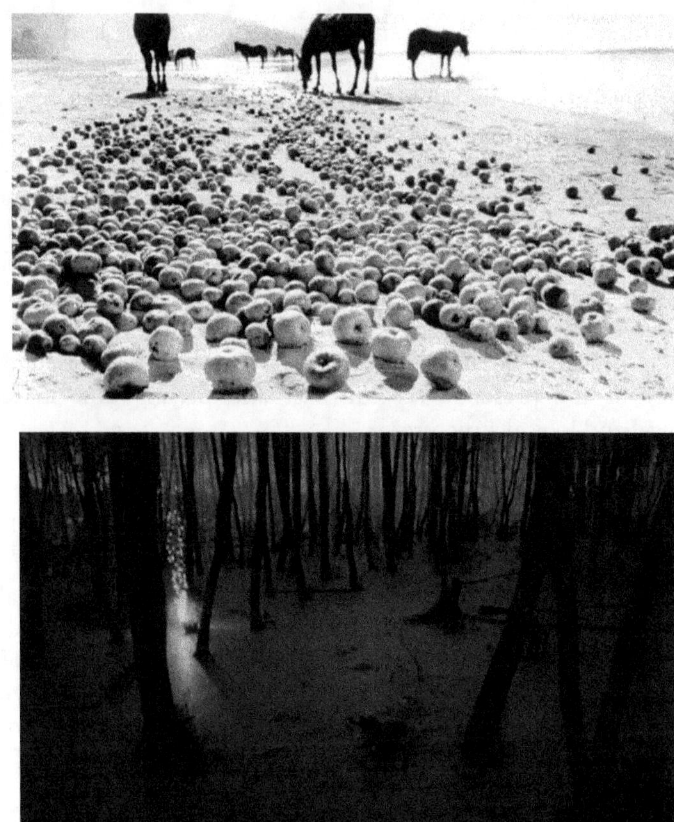

Figure 8 and 9 *Ivan's Childhood*: The nostalgic allure of memory stands in stark contrast to the nightmarish "reality" in which Ivan resides and the two are kept more separate than in many of Tarkovsky's later films.

Returning to the ground he sees a woman, his mother, collecting fresh water in a bucket from a well. He calls out to her, "Mama!" Like all Tarkovskian mothers she is beautiful, but distant, they do not touch, but they share an expression of tenderness as he drinks, wiping their brow in an identical fashion. The elegiac tone is short lived; the mood abruptly changes, as the camera suddenly zooms into his mother's face, jerking quickly more than ninety degrees as we hear his frightened voice cry "Mama" and a piercingly loud gunshot. Ivan is jarred awake, it has all been a dream; in reality Ivan is a twelve year old scout fighting for the Soviet Union during the Second World War. His mother and his entire family have been killed by the Nazis.

The dreams/memories, which populate the film, recall a time before the conflict, evocative of family, harmony, nature, the sweetness of the maternal bond, an Arcadian ideal of an idyllic past, which will be explored in many Tarkovsky films. Each dream is clearly recognizable as such: the recurring motif of the sound of dripping water acts as a distinct link between the unreal dream world and his present reality. *Ivan's Childhood* is one of the many more challenging depictions of the Second World War—in Russian referred to as "The Great Patriotic War"—that emerged during the Thaw period, which saw the conflict approached from a more humanist perspective, avoiding the glamorous, epic sweep of traditional heroic Soviet cinema. Denise Youngblood suggests that "rather than making stylised epics in the Socialist Realist fashion, a daring few fomented a quiet revolution, both in the style and content of the war film."[224] Despite this "quiet revolution," on its release *Ivan's Childhood* was criticised by, among others, the Italian newspaper *L' Unità* for its supposedly distinctly western brand of individuality and subjectivity, they even went so far as to call Tarkovsky a "petty bourgeois." They were particularly vociferous in their condemnation of Tarkovsky's use of dream sequences, which went on to be a staple of his work: "Dreams! *We*, in the West, stopped using dreams long ago! Tarkovsky's slow on the uptake – Those were all right between the wars!"[225]

Ivan's Childhood, however, presents a partial challenge to the *L' Unità* critique. The film simultaneously adheres to conventional representations of space and time and breaks them. Many of the reviews register this dichotomy between convention and experiment. Bordwell and Thompson commented on its "ambiguity characteristic of 1960s Art Cinema,"[226] which for David A. Cook even "approaches the avant-garde in its surreal rendition of the horrors of war."[227] Yet David Thomson saw fit to describe it as Tarkovsky's "most conventional, his most Sovietized and his most successful [film]."[228]

Somewhat surprisingly, it was Jean Paul Sartre who led the passionate defence of the film against the criticisms of *L' Unità*. He did not see the film as a personal, subjective account of one young man's experience, but rather a more ambiguous social and symbolic cultural artifact. For him the dreams are not distinctly separated from reality or visions of the past:

> His hallucinations have nothing gratuitous about them. They are not bits of bravura, or practised examples of a child's 'subjectivity': they remain perfectly objective. We continue to see Ivan from outside, like in the 'realistic' scenes; the truth is that the whole world is a hallucination for this child.[229]

---

224. Denise Youngblood, "Post Stalinist Cinema and the Myth of World War Two," *Historical Journal of Film, Radio and Television* 14.4 (1994): 415.
225. Quoted in Jean Paul Sartre, "Letter on the Critique of *Ivan's* Childhood," in *Tarkovsky,* 36.
226. Bordwell, David, and Thompson, Kristin, *Film History An Introduction* (Columbus: McGraw-Hill, 1994), 537.
227. David A. Cook, *A History of Narrative Film*, 791.
228. David Thomson, *The New Biographical Dictionary of Film* (London: Little, Brown, 2003), 858.
229. Jean Paul Sartre, in *Tarkovsky,* 39.

As the dreams progress, they reflect a distorted mirror of the "reality" of Ivan's existence. The dirty water and oppressive rainstorms of his waking life become the idyllic summer rain of his dreams; his starvation is manifested in memory of an abundance of apples on the back of the cart; the childhood games of hide and seek perversely reflect his tortuous combat experience. Ultimately, Ivan retreats to his dream world but cannot remain there: the return to the past is impossible, as he is continually pulled back to his present, until, finally, he is murdered.

There is a sense that as Tarkovsky's career progressed, he found the strict dichotomy between reality and memory unsatisfactory and sought other cinematic techniques to illustrate his much more ambiguous narratives onscreen.[230] His more challenging attitude to temporality and space required a different form:

> It occurred to me then, that from these properties of memory a new working principle could be developed, on which an extraordinarily interesting film might be built. Outwardly the pattern of events, of the hero's actions and behaviour, would be disturbed. It would be the story of his thoughts, his memories and dreams.[231]

By the time of *Mirror*, and later *Nostalghia*, his directorial style had evolved into something more personal and experimental; he even defined his own concept of the way memory should be represented in the cinema and called it "time memory."

2.2 Memory and Experience

I wanted to make a film about Russian nostalgia – about that state of mind peculiar to our nation, which affects Russians who are far from their native land.... I wanted the film to be about the fatal attachment of Russians to their national roots, their past, their culture, their native places, their families and friends, an attachment which they carry with them all their lives, regardless of where destiny may fling them.... How could I have imagined as I was making *Nostalghia* that the stifling sense of longing that fills the screen space of that

230. This more provocative portrayal of dreams is anticipated in the final dream of *Ivan's Childhood* which takes place after Ivan's death and cannot therefore be his own dream in the conventional sense. It is one of the most poignant moments of the film and rather than give the film a conventional happy ending it is enigmatic and suggestive, portraying a young life wasted, cut off in its prime by a brutal war.

231. Tarkovsky, *Sculpting in Time*, 29.

film was to become my lot for the rest of my life; that from now until the end of my days I would bear the painful malady within myself.

~Andrei Tarkovsky

The choice to call his first film made abroad *Nostalghia* was incredibly significant. As Tarkovsky undertook its production, the task must have been a daunting one: making a film without the usual network of friends and colleagues, in a language which he hardly knew, with a foreign cast and crew, and being separated from his family. In interviews he went to great lengths to distinguish the Russian concept of "nostalghia" from western nostalgia. For Russians "nostalghia" is inherently connected to cultural identity and to the ethereal concept of the "Russian idea," that of Russia's unique role in world history, its past and its future. Tarkovsky stated:

> Our 'nostalghia' is not your 'nostalgia.' It is not an individual emotion but something much more complex and profound that Russians experience when they are abroad. It is a disease, an illness, that drains away the strength of the soul, the capacity to work, the pleasure of living.[232]

The use of the word soul, in Russian *dusha*, is indicative of Tarkovsky's spiritual beliefs, which are of considerable importance to his cinema. In another interview he continued to describe "nostalghia" as an emotion, "that binds us not so much with our own privation, our longing, our separation, but rather with the suffering of others, a passionate empathy."[233] For Tarkovsky one of the primary goals of art was communication. The great Russian author Alexander Solzhenitsyn, who shared much of Tarkovsky's experience and his lament, described exile as "spiritual castration."[234] For Tarkovsky "nostalghia" is not the pleasurable experience of reminiscence, but a painful recollection of a time that can never be returned. Tarkovsky's ardent explanation of these concepts must, in some ways, mirror his internal feelings of being alienated from his own country and family. It is these feelings that permeate *Nostalghia* from its very opening shot to its closing frames.

Nostalghia is about a Russian academic and poet, Andrei Gorchakov, living in Italy while writing a book on another Russian exile, the 17th Century composer Pavel Sosnovsky. It is unclear how long Gorchakov has been in Italy, but it is evidently a long time. He has powerful feelings of nostalgia for his native country, but for unspecified reasons he is unable to return. The

---

232. Quoted in Maurizio Porro, "Cannes Tarkovsky," *Corriere della Sera*, May 16, 1983, trans. David Stringer, para 1, (n.d.) <http://www.acs.ucalgary.ca/~tstronds/nostalghia.com/TheTopics/Tarkovsky_Porro-1983.html> (10th September 2008).
233. Quoted in Natalia Aspesi, "That Gentle Emotion that is a Mortal Illness for us Russians," *La Repubblica*, May 17, 1983, trans. David Stringari, para 4, (n.d.) <http://www.ucalgary.ca/~tstronds/nostalghia.com/TheTopics/Tarkovsky_Aspesi-1983.html > (10th September 2008).
234. Quoted in Hedrick Smith, *The Russians* (Aylesbury: Sphere Books, 1976), 516.

nature of his exile and whether it is voluntary or not is never revealed. His subject, Sosnovsky, had considerable success abroad, but also felt such a sense of loss for his homeland that when he finally returned to Russia, he committed suicide. Gorchakov becomes obsessed with a local man whom he meets through his beautiful Italian translator Eugenia; it transpires that the man imprisoned his family in their own home for years, waiting for the apocalypse. Gorchakov comes to see in this man, Domenico, a reflection of his own search for faith and identity. In fact, Tarkovsky uses similar cinematic techniques to emphasise their connectedness. They appear as reflections of one another in a mirror, they impossibly share the same dog and both meet the same fate. In the documentary *Tempo di Viaggio*, Tarkovsky revealed how similar his own thoughts were to Gorchakov's. Talking to Tonino Guerra, the film's writer, he suggested, "I've got a complicated impression. I am confused, you see? The things that I saw yesterday seem as if I saw them a week ago. About our journey that was a month ago, I feel that it was just a moment ago. Everything got mixed up, the time and the space." Tarkovsky's articulation of his own spatio-temporal dislocation becomes dramatised in Gorchakov's mental state and the film itself.

Like in many of Tarkovsky's films, plot is marginalized in favour of atmosphere, imagery and the exploration of ideas. Thompson and Bordwell describe the film as a "melancholy, virtually non-narrative meditation on memory"[235] and their choice of words is apt; the film is as much about the memory process as it is about the memories themselves. There is an absence of strict causality in the narrative, little actually happens in terms of plot, and the behaviour of characters often seems illogical when viewed from a naturalistic perspective. The film sometimes has the air of a parable, which is accentuated by the repeated and unsubtle prelapsarian metaphors and the naming of two of the main characters Andrei and Eugenia.

Memory is at the very core of the film, and it is Gorchakov's thoughts, memories and dreams which are on display, as well as his psychological and spiritual malaise at being alienated not only from his country, but from other human beings, and his belief that the world is being consumed by superficiality and desire for material goods over the heavenly. It is in the representation of Gorchakov's memories that *Nostalghia* departs from the likes of *Ivan's Childhood*, *Andrei Rublyov* and even to a certain extent, *Mirror*. *Nostalghia* visualises Tarkovsky's interpretation of Proust's "Sensuous Signs," as Gorchakov is "crushed by the recollections of his past, by the faces of those dear to him, which assail his memory together with the sounds and smells of home."[236] In *Nostalghia* the boundaries between reality, memory, dream and fantasy—borrowing the Deleuzian term an "actual" and a "virtual"—are frequently indistinguishable. Unlike conventional flashbacks, memories emerge without

235. David Bordwell and Kristin Thompson, *Film History An Introduction*, 750.
236. Tarkovsky, *Sculpting in Time*, 203.

being prompted; they are cut into the action without context and they are frequently not codified as memories through narrative or *mise en scène*. This has led some to conclude, as David Cook does, that *Nostalghia* is Tarkovsky's "most mysterious and inaccessible film."[237]

This particular stylistic approach is well suited to the narrative of *Nostalghia*: as Gorchakov becomes overcome by memories of his past, so intense are these feelings and involuntary memories that they begin to invade his waking life and he loses control over them. As the film progresses, Gorchakov faces stronger and stronger "disturbances of memory and the failures of recognition,"[238] and the audience share his experiences, as they, like Gorchakov himself, find it harder and harder to discern what is memory, what is past and what is present.

Writers on Tarkovsky have often found this intentional ambiguity obfuscatory, failing to register that it is a key element of Tarkovsky's film theory and his poetic aesthetic. The usually astute Johnson and Petrie fail to adequately process these sequences. Without taking into account the Bergsonian/Deleuzian approach to the cinema of perception, they flounder: "His [Gorchakov's] dreams and memories are self-enclosed, circular, and repetitive, and seem to be an excuse for avoiding any commitment to his existing reality rather than as a force for emotional and psychic liberation and self-understanding."[239] While it is true that the dreams and memories are a symbol of Gorchakov's spiritual and psychological *ennui*, they are far from enclosed; in fact, they are remarkably open, as we are witness to the past bleeding into the present and vice versa with remarkable fluidity. In one of the numerous sequences set in the hotel where Gorchakov is staying, one of Tarkovsky's most potent zones of temporal and spatial ambiguity, he sits with his interpreter Eugenia and refuses to see any more Italian ruins: the superficiality of Italian beauty has become an anathema to him. Involuntary memories of his home burst from nowhere, perhaps inspired by the sound of a dog barking or the rhythmic movement of a woman's hair.

These involuntary memories become more and more frequent, as it becomes apparent that Gorchakov has a precarious grip over his own sense of reality; he "becomes the prisoner of an illusory existence; falling out of time he is unable to seize his own link with the outside world—in other words he is doomed to madness."[240] Tarkovsky had flirted with ambiguous representations of interior and exterior prior to *Nostalghia*; the ravaged and war-torn landscapes of *Ivan's Childhood* seem to emerge from Ivan's fractured psyche and the dream-like world of *Stalker* almost appears from the eponymous Stalker's imagination, just as Hari in *Solaris* emerges from Kris Kelvin's memory. However, in the exile films it becomes harder and harder to discern which is which. Gorchakov

237. David A. Cook, *A History of Narrative Film*, 792.
238. Gilles Deleuze, *Cinema Two: The Time Image,* 55.
239. Johnson and Petrie, *The Films of Andrei Tarkovsky,* 160.
240. Tarkovsky, *Sculpting in Time*, 57-58.

seeks refuge in the world of his memory, yet as for Ivan from *Ivan's Childhood* this is ultimately impossible: he cannot live either in the past or the present, and like Ivan before him he too will die.

Tarkovsky, continuing his taxonomic approach to cinema, had his own memory concept, which he referred to as "time memory," and it becomes an essential component of how "time pressure" is presented. Like the majority of Tarkovsky's theories "time memory" concerns itself with the spectator's relationship with the film experience, intrinsically connected to Tarkovsky's almost Bergsonian belief in the organic properties of film, in which the projected image itself is truly alive and given life through the spectator in much the same way that the memories are actualised through the body of the thinker. In principle, "time memory" is the relationship and the interaction between the spectator and film text: the spectator brings their memories and life experience to the act of watching the film and relates to the cinematic text in a unique fashion that has never been and will never be replicated (by other viewers or even by himself). By presenting the viewer with a range of remarkably open and archetypal images without an overwhelming narrative context, Tarkovsky allows the spectator to establish a profoundly dialogical relationship with the film in order to "complete" the image and provide it with meaning. The image itself then remains incomplete until filtered through the perception of the spectator, as each viewer becomes not only a witness to the event but a participator. In Tarkovsky's words, the viewer "becomes a participant in the process of discovering life, unsupported by ready-made deductions from the plot or ineluctable pointers by the author."[241]

Given such grand claims we are obliged to ask what is unique about Tarkovsky's cinema that makes this "time memory" apparent, especially when it is understood that viewers bring their experience to any film regardless of content and style. However, when seen through the prism of "time memory," Tarkovsky's preference for long takes and deep focus, his arguments against reductive symbolism are much more comprehensible. Through "time memory" Tarkovsky reasserts the uniqueness of a purely cinematic experience and its polysemic function. The techniques used are deliberate and modulate the "time pressure" accordingly as the film continues, ranging from his habitual use of the long take aesthetic to particular choices of narrative, theme, *mise en scène* and sound.

Tarkovsky's open approach to imagery is reminiscent of what Shohini Chaudhuri and Howard Finn call the "open image" in their work on New Iranian Cinema. Drawing on Pasolini, Deleuze's *Cinema Two: The Time Image* and Paul Schrader's *Transcendental Style in Film*, Chaudhuri and Finn speculate that a trend has developed in Iranian film in which directors explore the ambiguous properties of an image utilising many of the same techniques we have seen Tarkovsky use. They describe some of the properties of an "open

241. Tarkovsky, *Sculpting in Time*, 20.

image": they are often archetypal and universal, filmed in deep focus with long takes, they use a relatively static camera, but their primary characteristic is perhaps their lack of homogeneity. These "open images" "are not necessarily extraordinary images; they often belong to the order of the everyday,"[242] each deliberately designed to provoke associations in viewers, just as Tarkovsky's quotidian images of houses, water, animals, and his themes concerning memory and family are. "Open images" set off reverberations, "which try not to close down a narrative but rather to open it out to the viewer's consideration, to 'live on' after the film itself has finished."[243] While Chaudhuri and Finn concentrate on the echoes which continue after the film has finished, for Tarkovsky it is of the utmost importance that "time memory" sets off associations while the film is continuing. Thus, "time memory" uses a very emotive and correspondingly reflective style of visual aesthetic to encourage interaction and reflection through specific cinematic techniques conducive to the promotion of memory, which when combined, in Tarkovsky's words, "set off impulses within us, evoked associations; objects and circumstances [which] have stayed in our memory."[244]

The prologue of *Nostalghia*, the opening shot of the film, is one such "open image" seeking to engage directly with the viewer. Tarkovsky fades into a sepia coloured shot of a quintessential Russian countryside, very similar to those we have seen not only in *Mirror* but many of his other films. It is cloaked in mist, as if shrouded in memory and the past itself. Four figures emerge, an old woman, a younger woman and two small children. They move away from the camera very slowly as if in slow motion. In the background we can just make out a white horse, and as they move a dog follows behind them. The non-diegetic sound is initially a mournful, traditional Russian folk music song, which is then followed by a rendition of Verdi's *Requiem*, suitably setting the melancholic and threnodic tone that will continue throughout the film.

The image is immediately codified as being some sort of recollection. For many a prior knowledge of Tarkovsky filters through the perception of the image. Time and place are undetermined. Is it a dream? Is it a memory of the protagonist's family as they are now, or a memory of his own childhood? It even feels as if it might be a memory of one of Tarkovsky's previous films. Tarkovsky was very aware of the ambiguous and fertile properties of such an image: he stated on numerous occasions that they were not designed to be read or analysed in the traditional sense, but felt. Fellow travellers, who engage with the film in the way Tarkovsky intended, draw on their own past, either consciously or not, while watching the image; but, of course, what these associations will be is unique from person to person. Chaudhuri and Finn

242. Shohini Chaudhuri and Howard Finn, "The Open Image: Poetic Realism and the New Iranian Cinema," *Screen* 44.1 (Spring 2003): 38.
243. Ibid., 52.
244. Tarkovsky, *Sculpting in Time*, 23.

suggest: "While watching a film one might meet them [open images] with some resistance – yet they have the property of producing virtual after-images in the mind."[245] This "resistance" that Chaudhuri and Finn speak of is the reluctance of viewers raised on the codes and conventions of classical narrative cinema to process such a deviation from what they are familiar with. Tarkovsky was aware of the problems of such an approach as it moved too far away from mainstream cinema for the comfort of many. He wrote, "The way to poetic logic, however, is fraught with adversity. Opposition awaits you at every turn, despite the fact that the principle in question is quite as legitimate as that of the logic of literature or dramaturgy; it is simply that a different component becomes the main element in the construction."[246]

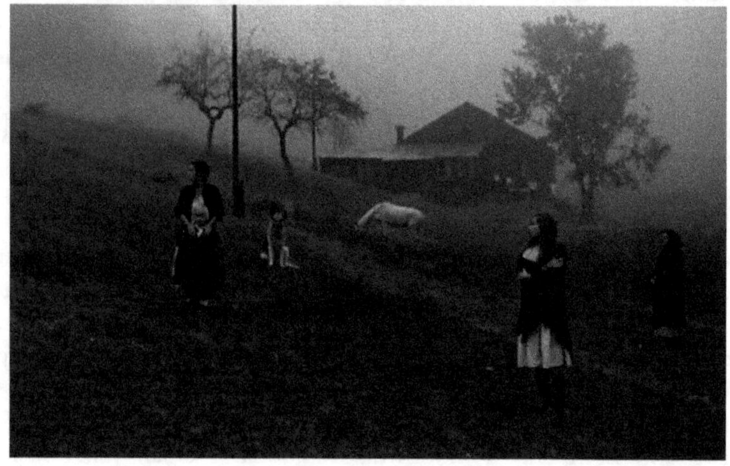

Figure 10 One of Tarkovsky's quintessential open images from *Nostalghia.* Is it a dream, a fantasy or a memory? What diverse range of associations might it spark in spectators?

In *Sculpting in Time* Tarkovsky discussed one particular "open image" from the end of Tolstoy's novel *The Death of Ivan Ilyich* (1886), which had a tremendous impact on him, an effect he strove to replicate with his own work. Ivan Ilyich is a judge, who discovers he has a terminal illness. With little time left, he contemplates how he has lived. While he initially concludes that he has lived a just life, later he begins to question whether he had thought of himself and his career too often and not helped others enough. After this epiphany he finds happiness and a sense of pity for those who have not achieved the same. Shortly after he dies in the middle of an ambiguous and prolonged sigh. It was this final image that had made such an impression on Tarkovsky:

To him all this happened in a single instant, and the meaning of that

245. Ibid., 38.
246. Johnson and Petrie, The *Films of Andrei Tarkovsky,* 29.

> instant did not change. For those present his agony continued for another two hours. Something rattled in his throat, his emaciated body twitched, then the gasping and rattle became less and less frequent. 'It is finished!' said someone near him. He heard these words and repeated them in his soul. 'Death is finished,' he said to himself. 'It is no more!' He drew in a breath, stopped in the midst of a sigh, stretched out, and died.[247]

What can Illyich's final words and his sigh possibly mean? Such is the openness and the ambiguity of their construction that they demand input from the reader. Does it represent a Tolstoyan affirmation of Christian values, as many have speculated, or the joy of becoming aware of the truth?[248] Tarkovsky suggested that "Clearly that image, which shakes us to the very depths of our being, cannot be interpreted in one way only. Its associations reach far into our innermost feelings, reminding us of some obscure memories and experiences of our own, stunning us, stirring our souls like a revelation."[249] What Tarkovsky experienced on reading the end of Tolstoy's novel is the effect which he is seeking to induce in his viewers, a distinctly personal and unique revelation and epiphany of their own.

In this respect, "time memory" gives us an insight into one of the most pervasive Tarkovsky paradoxes: how can his films be simultaneously so autobiographical and yet achieve such a profoundly personal effect on many of his viewers? There can be little doubt that he is one of the most autobiographical of directors; yet, despite this, the texts are frequently discussed with regard to their appeal to audiences on a distinctly intimate level, as if they in some way are able to reflect quite accurately the own emotional experiences of the individual members of the audience. This is evidenced in part by reviews of Tarkovsky's films and more significantly in letters from the public he included in *Sculpting in Time*. About *Mirror* one woman wrote,

> What is this film about? It is about a Man [….] It's a film about you, your father, your grandfather, about someone who will live after you and is still 'you.' About a Man who lives on the earth, is a part of the earth and the earth is a part of him, about the fact that a man is answerable for his life both to the past and to the future. You have to watch the film simply, and

247. Leo Tolstoy, *The Death of Ivan Ilyich* in *The Death of Ivan Ilych and Other Stories*, trans. Aylmer Maude and J. D. Duff (Colchester: Signet Classics, 2003), 152. It might also have been relevant for Tarkovsky that it all happened in a single instant,

248. The story has been loosely adapted twice, once by Akira Kurosawa in *Ikiru* (1952) and again as *Ivan's XTC* (Rose, 2000). About the ending Vladimir Nabokov said, "The Tolstoyan formula is: Ivan lived a bad life and since the bad life is nothing but the death of the soul, then Ivan lived a living death; and since beyond death is God's living light, then Ivan died into a new life- Life with a capital L." Vladimir Nabokov, *Lectures On Russian Literature* (Oxford: Harcourt Edition, 2002), 237. Such a spiritual epiphany is frequent in Tolstoy's short stories, especially his later works. See "Master and Man" (1893), "Repentance" (1886) and "What Men Live By" (1885).

249. Tarkovsky, *Sculpting in Time*, 108.

> listen to the music of Bach and the poems of Arseny Tarkovsky; watch it as one watches the stars, or the sea, as one admires a landscape. There is no mathematical logic here, for it cannot explain what man is or the meaning of his life.[250]

In Tarkovsky's finest moments there is no attempt to explain meanings or life, there is no fundamental argument or answer offered. The opening sequence of *Nostalghia* is one such fertile, aesthetic object, it pauses itself in a freeze frame, a moment of stasis, just like a memory, and the credits roll before fading to black. The single shot has lasted almost two and a half minutes and anticipates the narrative of the film which follows. *Nostalghia* is a threnodic lament for the past and an articulation of the memory process itself.

2.3 "Time Memory" and Gilles Deleuze's Time Image

Time, printed in its factual form and manifestations: such is the supreme idea of cinema as art, leading us to think about the wealth of untapped resources in film, about its colossal future.

~Andrei Tarkovsky

Time becomes the basis of bases in cinema, like sound in music, like colour in painting.

~Gilles Deleuze

Tarkovsky's characterization of a cinema with time at its foundation is markedly echoed in Gilles Deleuze's groundbreaking analyses of temporality in the cinematic art, in his *Cinema One: The Movement Image* and *Cinema Two: The Time-Image*.[251] Just as Tarkovsky sought for a new approach to film, one which embraces time rather than subordinates it, so did Deleuze. Close analysis of Tarkovsky's film theory reveals numerous parallels between the two, to such an extent, in fact, that we cannot be sure how much of an influence Tarkovsky had on Deleuze's writings. Some have commented on these similarities already: Robert Bird observes that "Deleuze's analysis of the time-image is of particular importance for understanding Tarkovsky, who consistently defined the basic element of his cinema as time."[252] Totaro went as far as asserting:

---

250. Ibid., 9.
251. Some of the ideas in this sub-chapter were initially proposed by the author in "Sculpting the Time Image: An Exploration of Tarkovsky's Film Theory from a Deleuzian Perspective," in *Through the Mirror: Reflections on Tarkovsky* (Newcastle: Cambridge Scholars Press, 2006), 79-99.
252. Bird, *Andrei Tarkovsky: Elements of Cinema,* 15.

> There are reverberations of Tarkovsky throughout Deleuze's *Cinema Two: The Time-Image* that lead me to speculate that Tarkovsky's writings left a formidable impression on Deleuze. In the least, there is a spiritual kinship between Deleuze's noted shift from movement-image to time-image, and Tarkovsky's views on cinema as 'sculpting in time.'[253]

However, neither Bird and Totaro, nor any other writer has satisfactorily clarified the theoretical connections between Tarkovsky's and Deleuze's exploration of time in film. They shared the belief that the cinema is far from being an inferior medium, as many have historically suggested, rather it was, arguably, the most important of all art forms; film-makers are able to philosophize as well as novelists, painters, poets and musicians. Tarkovsky's opinion on the erotetic role of cinema in this evolution is similar and equally well defined: film is a philosophical tool with the potential for revealing essential truths of consciousness and identity and the "Cinema should be a means of exploring the most complex problems of our time, as vital as those which for centuries have been the subject of literature, music and painting."[254] It is in the depiction of what Deleuze calls the time image that significant parallels begin to emerge.

For Deleuze the end of the Second World War acted as the catalyst for a progression of a new type of cinema, one with the capacity to confront our understanding of the world around us, as it has the possibility of revealing for the first time ever a direct image of time on screen. Deleuze asserted that Italian Neo-Realism heralded the beginning of the time image. He explained that the post-war period "greatly increased the situations which we no longer know how to react to, in spaces which we no longer know how to describe."[255]

---

253. Donato Totaro, "Art For All 'Time,'" *Film-Philosophy* 4.4 (2000), para 27. Totaro's use of the term "spiritual kinship" anticipates problems in the association of Deleuze and Tarkovsky. On one level such a juxtaposition might be considered antithetical, considering the fundamental role Tarkovsky's faith plays in his films when compared to the determinedly atheistic approach of the post-structuralist Deleuze. However, as Mary Bryden recently asserted in a challenging collection of articles examining the connections between Deleuze and spirituality entitled *Deleuze and Religion* (Edinburgh: Edinburgh University Press, 2004), "Since he [Deleuze] himself implemented radical and exhilarating encounters between apparent contrarieties or incongruities, it is not inappropriate to do likewise" (1). Contemporary scholars have found Deleuzian approaches to film useful for reinterpretations of a wide variety of areas; from Third World Cinema to gender, sexuality and perception. Barbara Kennedy reads a diverse range of contemporary films through a Deleuzian prism in *Deleuze and Cinema: The Aesthetics of Sensation* (Edinburgh: Edinburgh University Press, 2002). She reads films as diverse as *Strange Days* (Bigelow, 1995), *Orlando* (Potter, 1992) and even *Leon* (Besson, 1994).

254. Tarkovsky, *Sculpting in Time*, 80.

255. Gilles Deleuze, *Cinema Two: The Time Image*, xi. He suggested that there are a variety of reasons for its emergence that range from political, cultural, artistic and philosophical factors; citing examples such as the weakening of the American dream, the raised consciousness of minorities, the influence of new narrative modes in literature and growth of the European Art Cinemas among others.

It was, in part, these new experiences and new ways of thinking that led to a crisis of identity underlining the inadequacy of mainstream cinema, which he termed the movement image. The change is a reversal of centuries of Platonist causality and a shift from a classical external perspective to the internalised examination, reflective of emerging trends of twentieth century psychology. After the end of the Second World War, many film-makers started to interrogate the properties of time more than ever before. It is time itself and how it is perceived that plays the most important role in the formation of the time image. This period marks the transition from considering "time as the connection of homogeneous or equivalent units within some already given whole; we think of a world in which there is time, or a world that then goes through time,"[256] to, as identified by Deleuze and many others, an often indiscernible area, where irrationality frequently takes precedence and time becomes dominant over space, challenging our perception of the world around us and ourselves.

The movement image charts the progress of film from its so-called birth through the first fifty years of its life and even beyond. While the movement image is the formative period of the cinema, it has become the dominant mode of its construction, and one which is still very much apparent today. The defining characteristic of this movement image is montage. It is a cinema, which takes a voyeuristic delight in movement of the figures, the mobile camera and the power of editing: a highly spatialised cinema dependent on movement and space for action and reaction. From a temporal perspective, the techniques of montage, which link the shots together to form rational wholes, in many ways dispose of time by removing it, when editing sequences together.

If the movement image represents life, it is up to the time image to deconstruct the perception of life and reveal inherent truths in the process. Deleuze remarked, "The direct time image is the phantom which has always haunted the cinema, but it took modern cinema to give body to this phantom."[257] It is only if we disentangle ourselves from these preconceived notions that we are able to glimpse the world from outside our overwhelmingly subjective view; and the cinema is unique in its ability to do this. It is important to recognise that the time image does not replace the movement image, rather it evolves from it. The movement image remains the primary mode of expression for the cinema and will in all likelihood remain so, because this is how the majority of the world sees itself: "The greatest commercial successes always take that route, but the soul of the cinema no longer does."[258]

Deleuze's mention of the "soul" of film is especially significant, given the fundamental importance afforded to the "soul" of the Russian experience by Russian writers, dramatists, poets and film-makers. It is in the construction of

256. Claire Colebrook, *Gilles Deleuze* (London: Routledge, 2002), 41.
257. Gilles Deleuze, *Cinema Two: The Time Image*, 41.
258. Gilles Deleuze, *Cinema One: The Movement Image*, 210.

the "soul" of the time image that we begin to find extensive parallels to the work of Tarkovsky. The formative elements that make up this new style of cinema share many traits with the film-making style Tarkovsky developed in his films and wrote about in *Sculpting in Time*. Deleuzian concepts such as "irrational cutting," "the crystal image," "non-fixed perspectives," "transversal becomings" and "any-space-whatevers" find their corollaries in Tarkovsky's film form and his attempts to modulate the flow of "time pressure" throughout. Further to this, Deleuze placed memory, thematically and stylistically, at the centre of the time image; but it is a memory, like Tarkovsky's, far removed from the stereotypical representations of memory in mainstream cinema. What Deleuze terms "the crystal image" is, in purely memory terms, the interaction between an "actual" and a "virtual." In this respect, the "actual" is what we are experiencing at any given moment (a time that passes) and the "virtual" is a memory of an event, that has already occurred (a preserved time). Historically, mainstream cinema has depicted the "virtual" and the "actual" as distinctly separate. However, both Tarkovsky and Deleuze posit an interaction between these concepts which results in a more provocative perception of temporality and memory, one which challenges the idea that time is a linear construct. In this Bergsonian approach the virtual form has the potential to be accessed both voluntarily and involuntarily at any moment.

With such compelling imbrications between the two, it is perplexing why Deleuze only mentioned Tarkovsky briefly in his book *Cinema Two: The Time Image*. In 1985 he described Tarkovsky's article in *Positif*, December 1981 (a great deal of which would go on to be included in *Sculpting in Time*) as a "text with important implications."[259] Yet these implications were never identified by Deleuze in his writings, or, for that matter, by other scholars after their original publication. In the book he briefly registers Tarkovsky's relation to the time image,

> He [Tarkovsky] appears to subscribe to the classical alternative, shot or montage, and to opt strongly for the shot. But this is only a superficial appearance, because the force or pressure of time goes outside the limits of the shot, and montage itself works and lives in time.[260]

This compellingly brief analysis of Tarkovsky's work is as insightful as it is frustrating. He raises several notable concepts and displays an understanding of Tarkovsky's writing. Using the phrase "force or pressure of time," he implicitly refers to Tarkovsky's "time pressure," one of the cornerstones of Tarkovsky's

259. Gilles Deleuze, *Cinema Two: The Time Image,* 42.
260. Ibid., 42. Deleuze mentions Tarkovsky four times in total. On page 75 he describes *Mirror* as a "turning crystal" and suggests that it "turns in on itself, like a homing device that searches an opaque environment: what is Russia, what is Russia...?"

theory, and suggests the importance of the vibrancy of the shot in generating an awareness of time in film. Deleuze concludes with an awareness of the organic properties of time, something that is vital to an understanding of his own work, as portrayed in Tarkovsky's films: "[the film] itself works and lives in time." Yet Deleuze's paragraph is ultimately ambiguous and frustrating, and, like all his comments on Tarkovsky, it remains undeveloped. Once again the "important implications" are left unclear.

Deleuze's more challenging understanding of memory becomes effectively dramatised in both *Mirror* and *Nostalghia.* Gorchakov is plagued by involuntary memories over which he has no control. In one of the film's most potent sequences Gorchakov retreats to his hotel room and slumps on the bed, seemingly incapacitated, somewhere in the realm between dream and memory. The camera slowly zooms into him as the room darkens, a dog appears from the bathroom behind him and slowly sits at his master's feet. It is the same dog from his Russian memories, which has somehow been transferred into his reality. From a traditional dramaturgical perspective the incident is irrational, as the realms of the past and the present are conventionally distinctly separate, as in the flashback. Yet this actualisation of the "virtual" is symptomatic of Tarkovsky's move into a more challenging depiction of temporality. As for the protagonist of *Wild Strawberries* the memories become "alive" for him; as the memory moves from the ethereal to the corporeal, the memory *becomes* life, the "virtual" *becomes* the "actual," traditional representations of reality and the linearity of time are shattered. Just as memory stored in the mind requires the body to activate it, Gorchakov's memories are activated, and through his own perception they become "reality." In this arena Gorchakov now inhabits, the terms "reality" and "memory" become inadequate, as the distinctions between them become completely blurred. The concepts of present and past, for both Tarkovsky and Deleuze, are inadequate for describing the wealth of human perceptions and the cognitive experience.

Further adding to this complexity, Gorchakov's memories often seem not to be memories of real events that have passed, but rather they have elements of reconstruction or fantasy. This leads us to ponder whether our own memories of events in the past are accurate. Film has often been used to explore the limits and unreliability of memory, primarily because, as a visual medium, it can address the non-literal, non-linguistic, dream-like construction of memory so well.[261] In one of his dreams/fantasies/memories Gorchakov recalls his wife, who is then joined by Eugenia, and the two women engage in a conciliatory embrace and share a kiss. This event has not happened in the "real" world of the film, rather Gorchakov's unconscious mind is creating a kind of fantasy and a desired whole, which would bring his two worlds into

261. See films like *Rashomon* (Kurosawa, 1950), *Last Year in Marienbad* (Resnais, 1962), *Bladerunner* (Scott, 1982), *Memento* (Nolan, 2000) and *Eternal Sunshine of The Spotless Mind* (Gondry, 2004) for depictions of unreliable memory.

unity (in doing so it anticipates the final image of the film), but there can be no doubt that for him it has actually happened.

Like Tarkovsky's films, the time image harnesses these elements to show that time is a much more complicated concept than mainstream culture and cinema often implies. For Deleuze, as for Tarkovsky, there is no such thing as one all encompassing concrete version of reality. The time image is heavily critical of the western culture that has made this view pervasive. They posit that life is a multitude of subjective experiences; the world that we see is merely the result of perception filtered through our senses.

Tarkovsky's associative editing techniques, which I explored in *Mirror*, are similar to what Deleuze called irrational cuts: by disrupting the familiar, breaking down rational and logical links, the time image reveals the direct image of time. Deleuze felt that the time image was able to record the direct image of time, but to do this it needed to disrupt preconceived notions of how the world around us works. If the movement image was based on a system of images linked together by order and logic, for the time image to create its desired impact it would have to move towards the realms of irrationality. The images are no longer directly linked by causality, but are rather dislocated and fragmentary, forsaking narrative continuity and plot for a cinema of affect and sensation.

When Deleuze described the time image as a cinema of "subjective images, memories of childhood, sound and visual dreams or fantasies, where the character does not act or see himself acting,"[262] he could have been describing *Nostalghia*. Deleuze posits a new type of cinema, which is designed not to be a source of comfort or entertainment, but a generator of concepts and ideas with the power to shatter preconceived assumptions about life. Both Deleuze and Tarkovsky advocate a departure from the familiar inveterate processes of mainstream cinema, where master shots are followed by two shots, where cameras observe the one hundred and eighty degree rule, before moving in for a close up to gauge a character's emotional reaction to narrative events. These techniques, inculcated into the audiences' collective consciousness, have become the norm after a century of mainstream cinema. It is not a coincidence that Deleuze favoured both the long take and deep focus as they both are suggestive of recollection and embody separate regions of the past in a single shot. Both utilise the dichotomy of the present and past, viewing experience by constructing a "sheet of past," allowing all aspects of the image within the frame to be in sharp focus and visible, as opposed to the restricted planes of visibility used in the montage aesthetic of the movement image cinema. Therefore, a film using a deep focus/long take aesthetic can be suggestive of memory and evoke it, without necessarily showing memory onscreen.

Despite these compelling overlaps, one must be careful not to take the connections between Deleuze and Tarkovsky too far. While there are strong

262. Gilles Deleuze, *Cinema Two: The Time Image,* 6.

comparisons to be made between the two, there are elements of their approaches which are resolutely incompatible. Žižek asserts:

> Perhaps Tarkovsky is the clearest example of what Deleuze called the time-image replacing the movement-image. This time of the Real is neither the symbolic time of the diegetic space nor the time of the reality of our viewing of the film, but an intermediate domain whose visual equivalent are perhaps the protracted stains which 'are' the yellow sky in late van Gogh or the water or grass in Munch.[263]

In my opinion, Žižek states the case too far: one cannot reconcile several aspects of Tarkovsky's oeuvre with Deleuze's approach. Tarkovsky even at his most experimental, retains much more of a narrative than more deliberately experimental works like *Last Year in Marienbad*, *India Song* (Duras, 1975), Maya Deren's *Meshes of the Afternoon* (1943) and the films of Stan Brakhage.[264]

Deleuze's machinic eye of the cinema allows us to view an event from outside of our own subjective reality, giving birth to a new identity, a new concept of ethics, seen through the eye of a machine. For Deleuze the machine is not simply a metaphor; he views human beings as machines, which only function in association (or assemblage) with something else. Tarkovsky's oeuvre is still too representational and resolutely author-based to embrace the time image fully. Despite his progressive stylistics, he is one of the most autobiographical film-makers of the Twentieth Century.

---

263. Slavoj Žižek, *The Fright of Real Tears: Krzysztof Kieślowski: Between Theory and Post-Theory* (London: BFI, 2001), 102.

264. See Stan Brakhage, "Telluride Gold: Brakhage meets Tarkovsky," *Rolling Stock* 6 (1983): 11-4. Brakhage recounts a wonderful anecdote about Tarkovsky's incredulous and physical reaction to some of Brakhage's experimental films. Brakhage wrote, "Tarkovsky starts talking in rapid Russian, with Zanussi answering him, and whatever he's saying it's obviously angry. Finally, after a lot of these exchanges, Jane had the presence of mind to say, 'What's going on? What's he saying?' So Zanussi starts translating and he says, 'Well...' and we all wait, 'Well... he says,' and we wait some more, 'he says that Art must have a mystery to it and this is too scientific to be Art.' He ran, in the course of an hour and a half, through every argument against my work and any other individual's work that I have ever heard, from the Emperor's New Clothes argument through this-is-too-rapid-it-hurts-the-eyes, through 'this is sheer self-indulgence,' to 'film is only a collaborative art.' And in detail, 'the color is shit' and 'what is this paint? Why do you do this?' Then comes on *Arabic 3* and this maybe tripped him off the most. 'What is this? It doesn't mean anything, it's just capricious.' And I'm coming back and saying, 'shut up and look and you'll see there's a melodic line and shapes don't just occur anywhere in the frame, there's a balance.' 'But what does it mean?' 'What do you mean what does it mean? You have a lot of statements about music in your films...' 'But this isn't the same as music,' and it goes on and on."

2.4 The Living Past

There's an enormous difference, after all, between the way you remember the house in which you were born and which you haven't seen for years, and the actual sight of the house after a prolonged absence. Usually the poetry of the memory is destroyed by confrontation with its origin.

~Andrei Tarkovsky

We are constructed in memory; we are simultaneously childhood, adolescence, old age and maturity.

~Federico Fellini

Even though it possesses the capability of recreating events with supra-mimetic precision, film has long been considered an inferior medium for recording what we might term the lived life. Critics have, perhaps understandably, preferred to locate—as the etymological roots of the word suggest—the written form as the primary medium of the autobiographical text. It was not until the 1970s that theorists began to consider what other media could bring to the reproduction of an individual's life. It has been Philip Lejeune's definition of autobiography which has become the most widely used and it reflects the proclivity of theorists to reject cinematic autobiography. For Lejeune an autobiography is "retrospective prose narrative written by a real person concerning his own existence, where the focus is his individual life, in particular the story of his personality."[265] One might argue that what a film-maker can achieve with the cinematic medium is analogous and able to provide a distinctive and valuable alternative to the written form.

Critics of film's ability to record the lived life frequently concentrate on the structural difference between cinema and the novel: the written autobiography is a "pact of truth" between a creator and a text with only a single author, whereas film making is a much more collaborative process, where the artistic input of writers, designers, actors and other personnel needs to be taken into account.[266]

Yet this literary "pact of truth," where the writer recreates his life with unstinting veracity, is no more than a myth. It is, of course, impossible for a writer or anyone to recreate precisely how they felt at a particular moment in their childhood or any moment of their past. The narrated past is a complicated construction, fallible and selective, muddied by the waters of perception (as the recent rise in prosthetic memory studies seems to suggest).

265. Philip Lejeune, *On Autobiography* (Minneapolis: The University of Minnesota Press, 1989), 120.

266. These debates were anticipated by the auteur theory which came to dominate film theory in the post-war years from *Cahiers du Cinéma* in the 1950s and *Screen* in the 1970s.

The reality of absolutely truthful recreation of past experience is, therefore, an illusion: the "I" of the autobiographer is then a fictional construct, coloured with the benefit of hindsight and the knowledge of the person he or she is now.[267]

The strengths of the cinematic medium for presenting a personality are multifaceted: certainly, film has the ability to recreate the world with a Barthesian *chosisme* in a way that the written form cannot begin to approximate. As it was shown earlier in relation to *Mirror*, Tarkovsky recreated his childhood dacha with incredible precision from photographs and accounts of the period, using the correct wood and building styles, even planting the same crops to surround it that had not grown there for decades. The director is able to present images onscreen, avoiding the lexical ambiguity of words and their associations by bypassing an intermediary agent. As Tarkovsky wrote, "the interesting thing about literature is that however minute the detail which the author puts into each page, the reader will still 'read' and 'see' only what he has been prepared for by his own—and only his own—experience."[268] No matter how good the writer, his description of the dacha would offer significantly different images in the reader. While this does not make the text or the medium lesser, in the sense of an autobiographical reconstruction, a depiction of someone's life, such matters of perspective may be considered vital. All of Tarkovsky's films are grounded fundamentally in autobiography; primarily *Mirror* and *Nostalghia* for the direct correlations between his life and his art, but also the other films like *Solaris* and *Stalker*, which become autobiographical through their recreation of Tarkovsky's world view.

It is film's affective temporal power which differentiates it from the other arts. The fact that, unlike the written form, it does not rely on exact tenses in its generation of meanings, was effectively reiterated in Alain Robbe-Grillet's famous lament for the written form's inability to replicate the cinema's perpetual present tense. Viewing a film, regardless of when it was made or set, it happens for us only *now*. It is not a coincidence, that some of the richest autobiographical texts in film and literature of the last century were created during the decades after the Second World War. *Mirror* was made during the same period as Bill Douglas's trilogy of *My Childhood* (1972), *My ain Folk* (1973) and *My Way Home* (1978), Fellini's *Amarcord* (1973) and in literature Georges Perec's *W, or the Memory of Childhood* (1975), Oscar Zeta Acosta's *Autobiography of a Brown Buffalo* (1972), J. G. Ballard's *Empire of the Sun* (1980) and Akiyuki Nosaka's *Grave of the Fireflies* (1967). Many of the artists responsible were born

267. This pact of truth has been brought into debate recently after James Frey's "autobiography" *A Million Little Pieces* (2003) was revealed to be largely fictional. David Carr's *The Night of the Gun* (2008) takes an interesting approach to this issue by providing interviews and accounts of his life as a drug addict combined with his own autobiography. This provides different subjective accounts of events, each flawed in their own way but perhaps able to provide a composite and very relative truth as a whole.

268. Tarkovsky, *Sculpting in Time*, 176.

in the 1930s and had experienced the Second World War; during the sixties and seventies they began to write or make films about their experiences, having reached an age when they felt able to process them. All of these autobiographical works explore semi-fictionalised depictions of the past, where the "real" lives of the authors become filtered through memory and perception.[269]

If much of *Nostalghia*, and indeed all of his films, are the products of Tarkovsky's memory, then how much of him is invested in the character of Gorchakov? The parallels are extensive: just as *Mirror* featured a thinly veiled alter ego, so does *Nostalghia*; the character shares a name (Andrei), a profession (artist), political status (exile), separation from his family (wife and child in Russia), religious beliefs, patriotism and deep affinity for Russian culture. The relationship between Gorchakov and his subject Pavel Sosnovsky becomes a reflection of Tarkovsky's relationship with Gorchakov, acting as a sophisticated meta-narrative device akin to a *mise en abyme*. James MacGillivray confers, asserting "the making of *Nostalghia*, the nostalgia of Tarkovsky himself, is contained within *Nostalghia*." [270]

Tarkovsky's diary entry of 25th May 1983 is almost identical to Sosnovsky's letter contained in the film. Tarkovsky writes, "I cannot live in Russia, nor can I live here," an echo of Sosnovsky's, "I would die if I never returned to Russia, saw the birches, breathed the air of my homeland." Peter Green concurs on this issue of Tarkovsky using his work as an autobiographical enterprise: "There is a rare congruence between subject and object that goes beyond the usual autobiographical parallels artists draw in their work."[271] These associations between author and text were frequently recognised by Tarkovsky himself. Turovskaya observed about *Nostalghia*, "When Tarkovsky saw the first rushes, he was moved to tears of astonishment both at the quality of the material, and at the precision with which the dusky images reflected his own twilight inner state."[272]

Yet these autobiographical elements, while interesting in themselves, are only vital to Tarkovsky's film theory and his attitude to memory and how it functions in film. Tarkovsky's writings make it quite clear that cinema has

---

269. Fellini's *Amarcord* is one of the defining memory imbued texts of the post-war era. The title of the film literally translates into English as "I remember." Just like *Mirror* and *Nostalghia* the film is coloured by poetry and recollection. While what it depicts may not be factual, it is in many ways truthful. Fellini himself stated, "I have invented myself entirely: a childhood, a personality, longings, dream and memories, all in order to enable me to tell them." *Fellini on Fellini*, ed. Christian Strich, trans. Isabel Quigley (New York: Delacorte-Seymour Lawrence, 1976), 51. It depicts one year in the life of a seaside town much like the one Fellini grew up in. However, the year is not a normal year, rather the whole of childhood encapsulated into four kinetic and revelatory seasons.

270. James Macgillivray, "Andrei Tarkovsky's *Madonna del Parto*," *Canadian Journal of Film Studies/Revue canadienne d'études cinématographiques*, 11.2 (Fall 2002): 83.

271. Peter Green, *Andrei Tarkovsky: The Winding Quest*, 1.

272. Turovskaya, *The Films of Andrei Tarkovsky*, 122.

strengths that allow it to be more than the surface recreation of facts, but rather "the ability to present as an observation one's own perception of an object."[273] He also stated,

> Of course memory has to be worked upon before it can become the basis of an artistic reconstruction of the past; and here it is important not to lose the particular emotional atmosphere without which a memory evoked in every detail merely gives rise to a bitter feeling of disappointment.[274]

Autobiographical theorists may find fault with this concept of artistic reconstruction, but only if one accepts the veracity of the mythical pact of truth. If autobiography is the "artful construction" of one's personality, this presupposes that to recreate oneself truthfully one has to create oneself, and as long as this is the individual's perception of the truth, the result retains its truthfulness. Through the use of *mise en scène*, sound, modulation of actors' performances, choices of locations, camera angles, editing, casting, dialogue and narrative the director is able to use unique attributes of the cinematic palette to show not only what a past event *looked* like, but also what it *felt* like to be there. Tarkovsky's cinematic autobiographies capture life and life experience, as they continue to live in his recording of the "time pressure" flowing through the frame and beyond.[275] As Turovskaya commented about *Mirror*, "There he succeeded in something that few can achieve: giving life to the world of his childhood, recreating his home, peopling his memories, and

---

273. Tarkovsky, *Sculpting in Time*, 107.
274. Ibid., 29.
275. To find a film-maker with such an autobiographical approach to film as Tarkovsky and one who is as intrinsically connected to his culture we must look at Theodore Angelopoulos. It is no coincidence that Tarkovsky's co-writer Tonino Guerra on *Nostalghia* worked with Angelopoulos several times in films like *Landscape in the Mist* (1999) and *The Weeping Meadow* (2004). Their very titles could be unrealised Tarkovsky projects. Durgnat said "Angelopoulos' long takes approach, in their despair, their counterparts in Tarkovsky." Quoted in Andrew Horton, *The Films of Theo Angelopoulos: A Cinema of Contemplation* (Princeton: Princeton University Press, 1997), 4. Angelopoulos recounts an anecdote about when he met Tarkovsky, "Once, in Rome, I was staying in the same apartment building with Andrei Tarkovsky. He was shooting *Nostalghia* at the time. And we talked about 'Nostalgia,' the concept and the feeling, and he tried to tell me it was a Russian word, but of course I explained it was a Greek word, 'nostos,' meaning homecoming. So we argued over whether it was Russian or Greek! Finally, he said, 'Excuse me, I did not know it was a Greek word, but you see, nostalgia is so deeply a part of the Russian soul and spirit, that I feel it is we who developed it!'" Theo Angelopoulos quoted in *The Last Modernist. The Films of Theo Angelopoulos*, ed. Andrew Horton (Greenwood Press, 1997), 106. Angelopoulos is as connected to Greek history and national identity as Tarkovsky is to Russian. In all of the films Greece is much more than a backdrop, but a living tapestry. As for Tarkovsky strained and semi-autobiographical family relationships are at the centre of his narratives. Much of his life and experience filters through into his films: as a child he witnessed the Italian invasion of Greece in 1940, which later finds its way into *Voyage to Cythera* (1983). He dramatises the disappearance of his father during Red December in 1944 for not supporting the Communist Party in both *The Travelling Players* (1975) and *Ulysses' Gaze*.

capturing time itself."[276]

Nostalghia concludes with Gorchakov's death. After successfully carrying a candle across the bottom of the swimming pool in a metaphoric gesture of faith and hope, he collapses and dies of a heart attack. Tarkovsky ends the film with an epilogue, a splendidly evocative Bakhtinian chronotope of nostalgia and remembrance, another example of what it has been called an "open image." Gorchakov sits motionless in front of the dacha and next to him is the dog from the film. The camera slowly reverse zooms, revealing that he is also situated in the ruins of an Italian cathedral; Gorchakov is simultaneously both in Russia and in Italy. It is not clear how to decipher this image coming so shortly after his death. Whether it is his spirit returned to Russia in the afterlife or the vision he saw as he died, this contradicts the character's motivations: he, like Tarkovsky, had declared that he could not live in Russia or Italy. It is possible that Gorchakov achieved in death, what he could not achieve in life: a sense of spiritual harmony and reconciliation. The image at first seems harmonious, but it soon takes on a foreboding air, as snow begins to slowly fall. Just as the opening shot offers echoes of his previous films, so does this epilogue: in *Andrei Rublyov* a character remarked, "There is nothing more terrifying than snow falling inside a cathedral." Earlier the rain falling inside the dacha of *Mirror* had an equally foreboding air. For a director so strongly opposed to metaphorical readings of his films the image is strikingly loaded with symbolism; and Tarkovsky begrudgingly acknowledges this, "I would concede that the final shot of *Nostalgia* has an element of metaphor, when I bring the Russian house inside the Italian cathedral."[277] It is a profoundly effective image, designed to evoke a response in the viewer, much as the one Tarkovsky experienced at the conclusion of *The Death of Ivan Ilyich*. Tarkovsky's distinction between a metaphor and a symbol is a key aspect of his film theory, and firmly connected to his belief in the polysemic function of the artistic image.

276. Turovskaya, *The Films of Andrei Tarkovsky*, 152.
277. Tarkovsky, *Sculpting in Time*, 213-16.

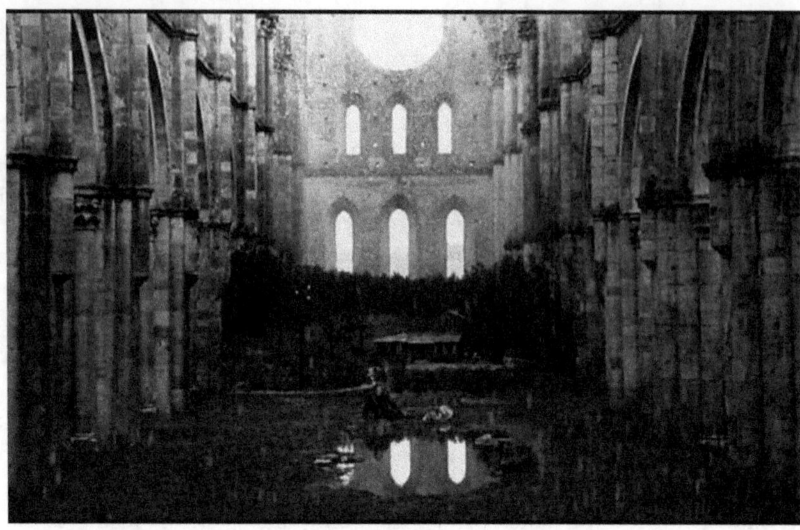

Figure 11 Gorchakov retreats into the final image of *Nostalghia*, once again blurring boundaries between past and present, reality and dream.

Chapter Three

Tarkovsky and Image

I don't like science fiction, or rather the genre SF is based on. All those games with technology, various futurological tricks and inventions which are always somehow artificial. The fact is when I was working on *Solaris* I was concerned with the same subject as in [*Andrei*] *Rublyov*. Human beings. These two films are only separated by the time the action is taking place.

~Andrei Tarkovsky

For a director with such a frequently expressed dislike of science fiction, it is somewhat surprising that two of Tarkovsky's films are firmly grounded in the genre and a third seems influenced by it. Tarkovsky's forays into sci fi appear to come about after his most turbulent productions; whether this is coincidental or not, one cannot be sure. After the protracted reception and release of *Andrei Rublyov* came *Solaris*, and after the much criticised and misunderstood *Mirror* came *Stalker*. This seems to support the opinion of many, who have regarded these choices as a deliberate move towards "safer" territory. Why else would Tarkovsky look to the future in a genre like science fiction, which was distinctly unappreciated by critics and the authorities in the Soviet Union? Turovskaya points out that "It seemed a strange choice; traditionally, science fiction is very much a popular genre, seeming to have no point of contact with Tarkovsky's style."[278] Synessios remarks that he was motivated by a "very tangible need for work and money."[279] Tarkovsky's production designer on *Solaris*, Mikhail Romadin, notes with some irony, that, "They [Goskino] viewed it as a genre which was hardly serious and intended for youngsters, so it was possible to entrust it to Tarkovsky!"[280]

Post-war Soviet science fiction films had tended to be either aimed at the youth market or constructed in a decidedly heroic "quest for space" template. Films like *Moscow Cassiopea* (*Moskva Kassiopeya*, Viktorov, 1973), *The Amphibian Man* (*Chelovek-amfibiya*, Chebotaryov and Kazansky, 1962) and *Ivan Vasilevich Changes Profession* (*Ivan Vasilevich menyaet professiyu*, Gaidai, 1973) provided formulaic and popular additions to the genre, which continued to be fuelled throughout the 1950s, 1960s and 1970s by both the space race and speculation about the possibility of communication with extraterrestrials, expounded by

278. Turovskaya, *The Films of Andrei Tarkovsky*, 51.
279. Natasha Synessios quoted in *Andrei Tarkovsky: Collected Screenplays*, 129.
280. Mikhail Romadin, "Film and Painting," *Tarkovsky*, 389.

scientists like Frank Drake and Enrico Fermi.[281]

Despite science fiction being regarded as a safe genre in the Soviet Union, in the wake of Khrushchev's secret speech in 1956 a trend of anti-utopian sci fi novels emerged from Eastern Europe. These texts could be more political in their metaphorical approach and reflected disenchantment with life and ideology which still remained largely inexpressible outside of allegory. Three of the foremost voices in this movement proved to be Arkady and Boris Strugatsky, authors of *Roadside Picnic* (1972), *Hard to be a God* (1963) and *Snail on a Slope* (1966-68) and Stanislaw Lem, the Polish author of *Solaris* (1961), *His Master's Voice* (1968), *Eden* (1959) and *Fiasco* (1987).[282] Given the serious metaphysical and socially critical themes of these works, it seems incredible that Goskino regarded them as fodder for the youth market, and even more surprising, that they believed Tarkovsky an appropriate director to make them.

Outside of the Soviet Union, science fiction had produced some of the most compelling films of the decade: *2001: A Space Odyssey* (Kubrick, 1968), *Alphaville* (Godard, 1965), *Planet of the Apes* (Schaffner, 1968), *Fahrenheit 451* (Truffaut, 1966) and *Der Große Verhaue* (Kluge, 1970). These films continued to do for science fiction cinema what serious science fiction literature had been doing for years, interrogating pertinent and complicated contemporary issues through the prism of the futures and other worlds in which they were set. So while many saw *Solaris* as a huge departure, Tarkovsky saw it as a continuation in its themes, values and especially in the emotional and spiritual journey of its lead characters. As he said: "It is obvious that there is a connection between them [Kris Kelvin in *Solaris*, Andrei Rublyov in *Andrei Rublyov* and Ivan in *Ivan's Childhood*], because all three characters in all three films are analyzed in a critical dilemma where either they die or abandon their beliefs. Or where they simply give up."[283]

Aside from the fact that both films are based on novels by prominent Soviet-bloc authors, the shared aspects of *Solaris* and *Stalker* are considerable. In both, Tarkovsky adapted the source material to fit his own philosophy, in the process alienating the original authors.[284] The relationship with Lem became so fractured that Lem refused to speak to Tarkovsky, calling him an "idiot" (which would become ironic, considering his later comments about the film being reminiscent of Dostoyevsky), and said:

281. "The Drake Equation" (1960) was an attempt to measure the number of extraterrestrial civilisations in the universe. "The Fermi Paradox" (1950) explored similar territory.

282. During this period novelists like Alexander Zinoviev who wrote *The Yawning Heights* (1976) and *The Radiant Future* (1978), and Ivan Efremov who wrote *Andromeda* (1957), *Razor's Edge* (1963) and *The Bull's Hour* (1968) emerged.

283. Quoted in "I Love Dovzhenko," *Filmwissenschaftliche Beitraege Hochschule fuer Film und Fernsehen der DDR Sektion*, no 14 (1973), trans. Karin Kolb, *Andrei Tarkovsky Interviews*, 41.

284. While this is true about Lem and Boris Strugatsky, Arkady remained involved with the project until the end.

> This has made me already quite mad. At this moment we were like two horses pulling the carriage in opposite directions... This is simply the type of person he is. When I understood that I stopped bothering. This director cannot be reshaped any more, and first of all one cannot convince him of anything as he is going to recast everything in his "own way" no matter what. [285]

Solaris and *Stalker* deal with similar themes, exploring familiar Tarkovskian motifs in their emotionally, psychologically and spiritually tortured protagonists. As ever, much of Tarkovsky's politics remains veiled, but not very far from the surface. The state is present in both films; in *Solaris* overly bureaucratic officials deny the existence of evidence which does not correspond to their rigidly dogmatic world view and then ruin the careers of those involved. The myopic scientists are so preoccupied with the pursuit of rational scientific knowledge over everything that it leads them to miss the opportunity of potential meaningful contact with extraterrestrials. In *Stalker* the state is personified by the nameless and faceless authorities, who persecute and harangue the stalkers (who themselves resemble survivors of the gulag) and the hundreds of people who mysteriously disappear from the Zone never to be heard from again. The shifting and fluctuating rules that must be carefully followed in the Zone are a compelling metaphor for the Soviet Union itself.

While *Solaris* and *Stalker* are two of Tarkovsky's most admired works, praise of them is not universal. David Thomson's droll criticism of *Solaris* is becoming more and more frequently quoted; Thomson is not one of Tarkovsky's "fellow travellers" and for him, "an episode of *Star Trek* explored this theme with more wit and ingenuity, less sentimentality, and at a third of the length."[286] This opinion on Tarkovsky's science fiction work was echoed by Janet Maslin in the *New York Times*, who stated: "However we may be doing in the arms race or the space race, we're winning the science fiction movie race by a mile."[287] Writing in 1982 she must be referring to the likes of *Alien* (Scott, 1979) and *Bladerunner* (Scott, 1982), conveniently ignoring or maybe actually referring to *Star Trek II: The Wrath of Khan* (Meyer, 1982), *The Empire Strikes Back* (Kershner, 1980) and *Superman II* (Lester, 1981), released around the same period, the bombastic excesses of which Tarkovsky strove to avoid.[288]

---

285. Quoted in "The Tolstoy Complex," para 2, ed. Seweryn Kuśmierczyk, trans. Jan Bielawski (n.d.), <http://www.ucalgary.ca/~tstronds/nostalghia.com/TheTopics/On_Solaris.html> (1st September 2008)

286. David Thomson, *The New Biographical Dictionary of Film*, 859.

287. Janet Maslin, *New York Times*, October 20 1982, in *The New York Times Film Reviews 1982-1983.* (Times Books and Garland Publishing Inc, 1984), 308.

288. However, it has been widely reported that on visits to the west Tarkovsky would actively seek out mainstream films rather than art cinema. He preferred to see science fiction and horror cinema and was known to have particularly enjoyed *The Terminator* (Cameron, 1984). See Jap Mees's interview with Layla Garrett. Garrett said, "He [Tarkovsky] wanted to see those films, not so much for the directors, but more to see the development of the technical side. He didn't have

The lead characters of *Solaris* and *Stalker* are tormented by recognizable Tarkovskian insecurities: they struggle to maintain their sanity, while events around them cause their preconceived ideas about life to unravel. Their outward physical journey is a manifestation of their more important emotional and spiritual journey within. In both films contact with extraterrestrial life is made; however, it is not the conveniently anthropomorphic aliens of *E.T: The Extra-Terrestrial* (Spielberg, 1982) and *The Day the Earth Stood Still* (Wise, 1951) or even the more ambiguous but still corporeal aliens from *The Thing* (Carpenter, 1982), *Invasion of the Body Snatchers* (Siegel, 1956) *Close Encounters of the Third Kind* (Spielberg, 1977). The alien life of *Solaris* and *Stalker* is a vague, amorphous entity, far outside the realms of human comprehension. Contact with it is much more problematic than translating human speech on some kind of super-computer or through a five-note melody composed by John Williams. The humans at the centre of the narratives are forced to question their own motives and values, as much as the intentions of the extra-terrestrials themselves. Even more specifically, both films contain an ambiguous zone, a Deleuzian any-space-whatever, which perhaps has the ability to grant the desires of individuals in its vicinity, not their conscious wishes or prayers, but their more troubling and hidden unconscious desires. In doing so they reveal truths about themselves that they would rather not confront.

This chapter looks at two important aspects of Tarkovsky's film theory very much connected to the way his work is experienced by spectators: firstly, how the presentation of imagery functions within his film theory and practice. Secondly, I consider how *Stalker* embraces what has been described by Laura Marks as a haptic aesthetic in order to bring about further powerful sensory connections between the spectator and the film. Both of these elements are vital to the way the films are designed to go "beyond the frame" in their reciprocal relationship with the viewer.

Tarkovsky's distinction between symbol and metaphor shows his attempt to move beyond a cinema with predefined, author-centred meanings, towards a more metaphoric approach, based on a fertile sense of ambiguity. The term poetic has frequently encircled debates on Tarkovsky's films and has often been used as a convenient way to describe his aesthetic. Maya Turovskaya's book *Andrei Tarkovsky: Cinema as Poetry* must be held partially responsible for this. The word poetic itself is certainly an overused term, not only in film studies, but also art in general. Peter Green questions the use of such a vague term and suggests that it "seems to stand for some undefined and effusive notion of beauty."[289] Reading through reviews of Tarkovsky's films, one notices that it is the word poetic that emerges most often, alongside puzzling,

much chance to see them in Russia. Once he recommended my husband to see [*The*] *Terminator* he was very surprised. Tarkovsky was interested in the theme of the film: travelling in time and space." "Andrei Tarkovsky: Profound, Majestic and Mysterious," para 14, http://www.talkingpix.co.uk/article_Tarkovsky.html (n.d.) (24th October 2008).

289. Peter Green, *Andrei Tarkovsky: The Winding Quest*, 10.

enigmatic, obscure, portentous and pretentious. While Tarkovsky himself never offered a specific definition as to what poetic cinema for him entailed, it becomes apparent through his writings that he was ambivalent about the classification as it is generally used, drawing a distinction between two types of poetic cinema. He stated that self-conscious Art films are as "contrived and pretentious as the meticulously made frames of "poetic cinema" with their empty symbolism."[290] This style of "so called 'poetic cinema' [is] where everything is made deliberately incomprehensible and the director has to think up explanations for what he has done."[291] Yet critics of Tarkovsky's work sometimes frame their criticisms of him in terms very similar to those.[292]

The second type of poetic cinema, to which Tarkovsky referred in *Sculpting in Time* is a "pure" (an equally vague word as "poetic" perhaps) poetic cinema, and this is how he defines his own work. Pure poetic cinema is film in its natural form: "Cinema in its essence, in its pictorial composition, is primarily a poetic art. For it is able to make do without maintaining any literal meaning, without normal sequential logic."[293] He suggested that "poetic" was an approach to art in general; in this respect any art form *can* be poetic, "Critics say that I'm a poet. Every art form can be poetry. All the greatest musicians, writers, and painters are also great poets."[294] Jeremy Mark Robinson goes even further, when he suggests, that the best way to approach Tarkovsky's films was as if they actually *were* poems. About *Mirror* he writes, "It's a cine-poem, complete with metaphors, allusions, references, historicity, lyricism, concrete and abstract images, a number of voices, motifs and symbols, autobiography, stanza and refrains."[295] Robinson's analogy is a striking one, not just appropriate for *Mirror*, but for all Tarkovsky's films with their clusters of images and allusions, abundant in their sense of association and ambiguity.

Turovskaya's definition of poetic cinema comes via the Russian Formalist Viktor Shklovsky to whom I will return later, revealing the formalist elements inherent in its construction. As usual she remains suitably vague: "In poetic cinema, elements of form prevail over elements of meaning and... determine the composition."[296] John Madden's *The Poetry of Cinema* offers a more specific definition of something with intangible and abstract qualities. According to Madden the characteristics of poetic cinema are open forms, ambiguity, expressionism, non-linearity, intuitive, non-rational, non literal, revision of

290. Tarkovsky, *Sculpting in Time*, 70.

291. Ibid., 224.

292. In 1983 Patrick Gibbs wrote "If there were a prize at the Cannes international film festival for the film most difficult to interpret, it would surely go to *Nostalghia*." *Daily Telegraph* (18th May 1983): 13.

293. Quoted in "The Twentieth Century and the Artist," *Iskusstvo Kino* 4 (1989), trans. Tim Harte, *Andrei Tarkovsky Interviews*, 132.

294. Quoted in "My Cinema in a Time of Television," *MassMedia* 5 (Nov.-Dec. 1983), trans. Ken Shulman, *Andrei Tarkovsky Interviews*, 99.

295. Jeremy Mark Robinson, *The Sacred Cinema of Andrei Tarkovsky*, 401.

296. Turovskaya, *The Films of Andrei Tarkovsky*, 101.

genre and subjectivity experiments.[297]

There is a considerable imbrication between these definitions of poetic cinema and those of another group to which Tarkovsky has regularly been equated, the *Film d' art* or the European Art Cinema of the 1960s and 1970s alongside film-makers, many of whom he professed his admiration for, like Ingmar Bergman, Michelangelo Antonioni and Robert Bresson. Bird suggests, that not only does Tarkovsky belong among the *Film d' art*, he also defines it, "His work may rank as the single most important influence on the style of contemporary European film."[298] In the crucial works on European Art Cinema, *The Art Cinema as Mode of Film Practice* (1979) by David Bordwell and Steve Neale's *Art Cinema as Institution* (1981), the defining characteristics are heavily reminiscent of Tarkovsky's work: the de-emphasis of action, deconstruction of stereotypical notions of plot and drama, introspective characters, the frequent use of the long-take and deep focus aesthetics. Neale suggests that, "Art films tend to be marked by a stress on visual style, by a suppression of action in the Hollywood sense, by a consequent stress on character rather than plot and by interiorisation of dramatic conflict."[299] He is echoed in Bordwell, who could have had in mind Alexei from *Mirror*, Gorchakov from *Nostalghia* or indeed any of Tarkovsky's protagonists, when he commented, "If the Hollywood protagonist speeds toward the target, the art-film protagonist is presented as sliding passively from one situation to

297. See John Madden, *The Poetry of Cinema* (Kidderminster, U.K: Crescent Moon Publishing, 1994), 2. Madden says "we allude often to the Russian/Soviet filmmaker Andrei Tarkovsky because his cinema seems to be a good example of the 'cinema of poetry'" (2). One could also turn to Pasolini's work on how film is more like poetry than prose in his "The Cinema of Poetry," in *Movies and Methods*, ed. Bill Nichols (Berkeley: The University of California Press, 1976), 556. Pasolini's speech in 1965 came at an important time in the evolution of Soviet cinema. By the mid-sixties the Thaw was coming to an end. When Tarkovsky entered the prestigious All-Union State Cinema Institute (VGIK) in 1954, the year after Stalin's death, it proved to be a transitional period for the institution and the Soviet Union itself. While of course it is a truism to suggest that art is a product of the time and culture in which it is produced, this is particularly true of Soviet art, as it is in other films produced under totalitarian regimes, so intrinsically connected is the state to the production process in every stage, from inception through to distribution and exhibition. Just a few years before, film production in the Soviet Union had hit an all time low, but the Thaw saw an almost unprecedented boom. In 1954 only forty-five films were produced, but in the next year there were sixty-five and by the early 1960s over one hundred feature films were being made per year. The number of cinemas in the country grew from fifty-nine thousand in 1955 to one hundred and eighteen thousand in 1965. The films produced began to win international recognition, gaining artistic and commercial success at home and abroad, such as Mikhail Kalatozov's *The Cranes are Flying* (*Letyat zhuravli*, 1957) and Grigori Chukhrai's *Ballad of a Soldier* (*Ballada o soldate*, 1959). Correspondingly, the combination of these factors resulted in the greatest number of opportunities for young Soviet film-makers since the revolution.

298. Robert Bird, *Andrei Tarkovsky: Elements of Cinema,* 10.

299. Steve Neale, "Art Cinema as Institution," *Screen* 22.1 (1981): 13.

another."[300]

3.1 Image and Identity in *Solaris*

It's difficult for me to explain. In this case I used water because it is a vital, living substance, that continually changes form, that moves. It's a very cinematographic element. And through this I tried to express an idea of the passage of time. The movement of time.

~Andrei Tarkovsky

Solaris was Tarkovsky's third film; and it has become one of his most culturally enduring texts, to the extent that it is now widely considered as one of the defining films of the science fiction genre. It has even received the dubious (and ironic, given the subject matter) honour of a Hollywood remake directed by Steven Soderbergh and produced by James Cameron, *Solaris* (2004). With a suitably organic metaphor, Soderbergh likened his own version to a "little bonsai" compared to Tarkovsky's "sequoia."[301] Steven Dillon dedicated an entire book to the relationship between nature and art, calling it *The Solaris Effect* in which he asserts that the film is "one of the most profound cinematic dreams ever conceived."[302]

The original novel and the two film versions of the story retain the same central premise, characters and, broadly speaking, the same narrative events. They revolve around the discovery of a mysterious planet known as Solaris. Scientists have speculated that it is sentient, but no meaningful, quantifiable contact has ever been established. However, those who stay in its proximity experience powerful, unexplained phenomena. A psychologist, Kris Kelvin (played by Donatas Banionis), is sent to the research space station orbiting the planet in order to ascertain exactly what is transpiring and make the decision whether the project should be discontinued. Despite his own decidedly rational approach, Kelvin too experiences events he cannot explain, including the mysterious reappearance of his deceased wife Hari (in the novel and the Soderbergh film, Rheya).

At the time many considered *Solaris* as the Soviet answer to that other iconic science fiction text of the 1960s, *2001: A Space Odyssey.* Tarkovsky saw Kubrick's film and it had a profoundly negative effect on him:

---

300. David Bordwell, *Narration in the Fiction Film* (Madison: University of Wisconsin Press, 1985), 207.
301. Steven Soderbergh quoted in Geoff Andrew, "Again, with 20 Percent More Existential Grief," *The Guardian* (13 February 2003).
302. Steven Dillon, *The Solaris Effect* (Austin: The University of Texas Press, 2006), 2. Dillon goes on to say that the film is an "extraordinary meditation on cinema" (7). The book also explores contemporary film-makers like Soderbergh, Aronofsky, Lynch and Spielberg.

> The film has made on me an impression of something artificial, it was as if I have found myself in a museum where they demonstrate the newest technological achievements. Kubrick is intoxicated with all this and he forgets about man, about his moral problems. And without that true art cannot exist. [303]

The concerns Tarkovsky had with *2001: A Space Odyssey*, were similar to the issues he had with Lem's source novel, which he admired, but had ideological problems with. The novel is characteristic of Lem's heavily epistemological and technological approach. Like much of Lem's work, *Solaris* is a search for truth and knowledge; exploration of space becomes a way to define the progress of human character, values, achievement and paradoxically its limitations. Lem's perennial theme is that man is little more than an insignificant speck of dust in the cosmos; notions of love, morality, honour and duty become superfluous in such a world. Yet his oeuvre is not pessimistic, rather, Lem establishes that there is strength to be gained in the recognition of one's insignificance. For Tarkovsky such an approach to humanity is suspect: man is far from insignificant in the cosmos, in fact, he *is* the cosmos. In Tarkovsky's words, "I am interested in man, for he contains a universe within himself."[304]

Tarkovsky takes the central narrative events, but changes the emphasis so profoundly that he makes the original text thematically almost unrecognizable. He is not interested at all in the technical progress of man; in fact, he is repulsed by it; it is the moral and spiritual issues which intrigue him. Tarkovsky sees the thirst for knowledge for knowledge's sake as symptomatic of man's turning away from spiritual values and ultimately towards his demise. The scientists in the film, apparently the best humanity has to offer, are egotistical, cold-hearted and, ironically, inhuman. In Tarkovsky's hands the film becomes an extended metaphysical meditation on identity, memory and spirituality, which almost coincidentally happens to be a science fiction film.

Tarkovsky's essential changes are characterised by the opening sequence of the film. Whereas the novel is set entirely in space, the film spends a significant portion of its running time, its first thirty-six minutes, on earth, both opening and concluding there. In early drafts Kelvin was even given a second wife, parents and aunt. This anthromorphisation of the story infuriated Lem, prompting him to exclaim, "And what was just totally awful, Tarkovsky introduced Kelvin's parents into the film, and even some Auntie of his. But above all the mother—because mother is *mat,'* and *mat'* is *Rossiya*, *Rodina*,

---

303. Andrei Tarkovsky quoted in "The Tolstoy Complex," para 1. On the DVD of *Solaris* there is an interview with Mikhail Romadin who states that Tarkovsky said *2001* was "exactly how you should not film science fiction...When you film science fiction it should be extremely down-to-earth visually. It must rigorously avoid the fantastic... let's make our space station look like a broken down old bus, and not like some futuristic space utopia."

304. Tarkovsky, *Sculpting in Time*, 204.

Zemlya. [Russia, Motherland, Earth]"[305]

On the day before he is due to leave for space Kelvin visits his parents' dacha, heavily reminiscent of the dacha from *Mirror* and those which frequently populate Tarkovsky's body of work. Tarkovsky sensuously frames the quotidian idyll of earth; the colours are verdant greens and they have a palpable texture; mist lingers in the garden much like the mist which will later fill the frames of *Nostalghia.* The shots linger over nature with an unhurried and deliberate pace, Johann Sebastian Bach's *Choral Prelude in F-minor* plays, with intensely spiritual associations, in the background of the sequence, which lasts eight minutes in its entirety. The vibrant sounds of water, the buzzing of flies and the singing of birds reveal a soundtrack that is almost alive itself. The images are imbued with a hypnotic quality, forcing the audience to consider them in more than a naturalistic vein. As the rain falls, children run for cover but Kelvin stands under it, not attempting to find shelter. He simply feels its life essence coursing over him. He silently and contemplatively observes a set of reeds—one of Tarkovsky's habitual microcosmic close ups—flowing gently and calmly beneath the surface of the water. Standing by the bank, Kris Kelvin holds a tin box, which he will take into space with him later; it contains earth and the seeds of a plant, a reminder of what he has left behind.

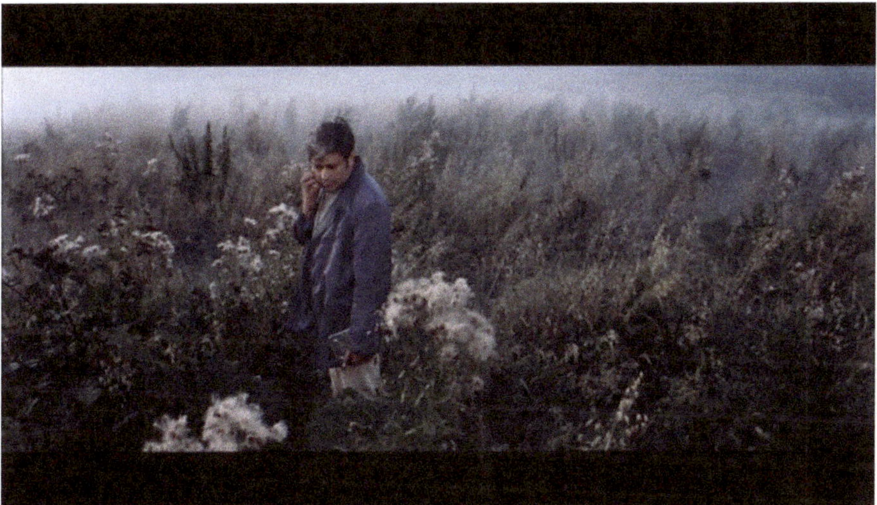

Figure 12 Kelvin's connection to the Earth and the natural elements is that which makes him human, yet this is what he must leave behind as he journeys into space in *Solaris.*

Despite his presentation amongst the natural world, Tarkovsky presents Kelvin's philosophical position as ambivalent; his values are firmly founded, as

305. Stanislaw Lem, quoted in "The Tolstoy Complex," para 2. Tarkovsky's portrayal of the mother in *Solaris* is an evolution from *Ivan's Childhood* and a precursor to *Mirror.*

his job as a psychologist requires, on logic, and not irrational, spiritual and emotional ties to objects and people. The battle his character will undertake is suggested by his name, Kris Kelvin, with its dual allusions both to science and Christian mythology. We later discover he is racked with guilt over his role in the suicide of his wife, Hari, who had killed herself as a result of his negligence and selfishness, his disconnection from humanity and people.[306] Even Kelvin's father has no illusions about his son's character: "It's too dangerous to send men like you into space. It's too fragile there! Yes, yes, that's exactly it – fragile. Earth has had time somehow to adapt to people like you – and God knows how much she has had to sacrifice!"

Yet by placing Kelvin amongst nature, Tarkovsky indicates that there is hope for him. With its vast array of properties, water takes a central place in Tarkovsky's canon of visual motifs; and it is to water that Kelvin's humanity is inextricably linked. Tarkovsky registered the importance of these scenes, which Lem so intensely disliked, for establishing the tone of the film:

> I needed the Earth for contrast although not only for that... I wished to make the Earth an equivalent of something beautiful in the viewer's mind. A subject of one's longing. So that after he plunges into the mysterious, fantastic atmosphere of Solaris, when he suddenly glimpses the Earth he again feels normal, at home. So that he begins to feel longing for this ordinariness. In other words, he feels the beneficial influence of nostalgia.[307]

Nostalgia, which so dominates *Nostalghia*, *Mirror* and *Ivan's Childhood*, is expanded in *Solaris*: not only is Kelvin nostalgic about his childhood, but when he voyages into space, he will be nostalgic about the earth itself. As Akira Kurosawa, Tarkovsky's contemporary and friend, said about the opening earth set sequence of *Solaris*:

> Without the presence of beautiful nature sequences on earth as a long introduction, you could not make the audience directly conceive the sense of having–no-way-out harboured by the people 'jailed' inside the satellite base. I saw this film late at night in a preview room in Moscow for the first time, and soon I felt my heart aching in agony with a longing to returning to the earth as quickly as possible.[308]

Tarkovsky's fascination with the cinegenic and metaphoric properties of water can be seen as early as the short films he completed at VGIK. In all his films,

306. Soderbergh shows the whole extended episode but Tarkovsky only alludes to it. This is a good indication of Soderbergh's approach to the material, a handsomely shot and intriguing mainstream Hollywood film but still resolutely classical in terms of narrative and exposition.
307. Andrei Tarkovsky quoted in "The Tolstoy Complex," para 2.
308. Akira Kurosawa, "Tarkovsky and *Solaris*," para 11.

without exception, water is used to examine notions of spirituality, purity, rebirth, motherhood, harmony, creativity and atonement. It is often associated with happiness or acts as a link to childhood through femininity or to motherhood. Tarkovsky's response to questions about this particular leitmotif and the metaphoric properties of his images, in general, is evasive: "Water is a mysterious element due to its monocular structure. And it is very cinegenic; it transmits movement, depth, changes. Nothing is more beautiful than water."[309] Despite Tarkovsky's recurring *topoi*, he repeatedly denied their symbolic value: "The rain in *Solaris* is not a symbol, it is just rain that grows in significance for the hero at a certain point."[310] However, water *is* more than "just" an image; it is central to Tarkovsky's film theory as well, to "time pressure" in its modulation and flow and to "time memory" in its ability to conjure up associations in the mind of the viewer. Water is a device through which "time pressure" is felt, in the "quivering of a reed"[311] that is the pulse of time as it flows through the screen.

Throughout his career Tarkovsky was often accused of hiding the true meaning of his films behind allegory and symbolism, a charge he vociferously denied. Nevertheless many consider that this was his and many other artists' way of dealing with the restrictions placed upon their creativity, as to what they were and were not permitted to show under the Soviet regime. He articulated understandable discontent about being repeatedly asked what his images were supposed to mean; what mattered to him was that they inspired feelings and associations in the spectator. One of the most compelling aspects of Tarkovsky's films is how he challenged these restrictions over the years; and one must wonder how much these disagreements powered his creativity. In his writings he draws a distinction between metaphor and symbol, which is perhaps key to a greater understanding of his work. As he stressed, he was "an enemy of symbolism. Symbolism is too narrow a notion for me, because symbols are there to be decoded. It is an equivalent of the world we live in."[312] This hatred of the term symbolism recurs many times in interviews:

> I prefer to express myself metaphorically. Let me stress: metaphorically, not symbolically. A symbol contains within itself a definite meaning, certain intellectual formula, while metaphor is an image. An image possessing the same distinguishing features as the world it represents. An image—as opposed to a symbol—is indefinite in meaning.[313]

---

309. Quoted in the Swedish Film Institute's English Programme Booklet for Offret, eds. Aina Bellis and Lars-Olof Löthwall.

310. Quoted in "An Enemy of Symbolism," *Tip* (March 1984), trans. Zsuzsanna Pal, *Andrei Tarkovsky Interviews,* 122.

311. Tarkovsky, *Sculpting in Time*, 120.

312. Quoted in "An Enemy of Symbolism," 122.

313. Andrei Tarkovsky, Swedish Film Institute's English Programme Booklet for *Offret*, eds. Aina Bellis and Lars-Olof Löthwall.

An image or a metaphor can stimulate varied associations for anyone; it draws on the spectator to provide an interpretation, whereas symbols have predefined meanings with little input required from the spectator. Paradoxically, however, he returns to the use of symbols when he calls the tree in *The Sacrifice* a "symbol of faith"[314] or when he discusses *Andrei Rublyov* with Michel Ciment: "We wanted to come back to the symbol of life, because for me the horse symbolises life."[315]

Tarkovsky was frequently criticised for his limited *topoi*, what Janet Maslin called his "tiny vocabulary."[316] Geoff Andrew states that "from *Solaris* on, however, Tarkovsky's pessimism and aloof mysticism led to increasingly portentous, turgid, even obscure narratives with woolly philosophizing couched in laboured dialogue, meticulous compositions featuring a hackneyed use of conventional symbolism, and long, often wordless scenes."[317] Tarkovsky was sure that if he explained his interpretation, it would devalue the essential mystery of the image; and in any case his interpretation would have no more value than anyone else's, because the film was as much about the audience's experience as his. When asked about *Mirror*, there is one delightful exchange that, for once, shows a more playful side of Tarkovsky's character:

> [Question from a member of the audience:] *Who is the woman in black? Why did you bring her in?*
> [Tarkovsky:] [Turning to the audience] What do you think, is it worth explaining?
> Unhesitating shouts of 'No! No!' from the hall.[318]

Tarkovsky's plea for openness of interpretation is central to not only his, but the poetic cinematic aesthetic. His attitude to imagery, space and narrative is as poetic as his attitude towards time and memory. Tarkovsky's cinema is built on poetic associations rather than formal, logical and rational connections:

> I find poetic links, the logic of poetry in cinema, extraordinarily pleasing. They seem to me perfectly appropriate to the potential of cinema as the most truthful and poetic of art forms. Certainly I am more at home with them than traditional theatrical writing which links images through the linear, rigidly logical development of the plot.[319]

---

314. Tarkovsky, *Sculpting in Time*, 224.
315. Quoted in "The Artist in Ancient Russia and in the New USSR," *Positif* 109 (October 1969), trans. Susana Rossberg, *Andrei Tarkovsky Interviews,* 25.
316. Janet Maslin, *New York Times*, January 8h 1984, in *The New York Times Film Reviews 1983-1984* (New York: Times Books & Garland Publishing, 1988), 175.
317. Geoff Andrew, *Film Directors A-Z. A Concise Guide to the Art of 250 Great Film-makers,* 217.
318. Tarkovsky, *Time within Time: The Diaries, 1970-1986,* 370.
319. Tarkovsky, *Sculpting in Time*, 18-9.

While on earth, one of Kelvin's father's friends, Berton, an astronaut who visited Solaris many years ago, comes to visit with an urgent plea to Kelvin. He begs him to keep an open mind about what he will experience when he visits the space station. While on Solaris, Berton experienced strange events, which he recorded on video camera. He saw a beautiful garden (which immediately links him to Kelvin despite Kelvin's protestations to the contrary) and, remarkably, a monstrously large human baby. When he returned to the earth the authorities refused to believe him, so far removed are his assertions from their own concepts of reality, and effectively put him on trial. The presentation of this trial, one of many films within the film itself, is abundant with associations. Not only is it evocative of the way Tarkovsky, and many film-makers who deviated from Socialist Realism were required to defend their films in front of the heads of the Soviet studios, but also the show trials which dominated the media during the late 1930s. The authorities of *Solaris* seem unconcerned with what actually happened, they have their own version of events.

When Berton shows the video he recorded there is no garden or baby; in fact, there is nothing to be seen but mist and clouds. The authorities accuse him of having had hallucinations. One of the men asks "Is that all? Is that the entire film? But we don't understand. We see nothing but clouds. Your film is nothing but clouds." These charges are evocative of many of the criticisms levelled at Tarkovsky throughout his career, that his films had no narratives and were a succession of beautiful but empty images. Kelvin has little time for Berton: he suggests, "I'm only interested in the truth, but you want to convince me of your point of view. I don't have the right to draw conclusions based on reasons of the heart, I'm not a poet." What Berton has told him moves too far away from his rational and logical understanding of life. Kelvin has not yet had his own epiphany, but later he will.

By immersing himself in the idyllic surroundings of his parents' dacha, Kelvin attempts to reconnect to his parents, nature, memory and life itself. He is already obviously isolated from those around him at the beginning of the film; he has a fractured relationship with his father, a deceased, distant mother, a wife who committed suicide and an unwillingness to come to terms with his past. Later, when Kelvin reaches the space station, he discovers that the scientists, even though they have turned their back on the spiritual values that nature has come to represent for Tarkovsky, have cut strips of paper and taped them to their doors, so the breeze from the air conditioner causes them to rustle like wind blowing through leaves. One of the scientists also has a butterfly collection, with all the resonance and irony of preserved dead butterflies hanging on his wall reminding him of the earth he has left behind.

"We don't need another world. We need a mirror. What man needs is man."[320]

The journey through space, usually a prerequisite for science fiction, is perfunctorily covered in moments, as Tarkovsky continues to self-consciously eschew the conventions of the genre; the passive and childish Kelvin is far removed from the glib and decisive heroics of a Flash Gordon or a Han Solo. There is no glory in the act of space exploration, no brave final frontier; it is a matter of routine and for some business, like for the capitalist astronauts of *Alien* and *Der Große Verhaue*. The film jump cuts directly into space via a close up of Kelvin's face, which begins to rotate with the screen. He asks, "When is lift off?" but is told "You are already under way." The film will test both his perception of reality and the audience's throughout. Tarkovsky does not even provide a conventional establishing shot of the space station, in order to further disorient the spectator prior to the unnerving and otherworldly events they are about to witness.

When he reaches the space station, the contrast between earth and space is immediate: dirty and unkempt, it hardly seems futuristic at all, and there are no advanced gadgets like in *2001: A Space Odyssey*. The narrow corridors seem claustrophobic compared to the open spaces of the dacha. Nobody even wears a space suit. They seem to prefer civilian clothing: leather jackets, tracksuits or laboratory coats. The scientists have been continuing to conduct their experiments on Solaris, with no success. For both Tarkovsky and Lem the planet is sentient, but in a way incomprehensible for humans. The contact it is attempting to establish (like the planets Eyrthro and Gaia in Isaac Asimov's novels *Nemesis* (1989) and *Foundation's Edge* (1982)) is unfathomable for the humans. It is no coincidence that Solaris is a water planet, a fact which is introduced by Lem, but heavily emphasised by Tarkovsky. Between scenes Tarkovsky frequently returns to images of the planet's surface, like poetic refrains. It pulses with energy and movement, like some sort of brain or living organism. Tarkovsky blames this failure to communicate on the scientists: their rational and logical approach is rigidly constrained and myopic, too firmly "human" to enable them to contact another life form. To make meaningful contact with Solaris would require a leap of faith that they are not willing, or perhaps even able, to make. One character asks, "How do you expect to communicate with the ocean, when you can't even understand one another?"

320. Snaut in *Solaris*.

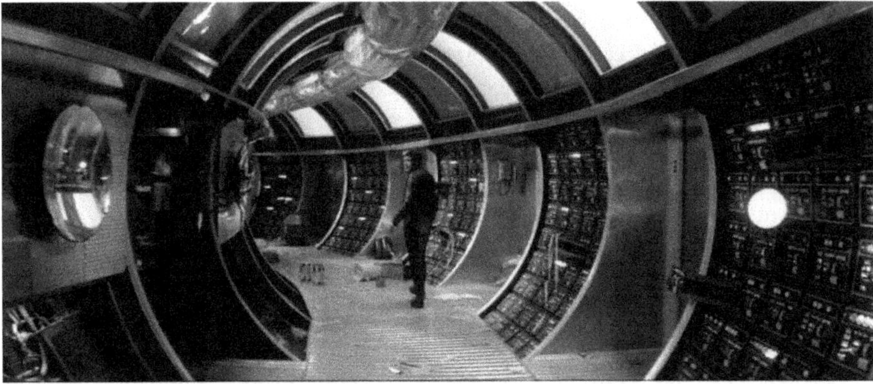

Figure 13 Kelvin finds himself physically, emotionally and psychologically adrift on the space station in *Solaris.*

Something approximating proof of the planet's sentient nature arrives in the form of "visitors," who miraculously appear. Each person who resides on the space station gets their own visitor, somehow materialised from their own memory or unconscious. The rational scientists question their sanity because it is impossible to comprehend that a living, breathing, anatomically correct organism can appear from nowhere. Nobody knows why the visitors have been sent. In the novel Kelvin speculates,

> You may have been sent to torment me, or to make my life happier, or as an instrument ignorant of its function, used like a microscope with me on the slide. Possibly you are here as a token of friendship, or a subtle punishment, or even as a joke. It could be all of those at once, or – which is more probable – something else completely.[321]

However, as is the norm for Tarkovsky's erotetic brand of narrative, he will supply no answers, only further questions. Of the three scientists on board, one, Kelvin's old friend and colleague Gibarian, has already committed suicide. It is unclear whether he killed himself because he was unable to understand what the planet had revealed to him or because he was ashamed of the truths he had been shown. There is perhaps something uncanny about the appearance of a very beautiful, very young girl that could have driven him to take his own life.[322] Turovskaya suggests that the visitors "are a physical embodiment of all the temptations, desires and suppressed guilt that torment

321. Stanislaw Lem, Solaris, [1961] trans. Joanna Kilmartin and Steve Cox (London: Faber & Faber, 2003), 152

322. Given the persistent echoes in Tarkovsky's film it might be important to relate that the Armenian actor who plays Gibarian, Sos Sarkissian, also played the Christ figure in the crucifixion scene in *Andrei Rublyov.* Sargsyan recently appeared as the grandfather in the distinctly Tarkovskian film *The Lighthouse* (*Mayak*, Saakyan, 2006).

the human mind."[323] It is hard to ignore the implications of, in Freudian terms, a "return of the repressed," exploring through the narrative what happens when those aspects of our ideology or our personality which we have sublimated re-emerge. In his video suicide note Gibarian wears a leather jacket, but appears naked underneath. He enigmatically comments, "It has to do with conscience," without telling Kelvin why.

The two other scientists Kelvin meets on the space station are even further removed from the natural world below than he is. Sartorius is an arrogant and small-minded misanthrope, for whom the visitors are just a pest to be experimented on and destroyed once they offer no further scientific value. Snaut is slightly more human than Sartorius, yet he is a man driven increasingly unbalanced by what he has experienced, as no amount of rational and scientific thought can explain it. He does not know where to turn when science cannot process what is occurring, and this knowledge is too much of a burden on him. Tarkovsky effectively dramatises this burden by having Sartorius's visitor a dwarf with palpable Nietzschean overtones that he will explore in later works.[324] Both scientists embody Tarkovsky's suggestion that "Modern man is too preoccupied by his material development, by the pragmatic side of reality… What good is it to go out into space if it's only to distance ourselves from the fundamental problem of man: the harmonizing of the spiritual and the material world."[325] Snaut's visitor is never actually shown, but he is frightened of it and has wounds that it has caused him. Both Tarkovsky and Lem are ambiguous about these creations, and the texts remain much the richer for it.

Kelvin's visitor is his deceased wife, Hari, or rather a reproduction of her, alike in almost every single way. She wears the same clothes, which happen to be the ones she was wearing the day she took her own life, down to the tear in the sleeves where she injected herself with an overdose; the tiny pin prick can still be seen on her skin. At first she is a monstrous creation for Kelvin. She is a threat, so he rejects her in the same way as Sartorious and the others have rejected their own visitors. He knows it cannot be her; confronted with guilt at his behaviour of ten years before, he almost instinctively ejects her in a rocket away from the space station. For him it is nothing less than a Freudian "face to face encounter with the materialisation of his own conscience."[326] To his even further surprise, she returns again, a different replica, but somehow the same. The shawl of the "original" Hari remains draped over his chair as a gentle reminder of the precarious nature of his new reality. Naturally Kelvin suspects

323. Turovskaya, *The Films of Andrei Tarkovsky,* 51.
324. For further work on the connections between Nietzsche and Tarkovsky see Gino Moliterno's "Zarathustra's gift in Tarkovsky's *The Sacrifice,*" *Screening the Past* (n.d.). <http://www.latrobe.edu.au/screeningthepast/firstrelease/fr0301/gmfr12a.htm> (March 2001).
325. Quoted in "A Glimmer at the Bottom of the Well?," *Andrei Tarkovsky Interviews,* 173.
326. Quoted in "Dialogue with Andrei Tarkovsky about Science-Fiction on the Screen," From *Andrei Tarkovsky Interviews,* 33.

he is insane; and Tarkovsky never gives us a firm anchor on reality throughout. Beginning with the refusal to have an establishing shot, Tarkovsky continually destabilises the audience with non-diegetic sounds, extended takes, three hundred and sixty degree pans, dreams, hallucinations and a remarkable slow zoom into Kelvin's ear, which all serve to question the sense of objective reality on display. [327]

Tarkovsky gives Hari's appearance a spiritual dimension. While Kris is sleeping (in a direct reproduction of Mantegna's *Lamentation over a Dead Christ*, 1480), the camera focuses on Kris's head as if she is being created directly from him. She appears against a white background, giving her what looks like a glowing halo. It is her presence which will act as the catalyst for Kris's possible emotional and spiritual redemption and rebirth. Despite her being a reproduction, Tarkovsky presents the replica Hari as firmly equated with the earth and the past, all those things that Tarkovsky considers most human. Even the warm browns and greens of her dress and her sensuously framed hair connect her to humanity. Here the name change from the original novel's Rheya (itself no doubt drawn from Greek mythology, where Rhea or Rheya was the mother of the Gods, an earth mother and embodiment of the fertility of the earth) to Tarkovsky's Hari becomes relevant, given its spiritual associations with, and its connections to, reincarnation and the divine.[328]

While ten years have passed since she committed suicide, impossibly, she is now before Kelvin again, a memory brought to life even more powerfully than the corporealised reveries of Gorchakov in *Nostalghia*. Hari is there in the flesh, somehow actualised by the planet Solaris, real and able to be touched and felt. Tarkovsky does not refer to the fact that she has not aged at all, leaving it to the audience to acknowledge, or not. Lem spells out the rebirth and immortality angle explicitly: "she had not changed since the day I had seen her for the last time; she was then a girl of nineteen. Today, she would be twenty-nine. But, evidently, the dead do not change; they remain eternally young."[329]

After his initial revulsion, Kris comes to love the new Hari; perhaps, she represents a chance for him to relive the past, something many Tarkovsky protagonists have wished for, but have never been able to achieve, from Ivan to Andrei Gorchakov. The space station becomes an Eden for them, outside

327. In the book Lem gives a different, much more sexual account of her appearance "It was Rheya. She was wearing a white beach dress, the material stretched tightly over her breasts. She sat with her legs crossed; her feet were bare, motionless, leaning on her sun-tanned arms, she gazed at me from beneath her black lashes: Rheya, with her dark hair brushed back. For a long time, I lay there peacefully gazing back at her. My first thought was reassuring: I was dreaming and I was aware I was dreaming" (54). Lem's evocation of lucid dreaming is an apt one for Tarkovsky's dream-like narrative, as we have previously observed.

328. Hari is a name for Hindu supreme God, the "essence of all things" beyond comprehension, in Sikhism one of the true names of god is Hari. Hari Krishna is able to transcend space and time. In Sanskrit it is the colour khaki. See *Faiths of Man* by James George Roche Forlong (London: B. Quaritch, 1906), 194.

329. Lem, *Solaris,* 54-5.

the bounds of space and time. Kelvin learns to love her even more than the original Hari, introducing her to the rest of the crew as his wife. Is it because she is the way he always wanted her to be? She is not the "real" Hari, but a projection of his wishes and memories, taken from his psyche, an expression of his own needs. Snaut is aware of the seductive powers of the mind and memory, even if Kelvin, ironically a psychologist, is not, when he suggests that she has come from "the recesses of your [Kelvin's] soul." In the book Lem has Snaut comment, "Remember that she is a mirror that reflects part of your mind. If she is beautiful it is because your memories are."[330]

From the start, this new Hari is presented as an ideal woman from within the diegesis and from without. Subordinate and dependent, beautiful and sexually available, she is both literally and figuratively virginal. Tarkovsky's representations of women have been detailed extensively by writers before. For Rosenbaum they are "Neanderthal,"[331] for Gianvito "disturbing,"[332] and, for Žižek, Tarkovsky portrays the sexual woman as an "inauthentic hysterical creature."[333] There have been apologists for Tarkovsky's sexism: "he once or twice stated that man should create and women should sacrifice."[334] Yet to consider these opinions as stated "once or twice" is simply not the case. His writings and his films are indicative of his well thought-out world view, and comments like "What is a woman's driving force? Submission, humiliation in the name of love. And a man's? Creation,"[335] are far from isolated; they occur

330. Ibid., 161. Lem frequently returns to the possibility of human contact with extra-terrestrials in many of his novels, often showing the limits of human intelligence and ability. The plot of *His Master's Voice* features a possible extraterrestrial message heard echoing throughout the galaxy. The sounds are captured and analysed by a sequestered group of scientists in a distant base reminiscent of the circumstances surrounding the Manhattan Project. They manage to interpret a tiny fraction of the message which enables them to build a curious organic substance which they call frog spawn. When the substance shows the potential of becoming a massively lethal and destructive weapon, the scientists are forced by the government to pursue these possibilities above all else. Lem satirizes the petty and warlike nature of humanity and concludes that the message was ultimately itself was an apophenic object in which human nature itself became reflected: "I began to suspect that 'the letter from the stars' was, for us who attempted to decipher it, a kind of psychological association test, a particularly complex Rorschach test. For as a subject, believing he sees in the coloured blotches angels or birds of ill omen, in reality fills in the vagueness of the thing shown with what is 'on his mind,' so did we attempt, behind the veil of incomprehensible signs, to discern the presence of what lay, first and foremost, within ourselves." Stanislaw Lem, *His Master's Voice*, [1968] trans. Michael Kandel (Evanston, Illinois: Northwestern University Press, 1999), 32. The experiment concludes in abject failure, the greatest minds of the world unable to glean information from the code, even finally unable to know for sure if it was a message after all.

331. Jonathan Rosenbaum, *Movies as Politics* (Berkeley: University of California Press, 1997), 282.

332. John Gianvito, *Andrei Tarkovsky Interviews*, xvi.

333. Slavoj Žižek, "The Thing from Inner Space," *Sexuation*, ed. Renata Salecl (Durham, NC, and London: 2000), 232.

334. See Daniel Jones, "The Soul That Thinks: Essays on Philosophy, Narrative and Symbol in the Cinema and Thought of Andrei Tarkovsky," 177.

335. Tarkovsky, *Time Within Time, The Diaries 1970-1986,* 89.

time and time again.

It is imperative that this sexism be considered in the context of his works and in the context of the culture in which they were created. Films made within the Soviet Union often followed a similar paradigm: valorisation and objectification of the virgin and the mother. Tarkovsky's world is populated and defined by men and relationships between men; women exist, but they are allowed to exist only through their men; they are mothers, daughters, wives or lovers "divine or dependent,"[336] but never equal. In death the mother or wife becomes sacred like in *Ivan's Childhood* and *Solaris*, or if they are safely away from reality, in dream or memory, they are valorised like Gorchakov's wife in *Nostalghia*. When women are alive, sexual and present, they prove problematic for Tarkovsky. As he proposed, "It would be difficult to deny the woman her world but it seems to me that this world is very strongly connected to the world of the man the woman is involved with. From this point of view the solitary woman is an abnormality."[337] Women like Adelaide in *The Sacrifice* and Eugenia in *Nostalghia* are framed as almost monstrous in their desire for independence and sexuality.

One of the most revealing interviews Tarkovsky ever gave was with the Swiss psychologist Irena Brezna. Brezna revealed how much she admired Tarkovsky as a film-maker, but could not reconcile herself with his limited portrayals of women. Tarkovsky's opinions come across as disappointingly reactionary and emblematic: several times he made almost the exact same comment, "Women don't understand that they only find their dignity in a male-female relationship in total devotion to the man."[338] In this respect Hari simultaneously provides an interesting embodiment and a contrast for Tarkovsky's characters, enough to problematize simplistic associations of Tarkovsky as a misogynist. She is "created through the power of the man"[339] made by and dependent on Kelvin, but ironically the narrative reveals her to be the most "human" character in the entire film.

"Rheya? But…I am not Rheya. Who am I then? And you, what about you?" Her eyes widened and sparkled, and an astonished smile lit up her face. "And you, Kris. Perhaps you too…."[340]

336. Mark Le Fanu, *The Cinema of Andrei Tarkovsky*, 13.
337. Quoted in "An Enemy of Symbolism," *Andrei Tarkovsky Interviews*, 106.
338. Ibid., 108.
339. Ibid., 106.
340. Lem, *Solaris*, 148.

Hari is the one who goes through an identity crisis, much more so than Kelvin, the ostensible protagonist and human centre of the film. When looking in the mirror, she is unable to recognise herself and asks Kelvin if he feels the same: "How do you know what you are?" Without any sense of introspection or sensitivity Kelvin answers that all humans do. He even has conveniently placed initials, reading K.K, on his pyjamas. While Turovskaya and most other writers on *Solaris* have accurately suggested that "Kris's meeting with Hari on the station is a means of gaining knowledge of himself and cleansing his soul,"[341] most have failed to identify that it is Hari who undergoes the most significant transformation. Kelvin is another of Tarkovsky's unsympathetic protagonists: he is self-obsessed and infatuated with his mother, much like Gorchachev from *Nostalghia* and Andrei from *Mirror*. He is reminiscent of Rick Deckard (played by Harrison Ford) in *Blade Runner*, adapted from Philip K. Dick's *Do Androids Dream of Electric Sheep*.[342] Both protagonists are, arguably, not as interesting as the non-human characters in the narratives. In the case of *Blade Runner*, Roy Batty (played by Rutger Hauer) and Rachel (played by Sean Young), the replicants, are individuals who are forced to confront what makes someone human with their very mortality at stake. The Christ-like Batty even gets to meet his own maker, but rather than a Tarkovskian imaginary reconciliation with a parent, he murders Dr Eldon Tyrell, who is both his father and his god-like creator. Both Kelvin and Deckard fall in love with a copy of a real woman, yet they do not entertain the notion that they themselves might be less than human, or consider what it means to be a human being, in the way Hari or Rachel do. For both, this love becomes an ill-fated second attempt at happiness. At the end of *Blade Runner* Deckard and Rachel flee the city looking for an Eden of their own in the wilderness, but, as the narrative has revealed, the replicants are far from immortal (unlike Hari) and Tyrell has built them to live for only a few short years.

---

341. Turovskaya, *The Films of Andrei Tarkovsky*, 53.

342. Memory plays a large role in Dick's work; *We Can Remember It for You Wholesale*, adapted into *Total Recall* (Verhoeven, 1990) features a protagonist trying to establish his identity through his memories, unsure whether they are true or false. In *Blade Runner* the debate still continues as to whether Deckard, the protagonist, is or is not human, the main evidence being a dream he has of a white unicorn running through the forest. In the Director's cut of *Blade Runner* Deckard's humanity is more ambiguous and the film is richer for it. After Stanislaw Lem's negative comments about the state of American Science fiction, Philip K. Dick was one of those who campaigned to have him thrown out of the SFWA (Science Fiction Writers of America). Dick sent a letter to the FBI in which he asserted that "Lem is probably a composite committee rather than an individual, since he writes in several styles and sometimes reads foreign, to him, languages and sometimes does not - to gain monopoly positions of power from which they can control opinion through criticism and pedagogic essays is a threat to our whole field of science fiction and its free exchange of views and ideas." Philip K. Dick "Frequently Asked Questions," para 5, http://www.lem.pl/cyberiadinfo/english/faq/faq.htm#dick. (n.d.), 24th October 2008. Ironically Lem was complimentary about Dick's work and wrote an entire chapter about him in *Microworlds* (New York: Harcourt Brace Company, 1984) called "Philip K. Dick: A Visionary among the Charlatans," 106-35.

Rachel and Hari are perfect replicas, but something remains absent; the thing that prevents them from being truly human is their lack of memory. Rachel's memories are fabrications, copied from a real girl to provide her with the illusion of identity; Hari's memories are vague and shallow. For Tarkovsky, as we have seen, it is memory which makes us who we are. The moment Hari comes closest to being human is one of the most powerful sequences in the film. She has already been shown to be evolving: at first she could not be apart from Kelvin, now she has gained some independence, she has started to think and even to sleep. The sequence takes place in the space station's library. While for Lem, the room is a resource centre with no windows, as if to represent the scientists' blinkered view of life, for Tarkovsky, it is something much more. Visually reminiscent of both a church and Kelvin's father's dacha from the beginning of the film, the room's wooden walls offer a stark contrast to the sterility of the rest of the space station. Books and works of fine art line the walls: a bust of Socrates, Pushkin's death mask, a series of Brueghel paintings, most prominently *Hunters in the Snow* (1565), Uccello's *Battle of San Romano* (1438-1440), and even an illustrated copy of *Don Quixote*.[343]

Hari has become more and more aware of her Pirandello-like status as the narrative continues.[344] She stares at the Brueghel painting (which itself was recreated in *Mirror*), presented as fragments rather than a whole, in much the same way as the paintings at the end of *Andrei Rublyov*. No other character has interacted with art in such a way throughout the film or has been so introspective. She sits away from the camera in a repeat of the pose from the opening of *Mirror*. Kelvin glances at the painting only momentarily, with a look of suspicion on his face. The sequence of shots which follows lasts almost two and a half minutes. There are whispers on the soundtrack as the camera slowly moves about the canvas, dissolving between the river, the landscape, the people and the animals. Intensely multi-layered sounds emerge, sometimes connected to the image and sometimes not. The sound of birds, dogs, a strange synthesiser, and the ringing of church bells are heard alongside Bach's choral music from the opening sequence. When Kelvin disturbs her, she utters a very human response: "sorry, I was lost in my thoughts." This may point towards her understanding of being human. For Tarkovsky being human means not just looking at, or "reading" art, but experiencing it, just as he wished spectators of his films to do. The others seem oblivious to the picture, and the whole room seems to have little more than a decorative function for them. So sure of their own place in the cosmos, they have had no such deliberation as what it means to really be a human being. At the end of the sequence, but very much a part of it, there is a brief live action shot of a boy dressed in red in a similar snow bound landscape, as if the painting has been

343. In *Fahrenheit 451* (Truffaut, 1966) *Don Quixote* is the first book to be burned.
344. See *Pinocchio* (Luske and Sharpstein, 1940), *A.I: Artificial Intelligence* (Spielberg, 2001), *The Purple Rose of Cairo* (Allen, 1985), *Sherlock Jnr* (Keaton, 1924).

brought to life in her mind.[345]

It is not a coincidence that moments later Hari and Kelvin embrace and levitate. The image is the symbolic opposite of the doctor's "fall" with the mother at the beginning of *Mirror*, with its sexual but primarily spiritual associations. In a remarkably Deleuzian statement Hari exclaims; "I'm becoming more human . . . I am human!" She is a matrix, a copy, a reproduction, but she is able to understand humanity in a way that Sartorius, Snaut and even Kelvin can never do. While Tarkovsky frequently criticises using paintings as a guide to *mise en scène*, he practically reproduces some of Marc Chagall's most famous images: *Au Dessus de la Ville* (1924), *The Lovers in the Red Sky* (1950), *L' Obsession* (1943) and *Three Candles*. (1938-40). These reproductions of works of art that permeate his work function as some sort of emotional "spike" for viewers, recreating a sensual experience that cannot be quite explained, all part of the way "time pressure" is manifested onscreen. Art becomes dislocated from its status as something with a predefined meaning and becomes an aesthetic object with no dramatic purpose other than to promote experience.[346]

Through Hari, Kelvin has been given the opportunity to relive the past, but of course it cannot be. The eternal return, as Mircea Eliade wrote, is nothing but a myth.[347] In an act born of love and self-sacrifice, Hari decides to kill herself because her presence on the space station can only be a burden for

---

345. Tarkovsky stated that, "Brueghel is close to Russians and makes a lot of sense for them. In the layering of levels, in the parallel actions which exists in his paintings, in the numerous characters, each caught up in his own activities, there is something very Russian. If Brueghel's manner did not resonate with the Russian soul, we would never have used it in our film - it simply would have never crossed our minds." "The Artist in Ancient Russia and in the New USSR," *Positif* 109 (October 1969), trans. Susana Rossberg *Andrei Tarkovsky Interviews,* 26.

346. Criticisms of Chagall's recurring motifs echo those routinely applied to Tarkovsky. When Walther and Metzger criticise Chagall for his limited topoi they state, "This suggests one of the fundamental problems of Chagall's pictorial language: a tendency for motifs to acquire an independent existence of their own, which threatens to rob them of their expressive power. Familiar elements in his work—all the loving couples, huts, animals, and later the religious images—are deployed in new combinations to determine the character of any new painting. Like words, they are strung together into ever new sentences, yet the many repetitions of them deprive them of specific meaning. Their symbolic value as representatives of another reality in a picture is levelled out: instead they become quotations from Chagall's own oeuvre. Parts of a seemingly mysterious world, they soon come to suggest nothing but their own exoticism, and the reality they are supposed to stand for becomes schematized." Ingo F. Walther and Rainer Metzger, *Chagall* (Cologne: Taschen Publishing, 2000), 68. Chagall himself echoed Tarkovsky's ideas about symbol and metaphor: "If a symbol should be discovered in a painting of mine, it was not my intention. It is a result I did not seek. It is something that may be found afterwards, and which can be interpreted according to taste" (Ibid., 78).

347. See Mircea Eliade, *The Myth of the Eternal Return: Cosmos and History* (Princeton: Princeton University Press, 1971). According to Eliade the Eternal return is the wish to become at one with the mythical age and return to the past. He reveals the contrast between the sacred and profane across both space and time.

Kelvin's sanity and life.[348] We have seen her commit suicide several times throughout the film, but she always comes back. There is also a suggestion that it has happened more frequently off-screen. Hari performs her duty as a Tarkovskian woman: she sacrifices herself so that Kelvin can live in peace without the manifestation of his guilty past before him. In doing so, she becomes more human than any of the scientists themselves. So while Tarkovsky has made her the most human character, he reaffirms the sexist trope of the woman sacrificing herself for her man. For Tarkovsky, "The meaning of female love is self-sacrifice. That is the woman's greatness."[349] Through Hari, Tarkovsky's perspective becomes slightly more understandable, it is in her choice to sacrifice herself that Hari becomes great (and human), not her duty. Gillespie emphasises this in his suggestion that the film is about "love and emotional contact, about the qualities of human life that can only be experienced and not explained by science or rational thought."[350]

In one of Tarkovsky's characteristic narrative devices, that of presenting key events off screen, we do not see the final suicide. When Kelvin wakes up in the morning after a feverish dream, which shows the space station and his parents' dacha somehow being united in space and time and Hari being a double of his mother (two motifs that will be dramatically recreated and expanded in his next film *Mirror*), she is gone. Here Tarkovsky takes a rare misstep. Kelvin asks Snaut to read the suicide note Hari had left behind: "Kris I'm sorry I had to deceive you. There wasn't any other way. This is the only solution for us both...Do not blame anyone for this. Hari." In Lem the note is even more heartbreaking: "'My darling, I was the one who asked him. He is a good man. I am sorry I had to lie to you. I beg you to give me this one wish – hear him out, and do nothing to harm yourself. You have been marvellous.' There was one more word, which she had crossed out, but I could see that she had signed 'Rheya.'"[351] The addition of the signing and crossing out of the name gets right to the heart of the centre of the film, the exploration of identity. While Hari is gone, her presence, like a memory, lingers. Her shawl remains draped over a chair in the library, the place where she was at her most human.

---

348. The comparisons between Scottie Ferguson from *Vertigo* (Hitchcock, 1958) and Kris Kelvin are so powerful that I am surprised no one has developed them before. Scottie is emotionally incapacitated by grief over his role in the death of a woman he loved and he attempts to recreate that love with another woman, who happens to be the same person. Both Scottie and Kelvin repeat the same mistakes they made in the past and lose love once again, when both of the new objects of their desire cannot stand being compared to the ideal of the previous love even though they are that same person. Just as Hari doesn't act Hari, she is her, "Judy was not *merely* acting Madeline – up to a point she *became* Madeline." Robin Wood, *Hitchcock's Films Revisited* (Second Edition) [1989] (New York: Columbia University Press, 2002), 121.

349. Quoted in "An Enemy of Symbolism," *Andrei Tarkovsky Interviews,* 108.

350. David Gillespie, *Russian Film*, 173.

351. Lem, *Solaris,* 199.

"I am interested above all in the character who is capable of sacrificing himself and his way of life—regardless of whether that sacrifice is made in the name of spiritual values, or for the sake of someone else, or of his own salvation, or of all these things together."[352]

The film concludes with an ambiguous epilogue. After the bombardment of the surface of the planet with lasers, all the visitors have disappeared; even the misanthropic Sartorius seems at a loss without his dwarf. With Hari gone, Kelvin goes back to earth, but, of course, the return is impossible. Kris has learned from his experience; it has given him some sense of self-realisation and hope for the future. When Hari confesses that he meant more to her than science ever could, he too becomes aware of his humanity in a way he had never been before. He realises that one cannot erase the past or forget it, but that it must be carried with us. Neither Lem nor Tarkovsky offer any answers.[353] Behind Kelvin the metal box he brought into space with him has miraculously sprouted a plant, anticipating his own growth and the tree of life, which will become the focal point of *The Sacrifice*. Kelvin has come to understand that life is impossible to understand: "We question life to seek out some meaning. Yet all the simple human truths are their own mystery. They are the essence of life."

The Lem novel ends with Kelvin staring at the surface of the planet Solaris, a being which perhaps understands him better than he will ever understand himself. In Tarkovsky's version, Kelvin returns to his father's dacha, where the film began. At first everything seems normal, but when it begins to rain inside the dacha the sequence becomes more and more dream-like. The father seems oblivious to the rain falling. We notice that Kelvin is wearing the exact same clothes from the start of the film; his own bonfire

352. Tarkovsky, *Sculpting in Time*, 217.

353. The endings of all three versions of *Solaris* show how different the approaches of the three respective authors are. In Soderbergh's *Solaris* Kelvin appears to return to earth but Hari appears once more. It seems he has remained on Solaris which has produced another incarnation of his heart's desire even after she was "permanently" erased. They are reunited in a familiar Hollywood fallacy, the affirmation of the primacy of love and its ability to conquer all, even time. The Dylan Thomas couplet echoes the myth, "Though lovers be lost love shall not; and death shall have no dominion." This is the very same myth that both Lem and Tarkovsky skewer; in Lem's words, "The age-old faith of lovers and poets in the power of love, stronger than death... is a lie, useless and not even funny" (Stanislaw Lem, *Solaris*, 194). At the end of the novel Lem has Kris sitting alone on the planet's surface after Hari's final disappearance: "I hoped for nothing. And yet I lived in expectation. Since she had gone, that was all that remained. I did not know what achievements, what mockery, even what tortures still awaited me. I knew nothing, and I persisted in the faith that the time of cruel miracles was not past" (Lem, *Solaris,* 214).

smoulders in the background and the same balloon can be seen floating in the air.[354] He embraces his father in a direct quote from Rembrandt's *The Return of the Prodigal Son* (1662). Above them the camera retreats slowly through the air to reveal that they are actually situated on an island on Solaris. Did they ever leave home at all? Was the whole thing a dream? Has the planet given Kelvin a new phantom, a new version of what he wants more than anything? Tarkovsky's interpretation of the ending is therefore problematic, "[*Solaris*] ends with what is most precious for a person, and at the same time the simplest thing of all, and the most available to everybody: ordinary human relationships, which are the starting point of man's endless journey."[355]

The autobiographical elements, which have resonated through all Tarkovsky's work, are present here. Tarkovsky's own guilt at leaving his first wife and child for another woman, something his father did to his mother when he was a child, and his fractured relationship with his own parents mirror Kelvin's:

> It's patently clear that I have a complex about my parents. I don't feel adult when I'm with them. And I don't think they consider me adult either. Our relations are somehow tortured, complicated, unspoken. It's not straightforward, any of it. I love them dearly, but I've never felt at ease with them, or their equal.[356]

The reconciliation of Kelvin and his father at the end of *Solaris* is an artificial one, and there is a sense that both Kelvin and Tarkovsky are aware of it. Tarkovsky himself never reconciled with his father, who outlived his son and died in 1989.

Despite winning the FIPRESCI prize and the Grand Jury Prize at Cannes in 1974 Tarkovsky was to look on *Solaris* as his least favourite film, going so far as to almost entirely remove it from *Sculpting in Time*. He stated: "I think that the idea of consciousness is fairly well expressed in it. The problem is that there are too many pseudoscientific gadgets in the film. The orbiting space stations, the technology, all of that aggravates me enormously. Modern, technological contrivances are symbols to me of human error."[357] But he did not always feel this way. In his diary entry for 16th February 1972 he described it as "more harmonious than *Rublyov*, more purposeful, less cryptic."[358] He never fully explained his dissatisfaction with the film, so we are only left with

---

354. About the balloon seen flying through the air at both the beginning and the end of the film, Tarkovsky states, "There is never anything left to chance in my films." "Faith Is the Only Thing That Can Save Man," *France Catholique* 2060 (June 20, 1986), trans. John Gianvito, *Andrei Tarkovsky Interviews,* 181.

355. Tarkovsky, *Time Within Time, The Diaries 1970-1986,* 364.

356. Ibid., 19.

357. Quoted in "A Glimmer at the Bottom of the Well?," *Andrei Tarkovsky Interviews,* 173.

358. Tarkovsky, *Time within Time: The Diaries, 1970-1986,* 53.

conjecture, but there is a sense that it was not the right direction he had wished to take after *Andrei Rublyov*. Perhaps, in his own opinion, he had come too close to what he had disliked about *2001: A Space Odyssey*? His next film was to be *Mirror*, arguably the fullest approximation of his own character and his own film theory. However, he returned to science fiction again just five years later, with a similarly themed project, *Stalker*.

When Tarkovsky handed his final cut of the film to Mosfilm, they demanded thirty-five changes in total, including removing all references to God and religion from the film, shortening the earth based sequences, cutting out the mother, making the scientists more human, clarifying the role of the planet Solaris and the mysterious visitors.[359] In short, removing everything in the film which made it Tarkovsky.

3.2 The Haptic Cinema of *Stalker*

I am often asked what does this Zone stand for? There is only one possible answer: the Zone doesn't exist.

~Andrei Tarkovsky

What was it? A meteorite? A visit by inhabitants of the cosmic abyss? One way or another, our country has seen the birth of a miracle – the Zone.

~The fictitious Professor Wallace, from the opening text of *Stalker*

In the summer of 1977 Andrei Tarkovsky discovered that most of the footage he had shot for *Stalker* (1979), the last film he would ever make in his homeland the Soviet Union, was worthless. For some reason the negatives had been rendered completely unusable. A variety of sources provide contradictory information about the cause: a chemical error, inadequate processing, out of date film stock, even sabotage.[360] Tarkovsky recorded his own response in his diary:

> Total disaster, so conclusive that one actually has the sense of a fresh stage, a new step to be taken – and that gives one hope. Everything we shot in Tallinn, with Rerberg, had to be scrapped twice over. First technically; for a start the Mosfilm laboratory processing of the negative (the last of the Kodak). Then the state of instruments and the gear.[361]

359. Ibid., 49-50.

360. See Stas Tyrkin, "In *Stalker* Tarkovsky foretold Chernobyl," *Komsomolskaya Pravda* (23 March 2001) (n.d.) <http://www.ucalgary.ca/~tstronds/nostalghia.com/TheTopics/Stalker/sharun.html> (1st September 2008).

361. Andrei Tarkovsky, *Time Within Time: The Diaries 1970-1986*, trans. Kitty Hunter-Blair

Was Tarkovsky mortified at the loss of only the fifth film he had been able to make in nearly twenty years? Or was he in fact relieved due to his dissatisfaction with the footage which had been shot? Nikolai Grinko, a regular member of Tarkovsky's ensemble and the actor playing the role of Professor, had overheard Tarkovsky say, after seeing early rushes, "This is not my film, I have to reshoot it."[362]

Regardless of Tarkovsky's feelings, the story might have ended there, as Goskino (The State Committee for Film Affairs) wished to write off the film as a creative accident. Film history is littered with the ghosts of unfinished films, scrapped because of the death of a leading performer: *Something's Got to Give* (Cukor, 1962), *Dark Blood* (Sluizer, 1993);[363] or funding being withdrawn: *I, Claudius* (Josef von Sternberg, 1937), *The Story of William Tell* (Cardiff, 1954), *The Deep* (Welles, 1967), *The Man Who Killed Don Quixote* (Gilliam, 2000). Even one of the great pioneers of Soviet cinema, Sergei Eisenstein, with whom Tarkovsky partook in a great quasi-oedipal struggle over film theory, had not one, but two unfinished projects of his own: *Que Viva Mexico!* (*Da zdravstvuyet Meksika!*, 1932) and *Bezhin Meadow* (*Bezhin lug*, 1937). Yet this was not to be the case for *Stalker*. Although Tarkovsky attacked the Soviet authorities repeatedly throughout his career, he was given the time and funds to rewrite the script and shoot the film again.[364] Several months later he went on to record in his diary, "I think *Stalker* really is going to be my best film."[365]

What Tarkovsky did not like about his previous science fiction film *Solaris*, he set out to remedy with *Stalker*, stripping the film of the distractions of the genre, which he believed had polluted the text, and moving even further away from conventions of narrative and iconography. This deliberate paring down of the material was to cause consternation among some critics, but is also what many find truly original and compelling about Tarkovsky's approach to science

---

(London: Faber and Faber, 2002), 146.

362. Quoted in *Andrei Tarkovsky: Collected Screenplays*, ed. Natasha Synessios, trans. William Powell and Natasha Synessios (London: Faber and Faber, 2003), 377.

363. However, advances in digital special effects have enabled films like *The Crow* (Proyas, 1994) and *Gladiator* (Scott, 2000) and *The Imaginarium of Doctor Parnassus* (Gilliam, 2009) to be completed despite the deaths of leading performers.

364. We find this term "authorities" crops up frequently in work written about film production in totalitarian regimes. In Tarkovsky's case it usually refers to those working at Goskino, or Mosfilm, the most powerful film studio and the place where Tarkovsky produced all of his Soviet films. In this state controlled film industry Goskino dealt with all cinema affairs: from production, distribution and exhibition, even film journals and magazines.

365. Tarkovsky, *Time Within Time, The Diaries 1970-1986,* 174. Over the years a variety of directors have taken the opportunity of remaking their own films for a diverse range of reasons. Michael Haneke remade *Funny Games* (1997) as *Funny Games* (2007) for the U.SA, as did Hitchcock for *The Man who Knew Too Much* (1934 and 1956). Woody Allen was so unhappy with *September* (1987) he filmed it again with a different cast. Lars von Trier set Jørgen Leth the intriguing challenge of remaking his own film five times in five different styles in *The Five Obstructions* (2003).

fiction. In many ways *Stalker* is an anti-sci fi film: it contains very little action, no dramatic futuristic sets or weapons. The technology in the film is old, decaying and broken. The closest the film comes to gadgetry is a rusted nut attached to a piece of cloth that the Stalker uses to feel his way through the fragmentary and fluctuating presence that is the Zone.

Stalker again saw Tarkovsky retain the central premise of the book on which it is based, *Roadside Picnic* by the Strugatsky brothers, as he had done with his other adaptations, *Solaris* and *Ivan's Childhood.* But with his fifth film he changed the narrative to an extent he had never done before. The plot concerns the appearance of a mysterious area reputedly with otherworldly abilities, enigmatically referred to as the Zone. Like the planet Solaris, it is an unfathomable space, which has been the object of considerable scientific scrutiny. Some characters speculate that it is the result of a nuclear catastrophe, a meteorite or even visiting extra-terrestrials, but its purpose and design remain unknown as much at the outset of the film as at its conclusion. The government has erected high fences around it, patrolled by armed guards, and rumours circulate about the myriad of dangers contained within. It is thought that somewhere in the Zone is hidden a strange room, which may have the ability to grant a person their innermost desires.

Tarkovsky asserted in interviews and in *Sculpting in Time* that *Stalker* was an evolution of the film-making aesthetic with which he had experimented in *Mirror.* Johnson and Petrie accurately call it, "the most visually and aurally complex of all Tarkovsky's films."[366] While the narrative is fairly chronological, from an imagesic perspective it is his most diverse piece. He stated that with *Stalker* he wished to make "a film with a unity of location, time, and action. This classic unity—Aristotelian in my view—permits us to approach truly authentic film-making, which for me is not action film, outwardly dynamic."[367] To do so, Tarkovsky embraced a range of devices, which effectively build on the way his films engage in a dialogical relationship with the spectator. These techniques are a deliberate concentration on the way "time pressure" is recorded through the film's *mise en scène* in order to create a very powerful

366. Johnson and Petrie, *The Films of Andrei Tarkovsky*, 153. I would suggest that after *Mirror, Stalker* is the most influential Tarkovsky film. Turkish auteur Nuri Bilge Ceylan's third feature film, *Uzak* (*Distant*, 2002), which won the Grand Jury Prize at Cannes in 2002, draws heavily on the film for inspiration. Tarkovsky returns to the screen when one of the characters Mahmut who is experiencing a distinctly Tarkovskian spiritual crisis puts on a DVD of *Stalker* to embarrass his uneducated cousin Yusuf. The irony reveals Ceylan as having an understanding of Tarkovsky's potency as a cultural and artistic symbol; not only does he address Tarkovsky's reputation as elitist and pretentious, but the film and scene are perfectly chosen. The plight of Stalker, Professor and Writer and their search for meaning reflects Mahmut and Yusuf's alienation from those around them and their struggle to establish identity. Later Yusuf, in his futile search for employment in Istanbul, comes across a rusted hulk in the harbour evoking the carcasses of the abandoned vehicles of the Zone. Here Ceylan lets the viewer make of it what they will, alluding to the moral, spiritual and economic battleground of modern Turkey.

367. Quoted in "*Stalker*, Smuggler of Happiness," *Andrei Tarkovsky Interviews*, 51.

cinema of affect and experience. Olivier Assayas suggests that the result Tarkovsky achieved was "not to film the real but to film perception."[368]

The overall effect is one of decay and age. The world of *Stalker* is in a permanent state of disrepair: buildings are crumbling, moss fills every corner, machines are rusted and broken, abandoned vehicles litter the landscape like carcasses, the detritus of a society in moral and spiritual decline. The appearance of the characters also reflects this sense of deterioration. Without exception they are dressed in dirty clothes and nothing in this world is new since everything has been used over and over again. Even the faces of the characters seem prematurely aged, deep lines are accentuated by the harsh lighting, a stark contrast to the radiant back lighting of *Mirror*, which had the effect of creating an aura indicative of the nostalgic allure of memory. This has several important implications for the text. It resonates with the film's eschatological themes, given that *Stalker* is the first of Tarkovsky's final three films, each dealing with the spiritual malaise of a contemporary culture obsessed with materialism. For post-millennial audiences this might offer profound resonances to their very own existential dissatisfaction with the stultifying effects of modern consumer capitalism. Maya Turovskya called *Stalker* the first film in his "late period," by which she means that from *Stalker* onwards the films become increasingly concerned with apocalyptic visions. In this respect, the environmental focus of *Stalker* seems strikingly prescient. In the years since its completion its reputation has grown and has even taken on a quasi-mystical prophetic air, considering its links to the Chernobyl nuclear meltdown, which happened just a few years later in April 1986.[369] Twenty years later the images of the abandoned city of Pripyat in Ukraine, part of the original Zone of Alienation 30km around Chernobyl, look eerily like Tarkovsky's abandoned Zone which, despite being covered by derelict buildings, is still a place of serene beauty. Some reports have suggested that after the initial devastation upon the area around Chernobyl, nature flourished there, able to recuperate without the intervention of man.[370] Its apocalyptic dystopian aesthetic has influenced a range of diverse cinematic visions of the future: from Lars von Trier's *The Element of Crime* (1984) to John Hillcoat's *The Road* (2009), an adaptation of Cormac MacCarthy's Pulitzer Prize winning book of the same name.

368. Olivier Assayas, "Tarkovsky: Seeing is Believing," 24.

369. Yet these interpretations conveniently ignore the details of the Zone which are firmly established in the Arkady and Boris Strugatsky Brothers novel and both they and Tarkovsky may have been influenced by a similar event which occurred in Cheliabinsk in 1957.

370. The same is true of other Zones where human interference has been removed, like the Demilitarized Zone between South and North Korea which is 155 miles long and 2.5 miles wide where no human beings or machines have set foot on it for fifty years. See Kwi-Gon Kim and Dong-Gil Chow's "Status and Ecological Resource Value of the Republic of Korea's De-Militarized Zone," *Landscape and Ecological Engineering* 1.1 (May 2005): 3-15.

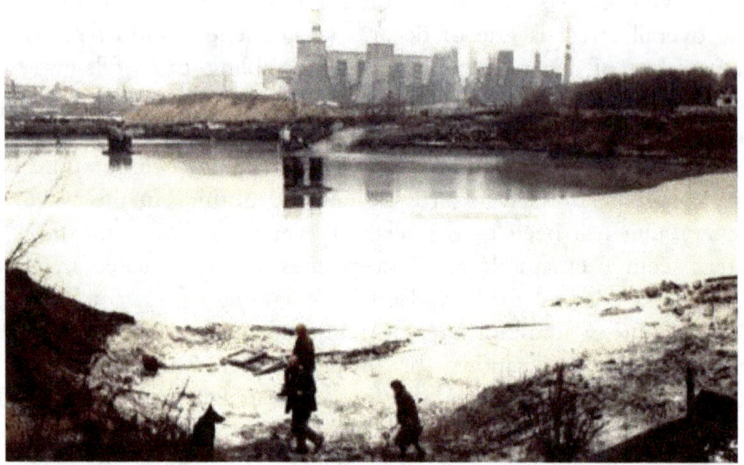

Figure 14 The aging and decayed world of *Stalker* reveals Tarkovsky's potent vision of the spiritual malaise of contemporary culture and it is one which resonates into the new millennium.

This decay is aesthetically significant too. The time present in the film feels different to the time witnessed in *Mirror*: it is not a nostalgic longing for a time that has passed, but a deterioration leading inexorably towards destruction, a time that has passed and is passing in front of our very eyes in every shot, what Tarkovsky referred to as a "lost time."[371] The images in *Stalker* are reminiscent of Godard's description of cinema as the only art form that "'films death at work'. Whoever one films is growing older and will die. So one is filming a moment of death at work. Painting is static: the cinema is interesting because it seizes life and the mortal side of life."[372] This aging process is something that had always fascinated Tarkovsky, and it is apparent in frequent references in his diary. He quoted the Russian journalist Ovchinnikov, who wrote about his visit to Japan:

> It is considered that time, per se, helps make known the essence of things. The Japanese therefore see a particular charm in the evidence of old age…To all these signs of age they give the name saba, which literally means 'rust.' Saba, then, is a natural rustiness, the charm of olden days, the stamp of time.[373]

This "saba" permeates every frame of the film: on the walls of the house in

---

371. Tarkovsky, *Sculpting in Time*, 83; 179.

372. Quoted from *Godard on Godard: Critical Writings by Jean Luc Godard* (Cambridge, MA: Da Capo Press: 1986), 181.

373. Johnson and Petrie, The *Films of Andrei Tarkovsky,* 59.

which the Stalker lives, in the glasses from which they drink at the bar before their journey, and on the train tracks that lead their way into the Zone. Tarkovsky registered the use of this "saba" in his work. Tarkovsky commented in his diary that *Stalker* "breaks with the traditional approach to the functions of film as such. What I am trying to do in it is tear apart the way we look at the present day, and turn to the past."[374]

This "tear" is most apparent in the quality of the images. In *Stalker* Tarkovsky experiments with manipulating the quality of the image from sequence to sequence, even shot to shot. By alternating between film stocks, clear or grainy images (which look as if they have become scratched through age) the shots are given a palpable sense of texture. This unconventional and challenging approach to the fabric of the images has been apparent in Tarkovsky's work to a certain extent throughout his career, but it reaches a climax in *Stalker.* There is a textured quality to the mud in *Ivan's Childhood* and *Andrei Rublyov* and to his water in *Solaris* and *Mirror.* This is part of Tarkovsky's distinctly poetic brand of cinema, which is designed to create "correspondences between materials, odours, colours and faces in the same way as poetry, by putting words together, allows us to reconstruct a particular feeling."[375]

This is echoed in Tarkovsky's film theory; by creating the sensation of "an aesthetic texture and emotional atmosphere,"[376] Tarkovsky interrogates the smooth and continuous images, which encourage the complacency of audiences in mainstream cinema. This more sensory and phenomenological approach to the construction of images has been described as a haptic cinema by Laura Marks in her study of the cinema of perception, *The Skin of the Film.* Marks asserts that "It is most valuable to think of the skin of the film not as a screen, but as a membrane that brings the audience into contact with the material forms of memory."[377] By describing the image as skin, she gives the screen an organic dimension evocative of both Deleuze and Tarkovsky. Marks discussed how this variation of texture can provide an essential and powerful stimulus to sensation and to memory, acting as a distinct contrast to how the "Ocular Centralism" of western cinema has prioritised sight over all senses. A haptic cinema embraces the discordance of grainy, unclear or differently textured images, which could be considered imperfect and less complete when juxtaposed with traditional mainstream cinema; yet it is such a look that provides a powerful stimulus and a sensuous engagement with the spectator.

At the centre of this haptic approach to cinema is a disconnection from narrative functionality in favour of creating a cinema of affect and perception, one not driven primarily by plot but by the generation of experiences, which is

374. Tarkovsky, *Time Within Time, The Diaries 1970-1986,* 159.

375. Olivier Assayas, "Tarkovsky: Seeing is Believing," 24.

376. Tarkovsky, *Sculpting in Time*, 60.

377. Laura Marks, *The Skin of the Film* (Durham and London: Duke University Press, 1999), 273.

almost Peircian in its "firstness." While concepts like firstness or haptic prove difficult to quantify, as they are outside of language and based on sensory experience, they become a tangible quality in art. A haptic cinema "may also encourage a more embodied and multisensory relationship to the image in films that use haptic imagery in combination with sound, camera movement, and montage to achieve sensuous effects."[378] The techniques Marks identifies are reminiscent of Tarkovsky's aesthetic: graininess, focus changes, manipulation of film stock or exposure, so called "illogical" camera movements, long takes and any process that seeks to disrupt the homogeneity of the film experience. The cumulative effect is that they "discourage the viewer from distinguishing objects and encourage a relationship to the screen as a whole."[379] Reviewers frequently noted this very deliberate texturing of the image, but remained unsure of what to make of it. In 1980 Gilbert Adair argued that the televisual aesthetic of *Stalker* was presented "in a preternaturally vivid style rendered Dostoyevskian by monochrome photography whose raspingly harsh textures suggest some grainy newsreel footage of the future."[380] Vlada Petric noted a similar quality and even suggested its impact on the viewer: "To experience all this one should search *beyond* the shot's narrative meaning, since it is beneath the images's representational aspect where numerous layers of ineffable transcendental signification can be found."[381] Both suggest that meaning, in part, resides beyond what normally constitutes meaning in mainstream film, and can be found in the sensuous relationship formed between the spectator and the images.

Without explicitly calling Tarkovsky's brand of cinema haptic, Žižek is very clear about Tarkovsky's approach to the presentation of imagery in *Stalker*:

> If *Stalker* is Tarkovsky's masterpiece, it is above all because of the direct physical impact of its texture: the physical background (what T. S. Eliot would have called the objective correlative) to its metaphysical quest, the landscape of the Zone, is a post-industrial wasteland with wild vegetation growing over abandoned factories, concrete tunnels and railroads full of stale water, and wild overgrowth in which stray cats and dogs wander. Nature and industrial civilization here again overlap, through their common decay – civilization in decay is in the process of again being reclaimed (not by idealized harmonious Nature, but) by nature in decomposition.[382]

This haptic approach can be discerned all throughout *Stalker*. As the three protagonists exhaustedly attempt to rest, Tarkovsky visualises the film's treatise

378. Ibid., 72.
379. Ibid.
380. Gilbert Adair, "Notes from the Underground," *Sight and Sound* 50.1 (Winter 1980/1981): 63.
381. Vlada Petric, "Tarkovsky's Dream Imagery," *Film Quarterly* 43.2 (Winter, 1989-90): 30.
382. Slavoj Žižek, "The Thing from Inner Space," *Sexuation*, 252.

in a remarkable sequence. The Stalker has led two tourists, only referred to as Writer and Professor, into the Zone. All three men are secretive about their reasons for wanting to visit the Zone, but it seems they are motivated by some sort of emotional, psychological and spiritual crisis. Writer is a man of talent who has achieved great success, but none of it has brought him happiness. He feels he has only written the work that others have wanted him to write, and never found the way to truly express himself. While outwardly successful, he is empty, cynical and sarcastic: he hates himself and his writing. The film first introduces him drinking and smoking, explaining to an attractive young woman, that there are no mysteries left in the world. He states, "There is no Bermuda triangle. There is a triangle a, b, c which is similar to x, y, z.... The world is ruled by cast-iron laws, and it's insufferably boring." His time in the Zone will force him to confront his rigidly prescribed formal preconceptions about the world, just as Kelvin was challenged by his experiences on Solaris. Professor is also largely unsympathetic; he too reveals very little about himself, until later in the narrative it transpires that he has brought a bomb with him into the Zone. He wishes to destroy the magical room, so no one will be able to use it for their own immoral purposes. However, it is their guide, the Stalker, who is the moral centre of the film, one of Tarkovsky's martyrs. He is a tragic and pathetic figure whose anguish is palpable. The Zone is the only place he feels worthwhile and the only place to which he belongs. He is referred to as both Chingachgook and Don Quixote by other characters, and in an interview Tarkovsky called him the "last of the idealists."[383] Like Kelvin, and many of Tarkovsky's protagonists, Stalker carries with him the burden of his past and his own needs: his child, Monkey, is mutated, seemingly the result of his repeated voyages into the Zone. On first arriving in the Zone Tarkovsky moves the film from sepia into colour for the first time. Stalker falls to the ground simply to be a part of it, as Kelvin sought to in *Solaris*, even letting a small caterpillar walk across his hand.

The camera tracks slowly over a fetid pool in a familiar Tarkovsky manoeuvre. Interspersed into this slow camera movement are shots of Writer, Professor and Stalker. The quality of the image changes from shot to shot: some are in black and white, some in colour, some in a sepia tone, though there seems to be no obvious pattern in their use. In a voiceover Stalker recites from the Book of Revelation 6:12-17. Under the stagnant water there are objects, symbols of the moral decomposition of society: a gun, a discarded religious icon, a date that reads the 28th, some gold coins, a box, a part of a clock, and a hypodermic needle. The religious icon, on closer scrutiny, is Jan van Eyck's *Ghent Altarpiece* (1425-32), which shows the predicted second coming of Christ. Some shots show strange foam in the air, in others the image is distorted by a heat haze. A dog is cut into the sequence and it moves to sit

383. Quoted in "*Stalker*, Smuggler of Happiness," *Andrei Tarkovsky Interviews*, 51.

by Stalker, as if it has emerged from his psyche or memory to become real as Gorchakov's does in *Nostalghia*.

This detritus calls to mind the name of the original novel by the Strugatsky Brothers, *Roadside Picnic*. The Strugatskys explored how the debris left behind by extra-terrestrials may leave no value to them, but for a less developed civilisation even this simple refuse would be remarkable:

> A car drives off the country road into a meadow, a group of young people get out of the car carrying bottles, baskets of food, transistor radios, and cameras. They light fires, pitch tents, turn on the music. In the morning they leave. The animals, birds and insects that watched in horror through the long night creep out from their hiding places. And what do they see? Gas and oil spilled on the grass. Old spark plugs and old filters strewn around. Rags, burnt-out old bulbs, and a monkey wrench left behind. Oil slicks on the pond. And of course, the usual mess – apple cores, candy wrappers, charred remains of the campfire, cans, bottles, somebody's handkerchief, somebody's penknife, torn newspapers, coins, faded flowers picked in another meadow.[384]

Several of the shots are very close to the characters' faces, yet Tarkovsky's use of the close up is profoundly different to mainstream cinema and emblematic of his profoundly affectual approach. His close ups of faces are not reaction shots in the traditional sense, as the images do not progress narrative or develop characterisation, rather they are integral to the consideration of the way "time pressure" is integrated into the cinematic experience. In Tarkovsky's oeuvre it is not only the face which appears in close up, but objects like water, shrubs, milk, fire and icons, even a ring of condensation disappearing from a table. With no direct literal meaning in the interpretational sense, the images take on a vivid and organic life of their own. Craig Brown describes Tarkovsky's microcosmic close ups as "the innocent, inquisitive camera, always seeing normal things anew—a fish, a bowl of milk, a hand—becomes an indefinable part of the metaphysical yearnings of the characters."[385] For Tarkovsky they generate a palpable resonance that promotes ambiguity and intensity, what might be termed a poetical estrangement: "The artistic image is always a metonym, where one thing is substituted for another, the smaller for the greater."[386] By giving familiar objects qualities of otherness, Tarkovsky is able to reach "beyond the frame," demanding that the audience provide a sense of context or meaning for them. They are a part of Tarkovsky's desire to create associations and stimulation to not just the eye but the body itself.

---

384. Strugatsky Brothers *Roadside Picnic*, [1971] trans. Antonina W. Bouis (London: Gollanz Publishing, 2007), 102.
385. Craig Brown, "Making New," in *The Times Literary Supplement* (27th February 1981): 228.
386. Tarkovsky, *Sculpting in Time*, 38.

Tarkovsky, like the Russian Formalists, saw the close up as one of the defining aspects of the cinema: one of the components it possesses, which cannot be replicated outside film. Balázs wrote that "Not even the greatest writer, the most consummate artist of the pen, could tell in words what Asta Nielsen tells with her face in close-up as she sits down to her mirror and tries to make up for the last time her aged, wrinkled face, riddled with poverty, misery, disease and prostitution."[387] Similarly Stalker's face reveals his burden without words as meaning is etched in the lines that cover his face. The close up is part of film's unique relationship with time. Yuri Tynyanov stated that "The specificity of time in cinema is revealed by a device such as the close-up. A close-up abstracts a thing, a detail, or a face from its spatial relations—and from the temporal sequence."[388] This notion of abstracting a thing becomes a key device in Tarkovsky. By removing from an object its explicit narrative function, withdrawing it from temporal and spatial planes, the familiar is turned into the unfamiliar, creating an object potent with affect, revealing the stoniness of the stone.

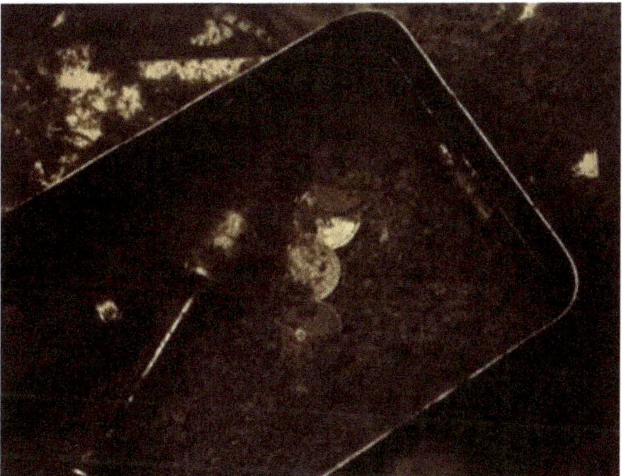

Figure 15 Tarkovsky's lingering close ups of artefacts within the Zone disconnect them from reality and reveal the stoniness of the stone.

The themes of decline and aging are reinforced by the soundtrack, which is a key ingredient of how "time pressure" is presented on the screen. Eduard Artemiev, who composed three of Tarkovsky's films, *Solaris*, *Mirror* and *Stalker*, used distorted sounds and musical fragments which suggest decay. Tarkovsky's soundscapes are at a distinct contrast to sound in mainstream cinema, where it has historically had a relatively formulaic function, primarily one of temporal

387. Béla Balázs, *Theory of the Film (Character and Growth of a New Art)*, 65.
388. Yuri Tynyanov, "On the Foundations of Cinema," ed. Herbert Eagle, *Russian Formalist Film Theory*, 88.

linearisation, where both diegetic and non-diegetic sound accentuates the action onscreen, increasing the emotional and dramatic weight of the images through corresponding sound effects and music.

Tarkovsky challenged this reassuringly familiar approach by using sound in a similar way to the image: links between sound and image are disrupted, delayed and distorted. Sound is no longer a separate entity used to reinforce the content onscreen but an essential tool in the creation of meanings. Techniques of temporal animation create experiential affects in the viewer, mismatching sounds with images, varying tonal quality, fluctuations in rhythm or using sounds that do not originate from the diegesis and have no logical connection to the action at all. Discussing his later films, Andrea Truppin writes that:

> Andrei Tarkovsky develops a compelling language based on sound's potential for ambiguity and abstraction. He probes sound's ability to function both literally—attached to an object—and abstractly—independent of any recognizable source. In these films, sound moves beyond its traditional role as secondary support for the image, at times surpassing the visual in its ability to convey certain types of meaning.[389]

Tarkovsky creates open aural images which are as associative as his visuals, "The main musical theme will have to be, on the one hand, purged of all emotion, and, on the other, of all thought or pragmatic intent."[390] Just as images are filtered through the gauze of personal perception so must sounds be: from the multi-layered aural images in the climactic scene in *Solaris* to the juxtaposition of classical and rhythmic synthesizers in *Stalker*.[391]

By 1967 Tarkovsky had tired of Ovchinnikov, who had composed his diploma work and his first two feature films, stating that he "must be held in check or else he'll write not a soundtrack but a talented opera."[392] Tarkovsky was demanding more and more expressive sound and sound effects for his unconventional image patterns. He required that "The notes had to convey the fact that reality is conditional, and at the same time accurately to reproduce precise states of mind, the sounds of a person's interior world."[393] In fact, Tarkovsky had expressed the idea that in the future films might need no music at all: "When I saw the rushes for the first time, I thought the film wouldn't need any music. It seemed to me that it could—that it must even—rely solely

389. Andrea Truppin, "And Then There Was Sound: The Films of Andrei Tarkovsky," *Sound Theory. Sound Practice*, ed. Rick Altman (New York: Routledge, 1992), 234.
390. Quoted in "*Stalker*, Smuggler of Happiness," *Andrei Tarkovsky Interviews,* 52.
391. For sound in Tarkovsky see David Beer's "*Solaris* and the ANS Synthesizer: On the Relations Between Tarkovsky, Artemiev, and Music Technology," in *Through the Mirror: Reflections on the Films of Andrei Tarkovsky*, 100-18.
392. Bird, *Andrei Tarkovsky: Elements of Cinema,* 158.
393. Tarkovsky, *Sculpting in Time*, 162.

on sounds. Now I would like to try muted music, barely audible, behind the noises of the trains that pass beneath the windows of the Stalker's home."[394] For an artist obsessed with the singularity of the medium he felt that film was at its most cinematic when it ignored other media entirely.

"There really is no time in the Zone."[395]

Stalker believes that the answers for Writer and Professor reside inside the Zone, and he has taken them there on a spiritual pilgrimage. Tarkovsky also intends for the film itself to be a pilgrimage for the viewers. The audience is never given a solid grasp of the Zone's physical presence and Tarkovsky withholds establishing shots to quantify the place. It is literally and figuratively an amorphous and shifting mass, a Deleuzian any-space-whatever, and perhaps the ultimate deterritorialised landscape in a body of work full of them. Like the Zone, any-space-whatever resides outside of space and time, where conventions of temporality and space lose their meaning. The dacha in *Mirror*, the planet Solaris in *Solaris* and Domenico's house in *Nostalghia* are similarly non-determinable, fluid and constantly changing Deleuzian spaces. Previously routine and stable objects, events and meanings are detached from fixed perceptions, indicative of an affectual cinema that no longer portrays. The Zone in *Stalker* is a resolutely ambiguous space, which modulates with experience. Stalker believes that the ground is so shifting and fluctuating that he ties small handkerchiefs to nuts and throws them in front, as if to test the temporal and spatial stability of the path ahead. Once the small party inadvertently leaves Professor behind and Stalker decides that it is too dangerous to turn back, so they journey forward over a stream and a waterfall. Yet in the next scene somehow they come across him again in the very same spot, as if the Zone has transcended boundaries of space and time. The Stalker *could* have engineered it all, a pretence to provide an illusion of the Zone's powers for his two companions. Tarkovsky offers some possible answers:

> Why do they find him in the same place? First of all they could have gotten lost. That's one answer. Furthermore, if the Zone has the powers that the Stalker says it does, then there could be a million explanations for this phenomenon. Finally, it's conceivable that he is leading them on these

394. Quoted in "*Stalker*, Smuggler of Happiness," *Andrei Tarkovsky Interviews*, 51.
395. Stalker in *Stalker*.

detours on purpose in order to create a magical atmosphere. You can never know for sure whether the Room exists or not.[396]

Questions of narrative cause and effect, which would be of paramount importance in more mainstream films, are left deliberately and provocatively ambiguous. Tarkovsky refuses to reveal where or even when the film is set and whether the Zone really has supernatural powers or whether it is all a product of Stalker's imagination. The mysterious practices of the Zone, which are self-evident in the book, are never objectively apparent in the film. When the Writer tires of Stalker's rules and regulations on how to behave in the Zone, he ventures off on his own, only to be stopped in his tracks by a mysterious voice, urging him to return. It is not clear whether it is the Zone speaking to him or this is a product of his own imagination. As Tarkovsky points out: "I entirely accept the idea that this world was created by the Stalker in order to instil faith—faith in his reality."[397]

This potency has lent itself to many allegorical interpretations: as in much of Tarkovsky's work the openness of its construction practically demands it.[398] What is the Zone? Is it freedom of social, political and religious beliefs, or liberation denied by the totalitarian regime and cordoned off by the state? Just as Kelvin speculated about why the visitors appeared on the Solaris space station, the Professor speculates that the Zone "Could be anything. A message to humanity, as the papers called it, or a present."[399] In interviews Tarkovsky deliberately avoided directly political interpretations, but writers have not. Le Fanu states that Stalker physically resembled one of Solzhenitsyn's "Zeks," survivors of the gulag or prisons.[400] The word "Zone" in Russian has become slang for prison, a form of purgatory outside of real life. In David

396. Ibid., 58.
397. Ibid., 61.
398. Such acausal pockets either literal or figurative have frequently appeared in literature and film. Godard's *Alphaville*, another of the defining science fiction films of the decade, saw a futuristic Paris divided into Zones (with political potency called North and South) and like *Stalker* the very film itself is a site of indeterminacy. One is even not sure when or where the titular Alphaville resides. Is it in the future? Or in space? Time there is incalculable; a clock on the wall reads 24:17. The protagonist, an ironic version of Humphrey Bogart called Lemmy Caution, says: "It seemed like centuries had passed but I had only been there for one day." Alphaville is governed over by a HAL-like super computer, which has gained sentience and thinks it knows what is best for humanity. Lemmy encounters a girl who is like Hari or Rachel, perhaps a clone. Like those who live in Alphaville she is losing her humanity a day at a time. The city is a place dominated by technology and logic at the expense of humanity, while displays of emotion have been outlawed and every day more words disappear from the dictionary.
399. This is one of the elements Stanislaw Lem liked about the novel and he comments about it in his *Microworlds*: "Preserving the mystery of the visitors. One does not know what they look like, one does not know what they want, one does not know why they come to this world, what their intentions were respecting/regarding mankind." Stanislaw Lem, "About the Strugatsky's *Roadside Picnic*," *Microworlds*, 253.
400. From the word *zakliuchyonnyi* in Russian, usually abbreviated to "з/к" or *z-k* in paperwork.

Cronenberg's visceral and melodramatic exploration of immigrant Russian life in contemporary London, *Eastern Promises* (2007), the protagonist Nikolai Lyuzhin (played by Vigo Mortensen), a gangster and member of the vory v zakone, or the thieves in law, comments "I am already dead. I died when I was fifteen. Now I live in the Zone all the time."[401]

The abandoned tanks that populate the Zone recall the Second World War, referred to by Russians as the Great Patriotic War. Visitors to Stalingrad (renamed Volgograd in 1961 during the Thaw as part of the de-Stalinization process) can still see abandoned tanks and buildings. Peter Green called the Zone "a place of terror, or the repository of dreams; a lost domain, another place or time."[402] Slavoj Žižek concisely sets out what for him are the possible allegorical meanings of the film very clearly:

> For a citizen of the defunct Soviet Union, the notion of a forbidden Zone gives rise to (at least) five associations: Zone is (1) Gulag, i.e. a separated prison territory; (2) a territory poisoned or otherwise rendered uninhabitable by some technological (biochemical, nuclear...) catastrophe, like Chernobyl; (3) the secluded domain in which the nomenklatura lives; (4) foreign territory to which access is prohibited (like the enclosed West Berlin in the midst of the GDR); (5) a territory where a meteorite struck (like Tunguska in Siberia). The point, of course, is that the question 'so which is the true meaning of the Zone?' is false and misleading: the very indeterminacy of what lies beyond the Limit is primary, and different positive contents fill in this preceding gap.[403]

Žižek is correct; there can be no definitive answer to the question. Like most images in Tarkovsky's cinema, the Zone is entirely what individual members of the audience take from it. Yet one indelible truth does remain: *Stalker* resonates as much now in the first decades of the twenty-first century as it did when it was originally made in 1979.

---

401. The Strugatsky brothers' work is no stranger to allegory. Their *Noon Universe Cycle* saw them emerge as the leading voices in Soviet cinema. *Hard to be a God* (1964) portrays a human populated world during a late medieval period. Groups of humans from a highly advanced earth of the future visit this world as observers who do not reveal their true identities. The medieval world, known as the Arkanar kingdom, is ruled by a merciless leader, a thinly veiled portrait of Stalin, called Don Rebar. Rebar has an army of grey troopers at his disposal who implement his iron rule across the kingdom killing all those who oppose him or who are educated. The culture of paranoia evokes the Soviet period. Don Reba's right hand man is very much a Beria figure, known as Father Kin, who writes a treatise on denunciation. He states, "My only goal is the good of the state. We need no clever people. We need loyalty."

402. Peter Green, *Andrei Tarkovsky: The Winding Quest*, 94.

403. Slavoj Žižek, "The Thing from Inner Space," *Sexuation*, 238.

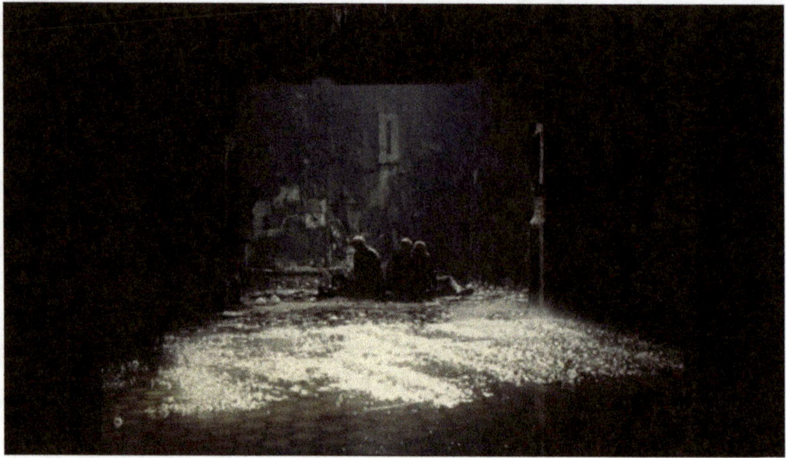

Figure 16 Like many of Tarkovsky's films, the imagery, characters and themes of *Stalker* are self-consciously designed to linger in the minds of audiences long after the film has finished.

When Writer, Professor and Stalker finally reach the end of their pilgrimage they do indeed find the mysterious room, but decide not to enter. They are afraid of what might happen if their innermost wishes come true. Earlier Stalker had recounted to them the story of one of his colleagues, a Stalker called Porcupine, who had entered the room wishing to save his brother's life, but was instead rewarded with riches beyond his wildest dreams. Like Gibarian in Solaris, he kills himself, perhaps, in realisation of the true nature of his character.

We discover that their real journey, like that of many of Tarkovsky's characters, has been psychological rather than physical. Although Writer had earlier wished to become a genius, the reality of the thought now repulses him: "If I change, if I become a genius, then why should I continue writing, as everything I'll write is always going to be perfect? The goal of writing is to overcome oneself, direct others towards the goal and the path to its realisation. What should a man who is a genius *a priori* write for? What can he offer? Creation is an expression of will." If he becomes a genius, then his work will be without merit, for it is only in the artistic struggle that meaning itself is created. He has realised these aspects of his identity without having to step into the room.

Professor had wanted to destroy the room in order to prevent anyone from using it for nefarious purposes, but he realises human beings are so petty and fragile that no one would ever want this in their heart of hearts: people "usually desire really primitive things: money, prestige, women." Tarkovsky interprets this failure to enter the room as a weakness on their part. He suggested: "They had summoned the strength to look into themselves and had been horrified; but in the end they lack the spiritual courage to believe in themselves."[404]

Even the camera does not move into the room. Greg Polin observes that "The inaccessible and prohibitive factors of the Zone are not strictly narrative in nature, but also apparent in the cinematography, and specifically the virtual space, which lies outside of the camera's scope…If it is not already clear, one goal this film is attempting is to not simply destroy the 'fourth wall,' but suggest that it doesn't exist."[405] One is forced once again to question whether the room's powers even exist or whether it is just a figment of Stalker's imagination, invented to give others hope or as a stimulus for self-evaluation. Tarkovsky suggested, "The spectator may doubt its existence or see it merely as a myth or a joke...or even as the fantasy of our hero. For the viewer this remains a mystery."[406]

With *Stalker* Tarkovsky returned to the themes of *Solaris* and attempted to realise the film he had tried to make before, but in his opinion had failed. *Stalker* is about a journey from the external to the internal, just as Tarkovsky's films themselves are such a journey. When the three men reach the final room, it does not actually matter that they do not enter, because the film has become much more than narrative; the external world has become almost irrelevant.

One interpretation of the film is a religious one. Still in the Soviet Union Tarkovsky's religious allusions remain suitably veiled, although in *Stalker* they become more pronounced than ever: the crown of thorns, the fish and Stalker's almost Christ-like status. Given these elements, it is surprising that the authorities asked for no changes or cuts to the film at all, which is ironic considering it was the last film he ever made in Russia. For his next films, those made in exile, he would be free to use as much religious imagery as he wished, and for some this would have an ambiguous impact on their realisation and their efficacy.

---

404. Tarkovsky, *Sculpting in Time*, 198.
405. Greg Polin, "*Stalker*'s Meaning in Terms of Temporality and Spatial Relations," para 49, <http://www.acs.ucalgary.ca/~tstronds/nostalghia.com/TheTopics/Stalker_GP.html> (n.d.) (1st September 2008). Bertolucci once suggested that "The camera has a dialectical relationship to the actors and is not merely recording the event, but is an invisible participant with its own soul. Sometimes the camera even enters into competition with the actor—while the actor moves, the camera moves independently." Daniel Bickley, "Bertolucci's *1900*: A Preview," *Cineaste* 7.4 (1976): 5.
406. Quoted in "*Stalker*, Smuggler of Happiness," *Andrei Tarkovsky Interviews*, 50.

Chapter Four

Tarkovsky and Spirituality

In art, as in religion, intuition is tantamount to conviction, to faith. It is a state of mind, not a way of thinking....In the case of someone who is spiritually receptive, it is therefore possible to talk of an analogy between the impact made by a work of art and that of purely religious experience. Art acts above all on the soul, shaping its spiritual structure.

~Andrei Tarkovsky

For the time it takes to screen the film, the film-maker is God.

~Louis Malle

While the Soviet Union officially enjoyed freedom of religious belief, the reality was very different. Under the Communist Party the USSR became a resolutely secular society and the church was branded a counter-revolutionary force allied to the decadent Tsarist regime. The state set about effectively eliminating religion from all forms of Soviet life: church funds, property and land were confiscated, Christians were prevented from rising in their careers and most significantly were not allowed to join the party, which made them political, social and artistic outsiders. Despite these conditions, Andrei Tarkovsky is widely considered as one of the great religious film-makers of the post-war era.[407] How could his films remain so resolutely spiritual under such conditions? David Robinson was aware of this paradox, when he observed, "The Soviet Union, traditionally dedicated to the aesthetic dogma of 'socialist realism' has produced two of cinema's greatest missionaries, Sergei Paradzhanov and Andrei Tarkovsky."[408]

The concept of a Hidden God or *Deus absconditus* in film was investigated in a conference at the Museum of the Moving Image in the Gramercy Theatre in New York in 2003, entitled *The Hidden God: Film and Faith*. The conference considered the depiction of the divine in a diverse range of films: from *Au hasard Balthazar* (Bresson, 1966), *Unforgiven* (Eastwood, 1992) and *Winter Light* (Bergman, 1962) to *Groundhog Day* (Ramis, 1993). The fundamental question was "how is it possible to portray faith onscreen?" Many concluded that

---

407. Some of the ideas contained in this chapter were initially proposed by the author in "'A State of mind, not a way of thinking': Spirituality in the Films of Andrei Tarkovsky." *Faith and Spirituality in Masters of World Cinema* (Newcastle: Cambridge Scholars Press, 2008), 58-72.
408. David Robinson, "Eccentrically dark defeatism," *The Times* (4th November 1983): 15.

spirituality could not be directly portrayed, only felt, hidden in "the Jansenist sense: absent, but present to those who seek Him—who in a Pascalian paradox, are those who have already found him."[409]

The films of Tarkovsky were included in the conference, but the contributors did not acknowledge some of the most intriguing contradictions at the heart of his work. Tarkovsky's position in relation to a *Deus absconditus* is problematised by the fact that faith in his films must remain doubly hidden: it is absent from the screen, because, of course, it is impossible to represent the divine, but also due to the limitations placed on film-makers in the Soviet Union where religion was effectively, if never formally, banned. How can one reconcile this with Tarkovsky's earnestly expressed belief that art is first and foremost an expression of religious faith? He wrote and seemingly sincerely believed that: "Art is born and takes hold wherever there is a timeless and insatiable longing for the spiritual, for the ideal: that longing which draws people to art."[410]

This chapter argues that part of the spiritual efficacy of Tarkovsky's films is ironically them being made under a totalitarian regime. Required to mask his religious themes and motifs in metaphor, the earnest struggle for faith in Tarkovsky's films becomes all the more resonant. In *Andrei Rublyov* the eponymous monk's spiritual journey is masked behind a search for artistic inspiration; in *Solaris* Kris Kelvin's religious epiphany becomes, on the surface, an emotional and psychological one, fundamentally connected to coming to terms with his past; the spiritual pilgrimage in *Stalker* is presented in such an ambiguous form, it could almost be a quest for anything. After leaving the Soviet Union his two final films were more explicitly about faith and spirituality which arguably results in a directness and lack of ambiguity when compared to *Mirror* and *Stalker*. It is perhaps this reason among others that *Nostalghia* and *The Sacrifice* are considered by some as two of Tarkovsky's lesser works.

In this respect this chapter suggests that the levels of spirituality apparent in Tarkovsky's films are twofold. Despite the context of their production, they are surprisingly full of unambiguously Christian imagery: from the fish and the crosses, to angels and even a conspicuously obvious crown of thorns worn by Writer at the climax of *Stalker*. However, in the realm of allegory, film holds for Tarkovsky, "the possibility of interaction with infinity, for the great function of the artistic image is to be a kind of detector of infinity."[411] This chapter will explore two of Tarkovsky's most religious texts. Firstly, *Andrei Rublyov* from his time in the Soviet Union where much of its religious content is veiled, yet ultimately all the more powerful because of it. Secondly, *The*

---

409. James Quandt, "*Au Hasard Balthazar* and *The Devil Probably*," *The Hidden God*, eds. Mary Bandy and Antonio Monda (New York: Museum of Modern Art Press, 2003), 17.
410. Tarkovsky, *Sculpting in Time*, 38.
411. Ibid., 109.

Sacrifice, his final film and his second made in exile, where the religious aspects are much more evident. Despite readily apparent failings which emerge from Tarkovsky's inability to adequately implement many of his own theoretical concepts, *The Sacrifice* emerges as profound summation of his career and his artistic legacy, bringing his body of work full circle, ending where it began.

It is important to note that Tarkovsky's films are not just about characters who have religious or transcendental experiences; they are intended to be transcendental experiences in themselves. Just as they are not exclusively about memory, but are memory artifacts in their own right. Tarkovsky strove to create an epiphany in the viewer by using very conscious techniques. In this respect Tarkovsky's cinema is very different from such explicitly religious films like *Passion of the Christ* (Gibson, 2004), *The Ten Commandments* (DeMille, 1956) and *The Nativity Story* (Hardwicke, 2006). Tarkovsky would not have been able to make films like this in the Soviet Union even if he had wanted to. When his work moved too close to overtly religious themes Goskino would respond with demands for changes or cuts.

This debate is reminiscent of Paul Schrader's influential *Transcendental Style in Film*, which explores a similar predicament. Schrader examines directors who consistently attempted to screen the numinous and express the transcendent in their work. The defining attributes of this transcendental style might be considered, with some qualification, a description of Tarkovsky's aesthetic strategies. Schrader states, "Transcendental style seeks to maximize the mystery of existence; it eschews all conventional interpretations of reality: realism, naturalism, psychologism, romanticism, expressionism, impressionism, and, finally, rationalism."[412] Schrader's language even echoes Tarkovsky's at times. Tarkovsky's notion that "The image is indivisible and elusive, dependent upon our consciousness and on the real world which it seeks to embody"[413] becomes Schrader's study of directors who strive "towards the ineffable and invisible."[414] Seeking to be more specific, one might define Schrader's cinematic techniques as a) the prioritisation of image over narrative, mood over narrative, ambiguity over logic/continuity and the preference for ambiguous chronological structures; b) irrationalism over rationalism, anonymity over individualization; c) sacred over profane, intellectual realism over optical realism, two-dimensional vision over three-dimensional vision.

While Schrader does not mention Tarkovsky by name (writing in the early seventies when Tarkovsky's reputation as a great spiritual film-maker had not yet been confirmed), the comparisons are clear. However, later Schrader suggested that Tarkovsky did not come under the rubric of a transcendental style, and chose to include the man many regard as Tarkovsky's heir, Alexander Sokurov instead. In a conversation with Sokurov, Schrader notes: "I always felt

412. Schrader, *Transcendental Style in Film*, 10.
413. Tarkovsky, *Sculpting in Time*, 106.
414. Schrader, *Transcendental Style in Film*, 3.

a little guilty because I thought I should like Tarkovsky more than I did. My head was telling me I should like it, but my heart wasn't going along. When I saw your [Sokurov's] films, my first reaction was, this is what I wanted from Tarkovsky."[415] Yet Schrader's suggestion, that "many film-makers have employed the transcendental style, but few have had the devotion, the rigour, and the outright fanaticism to employ it exclusively"[416] seems to embody almost Tarkovsky above all.

It is no coincidence that Schrader focuses on Yasujiro Ozu, Carl Theodor Dreyer and Robert Bresson, some of the film-makers who came to have a defining influence on Tarkovsky. These film-makers came from diverse cultures and backgrounds, and yet for Schrader they are united by a common spiritual goal. Schrader fails to take into account that Tarkovsky is distinguished from these directors by having made the majority of his films under a totalitarian regime. Japan, Sweden and France placed no such institutional restrictions on their artists. Although seeking to pursue such spiritually oriented films, which are frequently unpopular with mainstream audiences, they would have certainly faced other pressures, challenging their own sense of devotion, rigour, and fanaticism.

Tarkovsky's religious beliefs are not easily categorised. Despite his Russian Orthodox background, his films offer a multiplicity of perspectives: Christian, Humanist, Pantheist, Buddhist, Pagan, Hindu and Fideist. It is apparent from his films and his writings that his beliefs are very personal and difficult to define, and arguably this had a beneficial impact on his work. This might be seen "in the ease with which he maintained a consistency of vision through the varying Christian countries that he worked in: Russian Orthodox (Russia), Roman Catholicism (Italy) and Lutheran (Sweden)."[417] Tarkovsky himself suggested that, "I believe that it's truly not important to know if I subscribe to certain beliefs, whether pagan, Catholic, Orthodox, or simply Christian. The important thing is the work itself."[418] Tarkovsky's approach to the religious content of his films is as profoundly multivalent as his approach to memory, image and symbol. The films do not have to be experienced as religious, but these elements are present should the spectator seek them out. Just as Geraardus van der Leeuw suggested, art has no particular religious denomination: "Art can be religious, or it can appear to be religious; but it can be neither Mohammedan nor Buddhist nor Christian. There is no Christian art, any more than there is a Christian science. There is only art which has stood

415. Paul Schrader, "The history of an artist's soul is a very sad history: An Interview With Alexander Sokurov," *Film Comment* (Nov.-Dec. 1997): 20.

416. Schrader, *Transcendental Style in Film,* 10.

417. Donato Totaro, "Art for All Time," *Film-Philosophy* 4.4, para. 11.

418. Quoted in "Faith Is the Only Thing That Can Save Man," *Andrei Tarkovsky Interviews,* ed. John Gianvito, 179.

before the Holy."[419]

One might begin by asking, as the conference asked, how is it even possible to present such an intangible thing as religious faith onscreen? Of course, a director might film someone going to church and praying, but this is very different to the experience of prayer being felt in itself. It is perhaps poetic cinema, with its more associational qualities, which is more able to embody such a non-representational and incorporeal area on film than traditional cinematic narratives. I have attempted to argue that Tarkovsky's brand of cinema intentionally draws meanings as much from the spectator as from the text itself. When Joseph Campbell stated that "The symbol itself must be transparent to transcendence"[420] he was suggesting that the opacity of a symbol is the key to a multitude of meanings, an apophenic object for a spectator, who will find what they are searching for. This sense of metaphorical transparency is encoded into not only Tarkovsky's visual aesthetic, as we have seen in our discussion of open images, but also his narratives. There are critics of this style who argue that a film like *The Sacrifice* is "too opaque to yield concrete meaning, it offers itself as sacral art, demanding a rapt, even religious response from audiences."[421] Yet this opacity is only problematic for audiences who demand tangible and definite meanings from art; for some opacity and ambiguity is one of the strengths of the medium, as Tarkovsky frequently articulated in *Sculpting in Time.*

4.1 Narrative Poetics in *Andrei Rublyov*

Faith is a state of mind not a way of thinking.

~Andrei Tarkovsky

It is true that the theology of "the death of god" is extremely important, because it is the sole religious creation of the modern Western world. What it presents us with is the final step in the process of desacralization.

~Mircea Eliade

Following the remarkable success of *Ivan's Childhood* Tarkovsky found himself

---

419. Geraardus van der Leeuw *Sacred and Profane Beauty: The Holy in Art* (NY: Holt Rinehart and Winston, 1963), 279. Quoted in Paul Schrader, *Transcendental Style in Film*, 7.

420. Joseph Campbell, *The Inner Reaches of Outer Space: Metaphor as Myth and as Religion* (Novato, California: New World Library, 2002), 34.

421. G.C Macnab, "Andrei Tarkovsky" in *International Dictionary of Films and Filmmakers: Directors Vol.2*, 980. On the matter of opacity Tarkovsky suggested, "I would say that in cinema 'opacity' and 'ineffability' do not mean an indistinct picture, but the particular impression created by the logic of the dream" (72).

in a privileged position for a young, relatively inexperienced film-maker and had every reason to be optimistic about his future prospects. He had only just turned thirty years old and was already being acclaimed by critics all around the world. His next film was eagerly anticipated both inside and outside Russia; yet seven long years passed from his winning the Golden Lion at Venice for *Ivan's Childhood* in 1962 to the FIPRESCI Prize at Cannes for his second film *Andrei Rublyov* in 1969. The film's protracted struggle for release is reflected in the fact that it was still winning prizes as late as 1973, almost ten years after he had begun principal photography. The reason for this is certainly due to the subject matter of the film: the painter, monk and creator of "The Trinity," Andrei Rublyov (1360-1430), one of the most significant figures in Russian history. While it might seem unusual that a religious figure was held in such high esteem by an atheistic state, the Soviet Union had never been averse to using pre-Soviet icons when it was regarded as necessary to promote Russian identity and unity. During the Second World War Andrei Rublyov was one of a series of "great ancestors" like Alexander Nevsky (who defeated the Teutonic knights in 1242 during the Battle of the Ice on Lake Peipus) and Mikhail Kutuzov (for his heroic leadership during the Napoleonic War), who were conjured up, reinterpreted and politicised by Stalin.[422]

When Tarkovsky delivered his cut of *Andrei Rublyov*, Mosfilm was deeply troubled by what he had produced. Regarded by many as an allegory of the repression of the Soviet artist and the brutality of the Soviet state, it was criticised by many within the Soviet Union for being too violent, too religious, too experimental and most damning of all, un-Soviet in its construction. As was often the case, the paradoxicality of some of the criticisms emphasizes the film's inherent ambiguity. While screenplay editor N. V. Believa is able to classify it as being so far from the state ideology that it was "a crime against the nation,"[423] Alexander Solzhenitsyn suggested that it "besmirched" Rublyov's faith with its Sovietisms.[424] Critics almost all agree on the film's potent allegorical properties; Michel Ciment described the film as a "transparent allegory"[425] and Jacques Demeure classified it as "a serene allegory with no apparent connection to historical reality."[426] Adding to the film's resonance, it

422. During the war training colleges for priests reopened and the new patriarch described Stalin in *Pravda,* November 1942, as "the god chosen warrior." See William Husband's *"Godless Communists": Atheism and Society in Soviet Russia* (DeKalb: Northern Illinois Press, 2000). Kutuzov was featured in *Kutuzov* (Petrov, 1944) and Alexander Nevsky in *Alexander Nevsky.*

423. Bird, *Andrei Tarkovsky: Elements of Cinema,* 42. Originally cited in Transcript of a meeting of the Artistic Council of the [Sixth Creative] Unit to discuss the third version of the literary scenario *Beginnings and Ways* by A.S Konchalovsky and A. A. Tarkovsky (28 April 1963).

424. Ibid, 5.

425. Michel Ciment, *Dossier Positif,* 79. Quoted from Sean Martin, "Live in the House –And the House Will Stand: The Role of Autobiography and Lived Experience in Tarkovsky's Films," *Through the Mirror: Reflections on Tarkovsky,* 18.

426. Jacques Demeure, *Dossier Positif,* 81. Quoted from Sean Martin, "Live in the House–And the House Will Stand: The Role of Autobiography and Lived Experience in Tarkovsky's Films,"

has been suggested that Bergman saw it ten times[427] and called it, according to Bibi Andersson, the best film he ever saw.[428]

For audiences used to the rousing epics of Soviet Socialist Realism, Tarkovsky's introspective historical tapestry proved problematic. There were even rumours that Leonid Brezhnev ordered a private screening of the film and walked out before it had even finished.[429] *Andrei Rublyov* proved so controversial that it was refused international distribution, even when it was eagerly demanded by numerous film festivals impatient for the "new Tarkovsky." Instead they sent Sergei Bondarchuk's more ideologically conventional epic *War and Peace*.

The film itself is a poetic narrative presented on a grand historical canvas. Ostensibly a biopic, it is as much about 15th century Russian life as it is about the eponymous Andrei himself. Taking place over twenty-three years from 1400 to 1423, it is separated into eight named and dated parts with an additional prologue and epilogue. While it is mainly chronological, the plot recounts in a frequently ambiguous fashion his life and career, encompassing his travels through Russia, his experience of the internecine fighting between rival factions of royals, through to his vow of silence and his decision to paint his most famous work, one of the most celebrated works of art in Russian history, "The Trinity." While Rublyov's faith is certainly not at the centre of the narrative, which on the surface is much more about his struggle for artistic inspiration, it lingers in almost every scene.

Tarkovsky's comments reveal how he wished to move away from conventional narrative forms. The film was not to be connected by a traditional chronological line but by a more poetic connection between events and scenes,

> The episodes, each with its own particular plot and theme, draw their unity from that logic. They develop in interaction with each other, through the inner conflict inherent in the poetic logic of their sequence in the

---

Through the Mirror: Reflections on Tarkovsky, 18.

427. Tarkovsky, *Time Within Time, The Diaries 1970-1986,* 249.

428. Ibid., 77.

429. In the Soviet Union this was not a matter to be taken lightly. Stalin visited Sergei Eisenstein in 1947 when Eisenstein was filming the second part of *Ivan the Terrible*. Stalin was unhappy with the director's failure to show that Ivan's brutality towards his people had been justified and that it was necessary for a great leader to be ruthless. Stalin was reported to have commented, "I'm not giving you instructions but expressing the comments of a spectator." Eisenstein, who already suffered with a weak heart and constitution, died a few months later. Robert Service, *A History of Modern Russian,* 319. A slightly different account of this incident can be found in Ronald Bergan, *Eisenstein: A Life in Conflict* (Little, Brown and Company: London, 1997), 340-44. Even these actions were not a precedent in the life of the artist in Russia. See *Life Has Become More Joyous, Comrades: Celebrations in the Time of Stalin* by Karen Petrone (Bloomington and Indianapolis: Indiana University Press, 2000), 134, which compares the relations between Stalin and artists who worked during the 1930s and 1940s to the relationship between Alexander Pushkin and Tsar Nicholas I.

screenplay: a kind of visual manifestation of the contradictions and complexities of life and artistic creativity.[430]

Andrei Rublyov is an evolution from the aesthetic strategies of *Ivan's Childhood.* Where *Ivan's Childhood* took tentative steps away from Socialist Realism, but remained within mainstream conventions of narrative, *Andrei Rublyov* is a venture into much more poetic territory. It is Tarkovsky's erotetic style of narrative, which begins to come to the fore with *Andrei Rublyov* and much more so with the films that follow it. Tarkovsky suggested that "Through poetic connections feeling is heightened and the spectator is made more active. He becomes a participant in the process of discovering life, unsupported by ready-made deductions from the plot or ineluctable pointers by the author."[431] Again Tarkovsky is emphasising an experiential cinema that requires investment and engagement on the part of the spectator, rather than the "ready-made deductions" of mainstream cinema. Tarkovsky's narratives challenge and ask questions, always reluctant to provide answers about motivation and cause. As his career progressed, narrative became less and less a formative factor; in fact he commented that in his films "the story itself is never particularly important. The real significance in my works has never been expressed through the plot of the films."[432] This echoes the other key voices of the transcendental style, such as Ozu, who stated, "Pictures with obvious plots bore me now,"[433] and Bresson, who noted, "I try more and more in my films to suppress what people call plot. Plot is a novelist's trick."[434]

Andrei Rublyov is both elliptical and episodic. Andrei's journey is reminiscent of the Stalker's forays into the Zone and the seemingly inconsequential moments which come to define the life of the protagonist in *Mirror*. It loosely follows the protagonist towards his artistic epiphany, but the chapters do not all focus on what might be considered the most significant events of Rublyov's life, as would be the case in conventional biopics. Tarkovsky's interpretation as to what comprises these moments in an individual's life is very different; for Rublyov one might expect it to be his decision to paint "The Trinity" or his vow of silence, but Tarkovsky refuses to present these onscreen. In the course of the entire film Rublyov does not paint a single image, and for a film about Russia's most renowned artist not to paint must have been almost unimaginable for audiences. Like on the planet Solaris or the Zone, for Tarkovsky, the key moments of life remain beneath the surface in moments perhaps long forgotten: an unexpected rainfall, a simple

430. Tarkovsky, *Sculpting in Time*, 35.
431. Ibid., 20.
432. Quoted in "To Journey Within," *Chaplin* 193, para 56, (September 1984), trans. Trond S. Trondson (n.d.), <http://www.ucalgary.ca/~tstronds/nostalghia.com/TheTopics/Gideon_Bachmann.html.> (1st September 2008)
433. Ozu in Schrader, *Transcendental Style in Film*, 19.
434. Schrader, *Transcendental Style in Film*, 64.

conversation with a loved one, a momentary lapse of faith, or an illicit kiss.

Andrei Rublyov shows a striking disregard for conventional descriptions of time and place, a prerequisite for the genre in most biopics (and also mainstream cinema in general). While every chapter is given a date it is also presented with an ambiguous title. Within the chapters, dates and places are infrequently acknowledged. It is very difficult to ascertain how much time, if any, passes between scenes, where the characters are, where they have come from or where they are going. This demanding approach continues in the refusal to chart the logical progress of characters, who frequently disappear and reappear without explanation or motivation. Of course, this is perfectly reasonable if the film is presenting a fragment in time of an individual's life without the exposition of mainstream cinema, but it can confuse an audience not willing to undertake such a journey. When a missing character, presumed dead, reappears in a later episode, Tarkovsky remarked, "Let them make of it what they will."[435]

It might be suggested that central to Tarkovsky's films, if not to unlocking them, but to experiencing the world they are exploring, can be found in their prologues. Frequently narratively disconnected in the traditional sense, they seem to exemplify the principles and the themes in a more intangible, but highly resonant manner. They enable the viewer to enter into Tarkovsky's world, establishing an atmosphere or an idea, one that will "unfold more by associative laws of music and poetry than by the usual canons of cine-fiction."[436] We have already seen how the stutterer in *Mirror* introduced a motif of expression and identity, how Kelvin's trip to the dacha in *Solaris* embodied his desire to become at one with nature and earth, and how *Nostalghia* introduced Gorchakov's longing for an impossible return to his past. To these we must add what is often referred to as the "balloon sequence" in *Andrei Rublyov*.

With no date or a title, a dishevelled peasant is introduced, who has constructed a crude balloon from animal skins. The unnamed balloonist is the first artist in a film which will be full of them. The first lines of dialogue are a prayer, "Oh God. I pray we make it." A sweeping shot from the top of a church reveals that the balloonist is being pursued by both soldiers and civilians, but he manages to leap into the air just before they arrive. For a precious few moments he soars. "I'm flying. I'm flying" he yells, before crashing to the ground. The man is never identified, he and the place itself will not appear in the film again, nor will they be referred to; yet despite this lack of connection to the narrative on an explicit level, the scene establishes a setting and a mood. Tarkovsky presents an uneasy juxtaposition between realism and a dream-like atmosphere which characterises all of his films.

Tarkovsky often turned to the metaphorical realm of flight; whether it is

---

435. Johnson and Petrie, *The Films of Andrei Tarkovsky,* 96.
436. Bird, *Andrei Tarkovsky: Elements of Cinema,* 109.

representative of a search for religious, artistic or political freedom, or none of these, it is up to the audience to decide. Yet the authorities are trying to catch the balloonist, why? For daring to be free? For moving beyond what is expected of him? For threatening to be an individual? The film which follows relies more on associative connections, rather than firmly prescribed formulae of narrative causality and logic. Like many of the echoes in Tarkovsky's work it offers a link to the film which preceded it, and the films which follow.

Alain Robbe-Grillet, film-maker, novelist and screenwriter of *Last Year in Marienbad*, emphasised the nature of this more challenging approach to film narratives and the demands they place on audiences:

> It will be said the spectator risks getting lost if he is not occasionally given the 'explanations' that permit him to locate each scene in its chronological place and its level of objective reality. But we have decided to trust the spectator, to allow him...to come to terms with pure subjectivities. Two attitudes are then possible: either the spectator will then try to reconstitute some 'Cartesian' scheme—the most linear, the most rational he can devise—and this spectator will certainly find the film difficult, if not incomprehensible; or else the spectator will let himself be carried along by the extraordinary images in front of him, by the actors' voices, by the soundtrack, by the music, by the rhythm of the cutting, by the passion of the characters... and to this spectator, the film will seem the 'easiest' he has ever seen.[437]

The spectator reluctant to be "carried along" or to become a fellow-traveller, or an ally, will find it difficult to engage with *Andrei Rublyov* or films from Tarkovsky's oeuvre; for this type of spectator the films will appear long-winded, pretentious and abstruse. Yet, as Robbe-Grillet suggested, those who are prepared to make such a leap of faith will reap the rewards.

Andrei Rublyov does not appear in the prologue; in fact, he is off screen for large segments of the film. Even when he does appear he is not the dynamic force behind the narrative in any traditional sense. He only appears seven minutes into the film, in the first episode called "The Buffoon" (named after a very minor character who appears in the story, who has no more than a couple of minutes of screen time). He is not mentioned by name in the whole of the episode and it is not until a close up, twelve minutes and twenty seconds in, that he is revealed to be the protagonist. In the scene three monks enter a hut to shelter from the rain. Inside a fool, the titular buffoon, entertains the crowd with a vulgar, but vigorously satirical performance. Until the close up Rublyov is not especially prioritised through the use of *mise en scène*, he has no more or fewer words than the other members of this party, he is not a "star" nor does he look anything like one (a recurring motif throughout the film is the

437. Alain Robbe-Grillet, *Last Year at Marienbad* (London: John Caulder, 1962), 12-3.

fact that he is frequently mistaken for other people). This depersonalisation has been seen as Soviet by some: "[*Andrei Rublyov*] suffers from the rhetoric and depersonalization that has always hung over Russian cinema"[438] or ineffective cinematic practice by others, "I assume we are meant to share the passions, sorrows and doubts that shaped the artist, but since there always seems more going on in the head of the director than in the head of the man playing Andrei, the system did not work for me."[439] It is Grigori Kozintsev, the director of *Hamlet* (*Gamlet*, 1964) and *King Lear* (*Korol' Lir*, 1971), who came closest to determining Tarkovsky's intentions when he observed, "Rublyov comes to life not on the screen but in the viewer's consciousness and each has his own Rublyov."[440]

It is readily apparent that, like his previous films and those to come, *Andrei Rublyov* refuses to be confined to the narrative and stylistic tropes of its genre. This is far from a conventional biopic; Tarkovsky even stated his intention to move away from predefined concepts of genre, "I do not believe that the cinema has genres—the cinema is *itself* a genre. Once we start talking about genre, we are dealing with a systemization arising from the cinema as a commercial enterprise. But cinema is a high art, a deeply poetic art: it doesn't need any schemas to violate its potential."[441] Once again Tarkovsky turns to the adjective "poetic" to describe his approach to cinema, in which genre and convention are reductive. Perhaps Tarkovsky was drawn to Rublyov because of the lack of historical detail about his life, which gave him greater freedom to explore his own concerns, making changes as he saw fit as he did with the three novels he adapted to the screen.

The opening episode of the film ends with the law arriving and arresting the buffoon. They brutally smash his head against a tree for daring to offer criticisms of those in power. The artist often emerges as a martyr in Tarkovsky's work, making the ultimate sacrifice for their art. In *Andrei Rublyov*, we see this not only in the balloonist and the buffoon, but also the stonemasons, Boriska the bell-maker, the monk artists and even Andrei Rublyov himself, each of whom suffer for pursuing their art and their artistic freedom. It is the stonemasons' plight which offers one of the most affecting and resonating examples: master craftsmen, they are blinded by a Prince feuding with his brother in order to prevent an even more magnificent palace

438. David Thomson, *The New Biographical Dictionary of Film*, 859.

439. Vincent Canby, *New York Times*, October 10th 1973, *The New York Times Film Reviews 1973-1974* (New York: The New York Times & Arno Press, 1975), 115.

440. Grigori Kozintsev, *Sobranie sochinenii vpiati tomakh*, vol 2 (Leningrad 1982), 367. Quoted from Bird, *Elements of Cinema,* 194. Julian Graffy echoes Kozintsev when he suggests a similar thing about Tarkovsky's narratives, "All of us, perforce, must re-invent Tarkovsky to address our own concerns, but his world, of matter and spirit, is most surely our world." "Tarkovsky: The Weight of the World," *Sight and Sound* 7.1 (January 1997): 22.

441. Ian Christie, "Against Interpretation: An Interview with Andrei Tarkovsky," *Framework* 14 (1981), *Andrei Tarkovsky Interview*, 66.

being built. It is not immediately clear who informed on the buffoon, but it is implied that it was one of the monks who journeyed with Rublyov, Kirill. In the middle ages, as in the Soviet Union in the time the film was produced, one had to be careful what one said. In *Andrei Rublyov* the artist will be persecuted, harangued, starved, tortured and maimed for wanting freedom and independence, and this is why many read it as an allegory for the trials of the artist in Soviet Russia. The strands of this episode will only be picked up some twenty three years later at the end of the film, barely visible except to those looking for them. There will be no melodramatic disclosures, but as ripples flow outwards, moments we thought were inconsequential unbeknownst to us happened to be a vivid part of the tapestry of our lives.

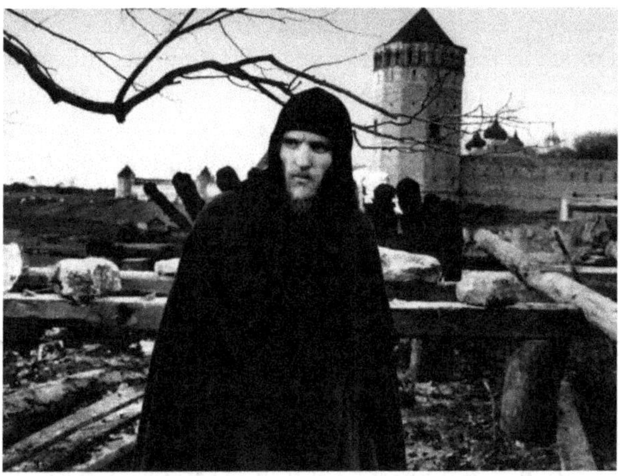

Figure 17 The eponymous itinerant monk and icon painter in the profoundly unconventional biopic *Andrei Rublyov*.

It is not too far-fetched to suggest that Tarkovsky saw something of himself in Andrei Rublyov, especially given the preponderance for alter egos in his work. Some have seen this as central to an understanding of the film.[442] Anatole Dauman commented in the documentary *After Tarkovsky* (Shepotinnik, 2003) that "When I met him [Tarkovsky] I was surprised at how much energy he had, and at once recognised him to be one of his own characters—Andrei Rublyov." It is not the real historical Rublyov that Dauman compares Tarkovsky to, but the Rublyov Tarkovsky had constructed as an image of himself. Tarkovsky's artistic ideals and motivation become filtered into his depiction of Rublyov: just as Tarkovsky rejected the assumptions of given artistic practices in favour of a more fluid interrogation of artistic principles, so does his Rublyov, both to potentially hazardous consequences. Tarkovsky

442. See Petur Petursson, "Mirrors in the Film *Andrei Rublyov*," *Through the Mirror. Reflections on the Films of Andrei Tarkovsky*, 188-199.

shows the great struggle and dangers Rublyov undertakes to produce something new. Both Tarkovsky and Rublyov work for God and mankind with a sense of determination, hope and faith. For Tarkovsky it is Rublyov's proximity to life and the people which make him a great artist: "The artist cannot express the moral ideal of his time unless he touches all its running sores, unless he suffers and lives these sores himself."[443] Rublyov is far from a perfect human being: in the course of the narrative he will be tempted and seduced by a pagan woman (though off-screen and ambiguous, it is implied they have sex), and he will even be forced to kill a man. But somehow it is this very fallibility that makes him the great artist and human being that he is.

This places Rublyov (and by extension Tarkovsky) at a great contrast to several of the other artists in the film; the esteemed Theophanes the Greek and Rublyov's colleagues Kirill and Danill. All three disconnect themselves from the people as much as they can, and their work becomes little more than a tool for the state. They unquestionably repeat the artistic traditions of their time with little thought or creativity. One sees echoes of Tarkovsky's criticisms of Sergei Bondarchuk in his depiction of this more conventional approach to art. Tarkovsky's view of these artists is similar to his view of Bondarchuk, whom he described as one of those "doomed to State and Lenin" destined to "win laurels in return for losing his self-respect and sense of individuality."[444]

Rublyov's journey is an arduous one, physically and emotionally, yet he is able to find a sense of faith within himself. While the film has ostensibly been about an artist searching for artistic inspiration, Tarkovsky has made a film about a man looking for God. The ambiguous presentation of Rublyov's journey allows spectators to formulate their own, very personal reactions to the film. On what a film is supposed to "mean," Tarkovsky quoted Engels: "The better hidden the author's views, the better for the work of art."[445] Like the Zone in *Stalker*, *Andrei Rublyov* has in it the meanings which people seek for themselves. Thus when the authorities criticised the film for its anti-Soviet message, it is perfectly logical, as this is what they sought to find. Though for many, above all, the film is a profoundly spiritual journey.

Many have noticed how similar some of the aesthetic qualities of *Andrei Rublyov,* and indeed Tarkovsky's other works, are to the techniques of medieval icon painting. Given that Tarkovsky wrote in his diary on 11th April 1986, that he "read Florensky with delight" and that he stated one could draw an analogy between "the impact made by a work of art and that of a purely religious experience"[446] such connections cannot be a coincidence. Throughout his work Tarkovsky showed a tendency to deliberately frame his characters as centrally positioned, gazing to the sides or beyond the camera, as is common in

443. Tarkovsky, *Sculpting in Time*, 68.
444. Tarkovsky, *Time within Time: The Diaries, 1970-1986*, 73.
445. Tarkovsky, *Sculpting in Time*, 47.
446. Ibid., 41.

medieval icons. In this respect Tarkovsky's visual aesthetic becomes reminiscent of many of the philosopher and theologian Pavel Florensky's ideas. Florensky suggested that in medieval icons there is more present than that which is depicted. He regarded superficial notions of realism to be reductive and rather ironically, lifeless. He asserted that, "For the task of painting is not to duplicate reality, but to give the most profound penetration of its architectonics, of its material, of its meaning. And the penetration of this meaning, of this stuff of reality, its architectonics, is offered to the artist's contemplative eye in *living contact* with reality."[447] The efficacy of the icon is not only connected to the painting itself, but to the contact it makes with an observer as it reaches "beyond the frame." Correspondingly, the icon is designed to open outward and envelop the spectator inside it. Robert Bird even suggested that "Viewing physical reality as rooted in a forcefield of spiritual energies, Florensky held the icon to be direct expression of divinity.... The surface of the icon is the locus of exchange between transcendent reality and the world, both a worldly window onto heaven and a heavenly mirror image of the world."[448] In Bird's and Florensky's analysis icons become more than real: they are a window onto truth and a "devotional aid" in the same way that Tarkovsky's films are.

Tarkovsky is deliberately influenced by icons, both stylistically and thematically. Tarkovsky has his own version of what in icon painting is called "simultaneous succession," where biblical scenes are depicted within the same icon without frames or markings to distinguish between scenes, time and space. As early as *Ivan's Childhood* Tarkovsky's films transgress classical film form by using a series of "illogical" camera movements and edits which transgress the codes and conventions of mainstream film. Characters disappear and reappear within the same shot, an action that is profoundly illogical if the film were a depiction of reality, but in the realm where Tarkovsky operates such actions appear regularly. In one of the dream sequences in *Ivan's Childhood* a young girl disappears and appears within the frame in what appears to be a single shot, and the same happens to the buffoon in *Andrei Rublyov* and the mother in *Mirror*. It happens most frequently in *Stalker* but the best example is perhaps in *Nostalghia*. When Gorchakov visits Domenico's house, in one extended shot Tarkovsky has him disappear from one side of the frame and emerge into the other. In Tarkovsky's films there is much life beyond the frame. Astrid Widding states that this possibility is a key part of Tarkovsky's aesthetic and his films often "revolve around the possibility to bridge over from the image to the non-representable, which has to remain off the frame."[449]

---

447. Pavel Florensky, *Beyond Vision: Essays on the Perception of Art*, trans. Wendy Salmond (London: Reaktion Books, 2002), 210-1.

448. Robert Bird, *Andrei Rublyov*, 76.

449. Astrid Widding, "Deus Absconditus – Between Invisible and Visible in the Films of Andrei Tarkovsky," *Through The Mirror: Reflections on Tarkovsky*, 165.

The narrative of *Andrei Rublyov* climaxes with the episode called "The Bell." Rublyov has not talked for fifteen years and he is scarcely even in the episode. He can be seen in the background observing the construction of a huge bell as it is orchestrated by the young Boriska (played by Nikolai Burlayev who played Ivan in *Ivan's Childhood*), but he is so moved by the young bell maker's plight and passion that he speaks again: "We'll go off together, you and me. You'll cast bells, I'll paint icons. That will give the people something to celebrate." Art brings about joy and epiphany for the people, not despite them. Painting is Rublyov's duty, despite the hardship and torment that it brings him, just as making films is Tarkovsky's.

Tarkovsky provides a moment of transcendence for Andrei Rublyov and those watching the film. It is presented as an artistic transcendence but also emphatically a religious one. After the conclusion of "The Bell" the epilogue is an eight minute long sequence in colour revealing Rublyov's original paintings, which until then have been totally absent from the screen. The sequence is presented in almost exactly the same way as Hari contemplated the Brueghel painting *Hunters in the Snow*, which corresponded to her moment of transcendence from replica to human being. Rublyov has had a similar epiphany. Tarkovsky shows the power of the artistic image and its capacity for expressing the divine. Angela Dalle Vache writes that "Divinity exists in human form through the presence of the icon itself, since the boundary between signifier and signified is so elastic that the beholder can relate to the representation as if it were the represented itself, to the image of God *as* to God."[450]

Andrei Rublyov is emblematic of Tarkovsky's depictions of spirituality onscreen while he made his films in the Soviet Union. If anything, Tarkovsky's religious beliefs become even more veiled in the three films which follow it, as if he were wary of showing his faith so close to the surface again after such sustained criticism. In this respect Astrid Widding is correct when she states that, "The divine in Tarkovsky is never associated with the fullness of representation, even though it may always be imagined as a possibility beyond the limits of representation. If God is present in these films, or if there is an inkling of the divine, it is only in his absence, in the void of the image. He remains hidden."[451] However, when Tarkovsky left the Soviet Union in the early eighties he became free to explore the issues which concerned him in a much more explicit fashion. As was to be expected, it was not politics that he turned his attention to but identity, philosophy and religion. In his final film, *The Sacrifice*, there is much more than an "inkling of the divine," as Tarkovsky audaciously provides proof of the existence of God to the believer.

---

450. Angela Dalle Vacche, *Cinema and Painting* (Austin: University of Texas Press, 1996), 138.
451. Astrid Widding, "Deus Absconditus – Between Invisible and Visible in the Films of Andrei Tarkovsky." *Through The Mirror: Reflections on Tarkovsky*, 160.

4.2 Endings and Beginnings in *The Sacrifice*

In my mind, if the viewer carries away the idea that life is a mystery then I am happy. Because for a huge number of people life today does not represent any sort of mystery.

~Andrei Tarkovsky

Is all that we see or seem, but a dream within a dream?

~Edgar Allan Poe

For what would be his final film Tarkovsky took up an offer from the Swedish Film Institute to make a film in Sweden. Scholars remain divided as to whether Tarkovsky was aware of his illness during the production of the film. Regardless, *The Sacrifice* has the air of a testimonial work. In the years since its release it has arguably become one of Tarkovsky's most criticised films, described by G.C Macnab as "a typically saturnine final testament from a film-maker overly aware of his own reputation,"[452] or "a stunningly beautiful film that holds your attention even while you feel slightly stunned, in a less welcome way, by what is going on... [there is] a certain silliness... those who stay with it, however, may find rewards in burst after burst of beauty and even a glimmer of meaning"[453] by Walter Goodman. However, many have praised it, describing the experience of watching it as "profound" and "elegiac."[454] Some reviewers are unable to decide whether it is successful or not: in May 1986 Philip French first called it "soporific, portentious, oppressively mystical,"[455] but six months later "one of the great films of Western Europe."[456]

There are elements of truth to these criticisms. Tarkovsky's propensity to polemicise rather than to debate or interrogate becomes more obvious, especially in *The Sacrifice*. He often seems more content to sermonize rather than contemplate, to explain "to those around him what man lives for, what is the meaning of his existence. To explain to people the reason for their appearance on this planet."[457] Many suggest that Tarkovsky had begun to believe what everyone had been telling him about his importance as both a prophet and a martyr rather than a film-maker. Sergei Selianov notes, "People came to ask Tarkovsky how to live, where to go, where to find the truth. And

---

452. G.C Macnab, "Andrei Tarkovsky," *International Dictionary of Films and Filmmakers: Directors Vol. 2*, 981.
453. Walter Goodman, *New York Times*, Sept 26 1986, *The New York Times Film Reviews 1985-1986* (New York: New York Times Books and Garland Publishing inc., 1988), 342.
454. Iain Johnstone, "*The* Sacrifice," The *Sunday Times,* 18th June 1986, 51.
455. Philip French, "*The* Sacrifice," *The Observer,* 25th May 1986, 14.
456. Philip French, "*The* Sacrifice," *The London Evening Standard* (3rd January 1987): 32. Could French have been influenced to change his mind by Tarkovsky's death?
457. Tarkovsky, *Sculpting in Time*, 36.

he was not shocked by these questions, because he acknowledged his teaching mission as his duty."[458]

Tarkovsky's intention with *The Sacrifice* is very clear, and it is this, above all, which detracts from the film's effectiveness. He was deeply disheartened with the state of the world and of contemporary film: "Modern mass culture, aimed at the 'consumer,' the civilisation of prosthetics, is crippling people's souls, setting up barriers between man and the crucial questions of his existence, his consciousness of himself as a spiritual being."[459] By designing the film as "a repudiation of commercial cinema"[460] Tarkovsky significantly impacts its ambiguity, which had up until then been one of the defining characteristics of a Tarkovsky text, a fact that he had frequently registered, and as a result he goes against one of the defining tenets of his film theory: "The greatness and ambiguity of art lies in not proving, not explaining and not answering questions."[461] The decision to give the film such an explicit and pre-meditated purpose is just one of the film's problems. It is perhaps an inchoate film: too theatrical, too self-consciously Chekhovian and Bergmanian. Despite these inherent flaws, which manifest themselves in a failure to adequately render "time pressure" on the screen, there is much to engage with: some of the imagery is remarkable, the themes are quintessential Tarkovsky, the quality of the performances, while theatrical, is effective, and the central dynamism at the core of the text remains intact. As a result it fits perfectly with his canon and brings much of it full circle, thematically and stylistically.

Despite being filmed in Sweden, with a primarily Swedish cast and crew speaking Swedish (including Bergman regulars Erland Josephsson and Sven Nykvist), like *Nostalghia* before it, the film feels authentically Russian. If anything, Tarkovsky appears freer to tackle the issues he wished to, without the imposing rubric of Mosfilm bureaucracy standing over him, which results in his most explicitly religious film by far.

The film's protagonist, Alexander, is a recognisable Tarkovskian, or even European Art Cinema archetype: a middle class intellectual, artistically minded, a writer and a critic, formerly an actor. He is experiencing a spiritual crisis and he has lost his faith in God. On the surface he has everything one might desire from life: wealth, a wife, children and a lovely home; but there is something missing. Alexander has become a passive observer in his own life and longs for a sign from God. These aspects of narrative are clearly shown to the audience through extensive and distinctly un-Tarkovskian scenes of expositional dialogue. Rather than the ambiguity of the prologue and opening sequence of *Andrei Rublyov*, *The Sacrifice* begins by providing an introduction to the characters and the themes that will dominate the narrative. Alexander's local

---

458. Sergei Selianov, "Cinema and Life," *Russia on Reels: The Russian Idea in Post-Soviet Cinema*, ed. Birgit Beumers (London: I.B Tauris, 1999), 44.
459. Tarkovsky, *Sculpting in Time*, 42.
460. Ibid., 228.
461. Ibid., 54.

postman and friend Otto helpfully sums up Alexander's life for the audience, "Here you are, a famous journalist, a theatrical and literary critic who lectures on aesthetics for students at the university." The narrative starts on the day of Alexander's birthday. He is celebrating with his wife, step daughter, beloved young son "Little Man" and two family friends, the Doctor, Viktor, and Otto. The gifts that his guests bring offer conscious echoes of *Andrei Rublyov*: Viktor's gift for Alexander is a skilfully bound book of icon reproductions; Otto's is an antique map from the 17th century. When Alexander attempts to refuse such an expensive present, Otto's suggestion prefigures what lies in store for him, "a true present *must* be a sacrifice." Instead of the understated associative imagery and dialogue of Tarkovsky's previous works the audience are assailed with philosophical musings from the characters. Otto talks about his interest in Nietzsche and discusses the eternal return, which will be dramatically embodied in the narrative itself. He asks Alexander, "How are your relations with God?" With no sense of mystery he answers, "Non-existent, I'm afraid."

Their gathering is interrupted by the announcement on the radio of an imminent nuclear war, just hours away. While the rest of the party are justifiably distressed at such news, Alexander separates himself from them, convinced that he has a part to play in the upcoming apocalypse; he believes that this has been the event he has been waiting for so he offers himself to God as a sacrifice. If God hears him and saves the world, he will give up everything:

> Lord, deliver us in this terrible hour. Do not let my children die, my friends, my wife... I will give you all I possess. I will leave the family I love. I shall destroy my home, give up my son. I shall be silent, will never speak with anyone again. I shall give up everything that binds me to life, if you only let everything be as it was before.

Alexander's prayer is sincere and powerful. He vows to give up everything, his family, his life, even his words. In Tarkovsky's previous films the religious conflict has never been so explicit. While his characters have suffered similar crises of faith, from Kris Kelvin to Stalker, they never revealed their feelings so gratuitously for all to hear. It is perhaps Rublyov's predicament that is closest to Alexander's, but he never gave such an impassioned, elaborate appeal; his plight was revealed in the expressions of his face. Alexander wants to sacrifice himself; he is given the opportunity and he does, there is no such dilemma. There is no arduous journey, physical and emotional, before he arrives at such a declaration. However, as ever, Tarkovsky seems aware of himself: the doctor comments about Alexander, "I don't like his monologues." Even Alexander himself states: "If only someone could stop talking and do something."

For Alexander the offer to give up speech is even more significant. Words have been especially important to him, since he has made his living as an actor, and then a teacher. Silence has been almost as important to Tarkovsky as a way of expression as sound, from Rublyov's vow of silence to the stutterer in *Mirror*. Alexander realises that words can prevent action. He quotes *Hamlet*: "Words, words, words."[462] Tarkovsky comments that for him language too has lost its value:

> The world is jam packed with empty chatter. All that information of which we pretend to have such need—consider radio and television—all those permanent infinite debates to be found in newspapers, all that is empty and meaningless.... We shall all die beneath the weight of this garrulous information.[463]

Yet the film is perhaps too self-consciously erudite and theatrical itself. Gone are the lingering, wordless close ups of characters' faces that punctuated *Stalker* and *Andrei Rublyov*. Throughout *The Sacrifice* the characters rarely stop pontificating, voicing almost their every thought. These elements impact on the "time pressure" present in the film, which frequently feels over elaborate. Tarkovsky's predilection for the long take, so effectively used in *Stalker* and *Mirror*, here becomes affected and almost contrived.

However this does not stop the powerful nature of Alexander's experience. Tarkovsky operates in a realm which it is impossible for modern culture to process. The concept of self-sacrifice is an anathema in a world where spiritual values have declined. He returned to this theme of sacrifice throughout his work; with Hari in *Solaris*, the Stalker in *Stalker*, Domenico in *Nostalghia*. Tarkovsky asserted:

> I posit that modern man, for the most part, is not prepared to deny himself and his interests for the sake of other people or in the name of what is Greater, of what is Supreme; he will more readily exchange his own life for the existence of a robot. I recognise that the idea of sacrifice, the Christian ideal of love of neighbour, enjoys no popularity—and nobody asks us for self-sacrifice.[464]

I suggest that Tarkovsky's films resonate as much as they do because they have never been unconditional acceptances of faith; rather they are deeply felt struggles for reconciliation and belief. His characters struggle with their convictions, and lose them as frequently as they find them. Part of the efficacy of the construction of *Andrei Rublyov* and *Stalker* is this unspoken search for faith. In *The Sacrifice* Alexander faces a critical test, but it seems to come too

462. William Shakespeare, *Hamlet* (London: Penguin, 2005), II.2, 192, 51.
463. Quoted in "Andrei Tarkovsky on The Sacrifice" from the programme booklet *The Sacrifice*, An Artificial Eye Release.
464. Tarkovsky, *Sculpting in Time*, 218.

easily to him. However, we shall see that he is rewarded with the ultimate prize, the acknowledgement of his faith and proof of God's existence.

The night of his prayer he experiences strange dreams. Dreams had long been a staple of Tarkovsky's visual and narrative aesthetic, yet they have continued to develop and evolve. Despite Tarkovsky's protests against allegorical interpretations of his work, they are redolent with powerful symbols which become almost overpoweringly pronounced. Freud's assertion that "Most of the artificial dreams contrived by the poets are intended for some such symbolic interpretation, for they reproduce the thought conceived by the poet in a guise not unlike the disguise which we are wont to find in our dreams"[465] seems more apt than perhaps it should be. By *Mirror* the boundaries between dream and reality were becoming harder to discern and in *Stalker* and *Nostalghia* even the characters were having problems telling which was which. *The Sacrifice* reaches the apogee of Tarkovsky's oneiric aesthetic. It is his most dream imbued text, to the extent that the audience is entirely unsure of what is dream and what is reality. In fact the entire film might just be a dream. It was this presentation of the dream-like nature of life and existence that Ingmar Bergman admired most about Tarkovsky: "He moves with such naturalness in the room of dreams... All my life I have hammered on the doors of the rooms in which he moves so naturally."[466]

The next morning Alexander wakes to discover that the world has returned to the day before and the apocalypse has been averted just as he had wished for as if nothing had ever happened. He asks himself the same question the audience is compelled to ask: what was real? Was the whole thing a dream or a fantasy? Tarkovsky offers no simple explanation for the viewer, as the film has presented the event as a bifurcation of reality. Alexander has experienced the defining moment of his life, but his family and the rest of the world remain completely oblivious of what has happened.

What Alexander has undergone is akin to the experiences of those who have visited the Zone in *Stalker* or Solaris in *Solaris*, except that he has had his conscious wish fulfilled rather than his unconscious desires. It could all be a figment of his imagination, and for those who do not have faith in their lives Alexander is a wonderful dreamer who has lost his hold on reality, where Gorchakov before him had only teetered on the brink. However for those who do believe Alexander has sacrificed himself and has been rewarded for his display of faith. Both interpretations are entirely valid in their own way, and both sides are able to take what they want from the film's narrative. It is this sense of mystery that is the beating heart at the centre of the film, an ambiguity which for some is its greatest weakness, yet for others the aspect which gives it its greatest resonance.

---

465. Sigmund Freud, *The Interpretation of* Dreams, [1899] trans. A. A. Brill (Ware, Hertfordshire: Wordsworth Editions, 1997), 189.
466. Bergman, *The Magic Lantern,* 73.

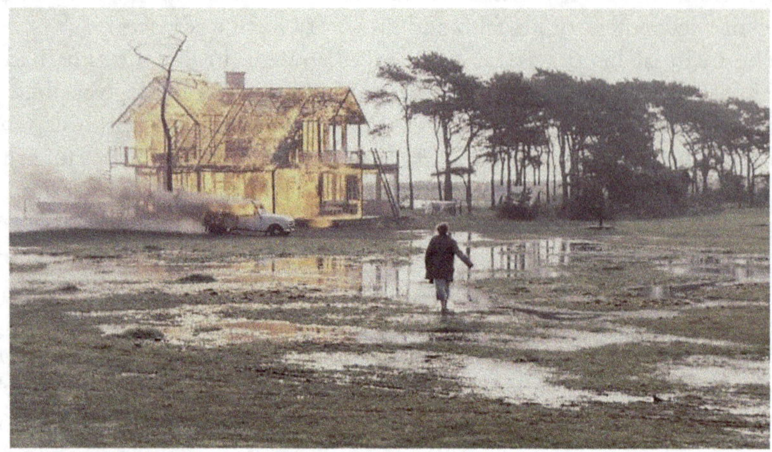

Figure 18 Faith is at the centre of the narrative of Tarkovsky's last film *The Sacrifice* made in exile in Sweden just a few years before his death.

Tarkovsky's films are never solely representations of faith. They are articles of faith in and of themselves; just as they have never just been about memory, they are memory artifacts. On this matter of interpretation Tarkovsky suggested that

> it's possible to interpret the film in different ways. For instance, those who are interested in various supernatural phenomena will search for the meaning of the film in the relationship between the postman and the witch, for them these two characters will provide the principle action. Believers are going to respond most sensitively to Alexander's prayer to God, and for them the whole film will develop around this. And finally a third category of viewers who don't believe in anything will imagine that Alexander is a bit sick, that he's psychologically unbalanced as a result of war and fear. Consequently many kinds of viewers will perceive the film in their own way. My opinion is that it is necessary to afford the spectator the freedom to interpret the film according to their own inner vision of the world, and not from the point of view that I would impose on him. For my aim is to show life, to render an image, the tragic, dramatic image of the soul of modern man.[467]

While Tarkovsky has previously been vehemently against interpretation, towards the end of his career he practically welcomed it. He suggested about *The Sacrifice* that "It's perhaps closest to the elegy, the parable, insofar as it functions on several different levels. Each of its episodes not only carries the

467. Quoted in "Faith Is the Only Thing That Can Save Man," *Andrei Tarkovsky Interviews,* 179.

weight of reality but offers more than one layer of meaning."[468] We must remember how he had vociferously criticised other artists for so explicitly presenting their themes or messages in their work; Larissa Shepitko's *Ascent* (*Voskhozhdenie*, 1977) was criticised for being such a blatant "parable."[469] If there is a distinction to be made between *The Sacrifice* and Tarkovsky's earlier work this is it. Tarkovsky quoted Vyacheslav Ivanov's assertion that "A symbol is only a true symbol when it is inexhaustible and unlimited in its meaning."[470] For Tarkovsky if an image "means" something, it is decipherable and therefore limited. He even criticised Raphael's "Sistine Madonna," stating, "the artist's thought is there for the reading: all too unambiguous and well-defined."[471] But the meanings of *The Sacrifice* are, for the most part, equally well-defined.

It is the reaffirmation of faith which distances Tarkovsky from his contemporaries like Bergman and "late" Bresson, where the presence of God is increasingly distant or even entirely absent. While *The Sacrifice* may well be "his most Bergmanian film,"[472] the difference between *Shame* (1968), *Winter Light* (1963), *The Silence* (1963) and *Through a Glass Darkly* (1961) and Tarkovsky's *The Sacrifice* is theologically profound. In Bergman God is decidedly absent or does not want to intervene; even the titles of Bergman's films evoke their perspective. Tarkovsky confirmed this distance: "Is Bergman's view of religion the same as Tarkovsky's? I don't agree at all. When Bergman speaks of God it is to say that he is silent, that he's not there. Hence, there can be no comparison with me."[473]

Despite their often alluded to formal similarities, Bresson's films also became progressively much darker towards the end of his career. The early work like *Diary of a Country Priest* (1951) and *A Man Escaped* (1956) saw Bresson suggest: "I want to make people who see [*Diary*] feel the presence of God in ordinary life" and "You can feel there is something, which, of course, I don't want to show or talk about. But there is a presence of something which I call God, but I don't want to show it too much. I prefer to make people feel it."[474] Both statements could have easily been uttered by Tarkovsky. By the time of *Mouchette* (1967), *Au Hasard Balthazar* (1966) and *Le Diable Probablement* (1977), culminating in *L' Argent*, the decline of faith is readily apparent. The masterful bleakness of *L' Argent* is almost breathtaking; the materialist world has taken over and God is for all intent and purpose dead; money has become "le dieu invisible."

---

468. Andrei Tarkovsky quoted from "Andrei Tarkovsky on *The Sacrifice,*" from the programme booklet *The Sacrifice*, An Artificial Eye Release.
469. Tarkovsky, *Sculpting in Time*, 151.
470. Ibid., 47.
471. Ibid., 48.
472. Mark Le Fanu, *The Cinema of Andrei Tarkovsky,* 135-6.
473. Quoted in "Faith Is the Only Thing That Can Save Man," *Andrei Tarkovsky Interviews,* 180.
474. Quoted *Robert Bresson,* ed. James Quandt (Michigan: University of Michigan Press, 1998), 487.

The Sacrifice concludes with Alexander fulfilling his promise: he burns his house down and offers himself in sacrifice so that his beloved son, and the rest of the world, can live. The dacha here has become the opposite of what it represented in Tarkovsky's earlier films, where it was a place of nostalgia and harmony; here it is a symbol of materialism, which has distracted Alexander from pursuing his spirituality and faith. Like Otto's map, the bigger the sacrifice, the bigger the reward, and Alexander is prepared to sacrifice everything. While the film appears to be set in the present day, like many of Tarkovsky's films there is a deliberately timeless quality about it. The house has a decor which evokes the fifties; the clothes appear deliberately designed to have nothing explicitly modern or culturally specific about them. Robinson called the final image timeless, "disregarding the boy's clothes, the image could be two million years old."[475]

The ambulance, which carries Alexander away from his former life, drives past his son, Little Man. The film had started with the tale of the monk Pamve who watered a dead tree every day, until it miraculously came back to life. The dead tree, under which Little Man now lies, has been the central motif of the film, modelled quite clearly on Leonardo Da Vinci's *The Adoration of the Magi* (1481-2), reflecting the decline of belief and spirituality in the contemporary world. However, in Tarkovsky's world there is still the opportunity of salvation; acts like Alexander's and the faith that comes with it *can* produce miracles.[476]

Jeremy Mark Robinson suggests that it is not just Alexander's act of faith that is being praised by the film, but "It is life itself that is being glorified – not the viewers, not the boy, not nature, but life as a whole."[477] Little Man, who has been silent throughout the narrative, speaks his first words, the final words of the film and the final words in Tarkovsky's body of work, "In the beginning was the Word. Why was that, papa?"[478] The camera moves gracefully up to the top of the tree, almost the exact same movement that had opened the film. The shot lingers in one of Tarkovsky's signature long takes for two and a half minutes, allowing audiences to engage with it as Tarkovsky has deliberately designed it to be. In the final shot Tarkovsky ever committed to film it is very clear he is still sculpting in time. While leaves have not grown on it, the iridescent water behind it makes it appear as if they have. The implication is clear, only through faith can man's salvation be achieved.

---

475. Jeremy Mark Robinson, *The Sacred Cinema of Andrei Tarkovsky,* 518.

476. The significant parallels between *The Sacrifice* and DaVinci's painting are explored in James Macgillivray's excellent "Andrei Tarkovsky's *Madonna del Parto," Canadian Journal of Film Studies/ Revue canadienne d'études cinématographiques* 11.2 (Fall 2002): 82-9.

477. Jeremy Mark Robinson, *The Sacred Cinema of Andrei Tarkovsky,* 523.

478. It is tempting to compare Little Man's inability to communicate with his father to Andrei Tarkovsky's estrangement from his son left back in Russia. This is further accentuated by the paratextual device of the dedication to Tarkovsky's son which reads "in hope and confidence" as the film concludes.

The Sacrifice, Tarkovsky's final film, has both opened and closed with the image of a young boy next to a tree, just as his *Ivan's Childhood* had twenty-four years before. These echoes or ripples can be felt throughout Tarkovsky's work, and it is entirely appropriate that the last ever image he created on film should be one too. In this way Tarkovsky's seven completed feature films form a harmonious circle, like the Ying and Yang symbols on the back of Alexander's robe.

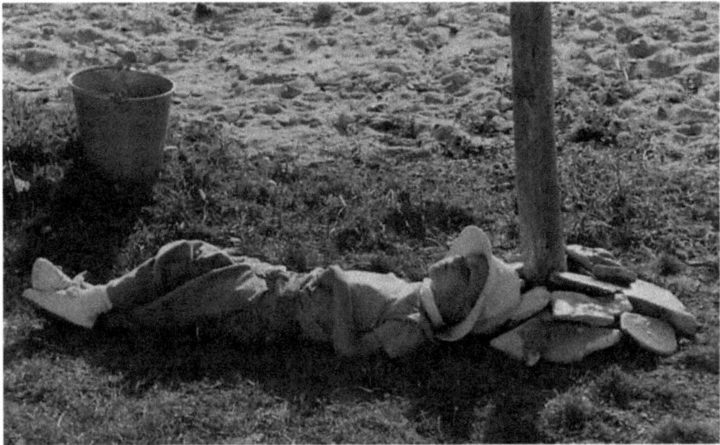

Figure 19 Tarkovsky's oeuvre ends as it began with a small boy beneath a tree: starting with *Ivan's Childhood* in 1962 and ending twenty-four years later with *The Sacrifice* (1986).

Conclusion

"Beyond the Frame"

Even now I am not sure I know what cinema is. To me it remains a great mystery.

~Andrei Tarkovsky

The opportunity to live through what is happening onscreen as if it were his own life, to take over, as deeply personal as his own, the experience imprinted in time upon the screen, relating to his own life what is being shown.

~Andrei Tarkovsky

Despite Johnson and Petrie erroneously asserting in 1994 that Tarkovsky "hardly wields any real influence on a new generation of film-makers,"[479] the number of those who have cited Tarkovsky as an inspiration is simply too vast to include in a study of this length. The most well known are from his contemporaries: Ingmar Bergman described Tarkovsky as "the greatest, the one who invented a new language"[480]; or Akira Kurosawa, who admitted that he felt that "probably there is no equal among film directors alive."[481] Less often recounted opinions are from the likes of Stan Brakhage and Krzysztof Kieślowski. Brakhage called Tarkovsky "the greatest living narrative filmmaker" and continued: "The three greatest tasks for film in the twentieth century are 1) To make the epic, that is to tell tales of the tribes of the world. 2) To keep it personal, because only in the eccentricities of our personal lives do we have any chance at the truth. 3) To do the dream work, that is, to illuminate the borders of the unconscious. The only film-maker I know that does all these three things equally in every film he makes is Andrei Tarkovsky."[482] In interviews Kieślowski suggested Tarkovsky was "one of the greatest directors of recent years. He's dead, like most of them. That is, most of them are dead or have stopped making films. Or else, somewhere along the line, they've irretrievably lost something, some individual sort of imagination, intelligence or way of narrating a story. Tarkovsky was certainly one of those who hadn't lost this."[483]

---

479. Johnson and Petrie, *The Films of Andrei Tarkovsky*, 4.
480. Ingmar Bergman, The Magic Lantern, 73.
481. Akira Kurosawa, "Tarkovsky Was a Real Poet," para 9.
482. Quoted in "Telluride Gold: Brakhage meet Tarkovsky," *Rolling Stock* 6 (1983): 11-2.
483. Quoted in *Kieślowski on Kieślowski*, 33-4.

Many of the directors and the theorists who have appeared in this book, share Tarkovsky's passion for the uniqueness of the cinematic experience, and have sought to define what separates film from other media in their own work. After Tarkovsky's death, the obituaries were uniformly laudatory. Peter Green's in *Sight and Sound* is representative of most:

> This handful of completed works is individually of such weight and vision that each of them alone might have secured him a place in film history. It was his ambition to raise the art of cinema to a level achieved in the other arts; in literature, for example, by poets such as Dostoevsky or Tolstoy... A successor to his own Rublyov, a commentator on our modern condition, an icon painter in film, and a man of profound belief, it was Tarkovsky's aim to bring the inward spiritual world into a state of harmony with the outward, material world. Perhaps more than any other, he perceived the potential of film for charting the modern space-time dimension we inhabit.[484]

As Green suggests, much of Tarkovsky's film theory can be regarded as an extended and insightful meditation on film specificity, which is then put in practice, often with startling precision, in the films themselves. On the opening page of *Sculpting in Time*, Tarkovsky asks, "What are the factors that distinguish film from the other arts"?[485] Later he speculates, "What are the determining factors of cinema, and what emerges from them?"[486] For Tarkovsky, film is a uniquely powerful apparatus, in every sense a medium through which experience is filtered and facilitated. It is able to function as both a means of communication and as a philosophical tool for epiphany, inspiration, debate and provocation. Tarkovsky stated,

> There's another kind of language, another form of communication: by means of feeling and images. That is the contact that stops people being separated from each other, that brings down barriers[....] The frames of the screen move out, and the world which used to be partitioned off comes into us, becomes something real.[487]

It is the immediacy of film which makes it perfectly suited to establishing this kind of contact. By moving "beyond the frame" and interacting directly with the viewer, a relationship is formed, the likes of which mainstream cinema does not want, or is unable to achieve. Tarkovsky believed that it was this relationship which gave film its affectual power and distinguished it from

484. Peter Green, "Andrei Tarkovsky (1932-1986)," *Sight and Sound* 56.2 (Spring 1987): 108-9.
485. Tarkovsky, *Sculpting in Time*, 7.
486. Ibid., 62.
487. Ibid., 12-3.

literature, theatre and the other arts. However, in his life, Tarkovsky ultimately wondered if film had yet achieved parity with literature in its ability to move an individual:

> Whether up until now cinema can actually claim any authors to stand alongside the creators of the great masterpieces of world literature is extremely doubtful. I don't think it can. And my own feeling is that this could be because cinema is still trying to define its own specific character, its own language, at times becoming quite close to doing so.[488]

For Tarkovsky, cinema finds its true purpose when it tries not to entertain, but to interrogate and debate the essential questions of human existence: "Cinema should be a means of exploring the most complex problems of our time, as vital as those which for centuries have been the subject of literature, music and painting."[489] Yet the medium itself, Tarkovsky felt, was still in its formative years: while its role in culture and society was singular, it had not yet fulfilled its potential. To do this required it to break free of the bounds of rationality, banal conventions of narrative and image and especially its links to other art forms. For it is only when cinema embraces what is truly cinematic about its construction that it will become the pre-eminent art: "Trying to adapt the features of other art forms to the screen will always deprive the film of what is distinctively cinematic, and make it harder to handle the material in a way that makes use of the powerful resources of cinema as an art in its own right."[490] In so doing the cinema would be able to reach its potential and become "the most truthful and poetic of art forms."[491]

I would argue that, in his finest films, Tarkovsky is one of those directors who enable film to come closest to achieving this. This is an opinion shared by the likes of Sergei Paradzhanov, director of *The Colour of Pomegranates*, who, when asked, "Why do you make films?" replied, "To sanctify the tomb of Tarkovsky."[492] Lars von Trier said of Tarkovsky's *Mirror*, "What I saw was a long take without cuts, a camera tracking along a road. It was simply unbelievable—like a revelation to me! At the time I had of course seen a lot of films with different aesthetics and I was always interested in the divergent—in unusual things—but the images from this Tarkovsky film seemed to me to have come from another planet."[493] The long take that von Trier revered in

488. Ibid., 173.
489. Ibid., 80.
490. Ibid., 22.
491. Ibid., 18. Given such forceful comments another Tarkovsky paradox emerges; what then are we to make of Tarkovsky's frequent direct quotations of famous masterpieces particularly by Brueghel, Chagall, Mantegna and da Vinci?
492. John Gianvito, *Andrei Tarkovsky Interviews*, x.
493. Quoted in *Lars Von Trier Interviews*, ed. Jan Lumholdt (Jackson: University Press Mississippi, 2003), 7.

Mirror, and that both Bazin and Tarkovsky regard so highly, is the technique which has become so closely associated with Tarkovsky over the years, to such an extent that many contemporary directors who use long, slowly paced shots are often referred to as Tarkovskian.

Tarkovsky's hermetic approach to film proves problematic when attempting to position him alongside other film theorists. He emerges from the Soviet tradition of director-theorists embodied by the likes of Vsevolod Pudovkin, Alexander Dovzhenko and Sergei Eisenstein. Tarkovsky's aesthetic simultaneously embodies a reverence for his antecedents: "It's important to see the work of the great masters, and know it well, in order to not start inventing the bicycle. There aren't so many of them, perhaps five; Dovzhenko, Buñuel, Bergman, Antonioni, Dreyer, and perhaps one or two others."[494] And yet he is very much a part of the cinematic new waves which swept across the world during the 1960s; his win at Venice in 1962 for his cinematic debut came the year after *Last Year at Marienbad* (1961) by Alain Resnais and two years before *The Red Desert* (1964) by Michelangelo Antonioni. However, he was an iconoclast, who defined himself in opposition to evolving trends in film language to the extent that he even denied the existence of a new wave in the Soviet Union:

> In terms of a special trend in the USSR, there is no 'New Wave.' Being in my thirties, I simply belong to the youngest generation of Russian film-makers. My generation tries very seriously to explore the relationship between form and content. This issue was never addressed thoroughly enough in Russian cinema, and my generation is the first to really think about the fact that it can lead to vulgarisation if the topic has too much influence on the form.[495]

I have attempted to suggest that Tarkovsky's films are able to move "beyond the frame," but not in a mystical and esoteric sense, rather through the use of a particular set of recognisable techniques, which are refined and evolve over the course of seven films and the twenty-four years of his career. They are achieved through careful and deliberate consideration of time, memory and image and can be seen, in a variety of patterns, in every one of his films without exception.

There has been a desire by a minority of Tarkovsky scholars to keep his work, in some senses, sacred, as if too close a scrutiny might ruin what makes the films unique. I have endeavoured to show that while an analysis of what Tarkovsky's films "mean" is ultimately impossible, due to the multivalency on which they are based, a study of how this multivalency is achieved, rather than have a negative effect on an appreciation of Tarkovsky, in fact, provides a

494. Tarkovsky, *Time Within Time, The Diaries 1970-1986*, 361.
495. Quoted in "Encounter with Andrei Tarkovsky," *Andrei Tarkovsky Interviews*, 7.

greater understanding of his oeuvre.

However, to do so, one must experience the films as they are intended to be experienced. To pause a Tarkovsky film and then begin to analyse and decode it disrupts the sense of flow and life inherent in it, fundamentally altering its "time pressure" and changing it from a living artifact into an inanimate object, devoid of the very life essence that makes it Tarkovskian. This sense of temporality is central to Tarkovsky's cinema, as it is only film which is uniquely able to paradoxically capture time and yet preserve its living essence.

Tarkovsky's belief that film is an organic medium is a sincere one; yet it is only able to become alive in its interaction with the spectator. This approach to time is as divisive now as it was during Tarkovsky's career. For every fellow traveller there is someone not willing to enter Tarkovsky's Zone. The challenge that Tarkovsky's films offer is not one that everyone is prepared to accept; critics like David Robinson do not wish to enter Tarkovsky's world, and therefore it is entirely understandable that he wrote about *Nostalghia*, "Those who found *Mirror* and *Stalker* obscure will not be reassured to learn that beside his new film... they appear positively luminous and transparent."[496] Ironically, it is the transparency of Tarkovsky's films which is at the heart of their richness and their palimpsest-like nature. They are not transparent in the sense that they produce easily defined meanings, like mainstream cinema, rather in that they are able to generate different meanings for different spectators. The aesthetic Tarkovsky wrote about and practised offers a divergent experience, just as other films of European Art Cinema, Poetic Cinema or the Time Image do. It is a resolutely problematicised cinema, a site of contention and ambiguity, with its spatial and temporal coordinates frequently in crisis.

In 2003 Pulitzer Prize winning film critic Roger Ebert wrote his first review of a Tarkovsky film in the *Chicago Sun Times*. Many of his comments on *Solaris* are thoughtful, revealing Ebert as a reflective arbiter of mainstream taste:

> He [Tarkovsky] uses length and depth to slow us down, to edge us out of the velocity of our lives, to enter a zone of reverie and meditation. When he allows a sequence to continue for what seems like an unreasonable length, we have a choice. We can be bored, or we can use the interlude as an opportunity to consolidate what has gone before, and process it in terms of our own reflections.[497]

These comments seem to show an understanding of Tarkovsky's practices, but

496. David Robinson, "*Nostalghia*," *The Times* (19th May 1983): 15.

497. Roger Ebert, *Chicago Sun Times*, January 19th 2003, http://rogerebert.suntimes.com/apps/pbcs.dll/article?AID=/20030119/REVIEWS08/301190301/1023> (20th September 2008). Ebert's comments are very similar to Welles's criticisms of Antonioni. He went on to suggest that the remake was "clearer."

Ebert later added, "Tarkovsky's fault as an artist was complete indifference to his audience."[498] It has been my intention with this project to reveal this long held belief to be a fallacy. In fact, Tarkovsky's approach to the cinematic art is entirely the opposite. *Sculpting in Time* reveals that rarely has a director sought to involve the audience so much in their body of work. The foundations of Tarkovsky's film theory, time, "time pressure" and "time memory," engage the viewer in a compelling, powerful, associative and interrogative fashion. This is where the true nature of "beyond the frame" resides. When a young woman from Novosibirsk wrote to Tarkovsky, admitting that: "For the first time ever a film has become something real for me, and that's why I go to see it, I want to get right inside it, so that I can be really *alive*,"[499] she inadvertently replicated Tarkovsky's theory of "time pressure," seeing in it a more potent reflection of not only her life, but life around her.

Like time, to which it is inextricably connected, memory is also central to Tarkovsky's aesthetic. Tarkovsky's films are both memories and an inducement to remember on the part of the viewer. They fluctuate with experience and individuality and are very rarely stable, like memories themselves. Tarkovsky frequently talked of "authentic film-making," an internal cinema drawn from memory, dream and perception. Classical narrative cinema, for Tarkovsky, deprives film of what makes it truly cinematic. His are films which are about memory and *are* memories, films which are about transcendental experiences, but *are* transcendental experiences, films which are about time but *are* time themselves. Olivier Assayas describes the physical features of Tarkovsky's cinema, which go "beyond the frame," leading them to frequently induce physical reactions and associations in the viewer akin to the "sensuous signs" of Proust: "There are moments that convey that truth can only be expressed through sensations, for example the rotting wood you can almost smell—it leads to the sensuous presence of the land."[500]

Nathaniel Dorsky writes in agreement with Tarkovsky on the importance of time in film: "Time is one of the essential elements in film's alchemy. It is one of the most potent tools film has, yet few films connect profoundly with the plasticity of time and use the nature of time in their structure. It is the substance that, when handled properly, opens the door to the possibility of devotion."[501] Just as icons for believers open the window to divinity, this door has been opened by Tarkovsky through his films. However, it is not opened purely to religion (and this might be one of the reasons for Tarkovsky's enduring efficacy), but to memory, art and philosophy. Dorsky continued, suggesting that knowledge is ultimately about relinquishing control:

498. An email to Nostalghia.com, (n.d.) <http://www.ucalgary.ca/~tstronds/nostalghia.com/TheTopics/newsEbertRosenbaum.html> (20th September 2008).

499. Tarkovsky, *Sculpting in Time*, 12.

500. Olivier Assayas, "Tarkovsky: Seeing is Believing," 24.

501. Nathaniel Dorsky, "Devotional Cinema," *The Hidden God: Film and Faith*, 269.

> If we do relinquish control, we suddenly see a hidden world, one that has existed all along right in front of us. In a flash, the uncanny presence of this poetic and vibrant world, ripe with mystery, stands before us. Everything is expressing itself as what it is. Everything is alive and talking to us.[502]

Tarkovsky's films have always been a dialogue between the spectator and the text. For Tarkovsky everything is alive, even the very film itself.

When Tarkovsky was questioned about the nature of the soul, which is so prominent in much of his writings and interviews, he returned to the sculpting metaphor, with which I began this project. He was asked, "When you speak of the soul, do you mean it is a kind of sculpture which a man should secretly accomplish during his life?" To which he answered, "Man doesn't have to construct it, but rather liberate it. It is already constructed."[503] Like the sculpture Michelangelo saw in the block of marble, for Tarkovsky, the soul resides within. Tarkovsky has spent his career sculpting in time, revealing not only his own soul, but the souls of the viewers who watch or, rather, experience his films.

I have tried to suggest that the most effective way of experiencing Tarkovsky's canon is to see it, in some ways, as a single text. More than just seven individual films, they are an interlocking schema, rather, a cohesive and symbiotic body, which depend on each other and the spectator for the creation of meaning. They are alive in the relationship with one another and with the spectator. While this may be a standard auteurist notion, my approach is not particularly auteurist. I do not mean to suggest that the meaning resides in what Tarkovsky put into his body of work, although, of course, this is of paramount importance; rather, meaning resides, above all, in what spectators take from the films.

The quintessential Tarkovsky image, one which functions both as a metaphor and a *mise en abyme* of his work, is the Zone in *Stalker.* In fact it is useful to see Tarkovsky's films themselves as Zones, sites of indeterminacy, which modulate with experience and identity, apophenic objects of varying intensity. Tarkovsky's films reveal the truth in Heraclitus's assertion that "One cannot step twice into the same river, nor can one grasp any mortal substance in a stable condition, but it scatters and again gathers, it forms and dissolves, and approaches and departs."[504] The Heraclitan metaphor is particularly apt given the Tarkovskian associations with water. For Tarkovsky, water is a central motif due to its organic and opaque construction. It can both reflect

502. Ibid., 273.
503. Quoted in "Nostalgia's Black Tone," *Le Monde* (12 May 1983), trans. John Gianvito, *Andrei Tarkovsky Interviews,* 87.
504. Heraclitus, *The Art and Thought of Heraclitus: A New Arrangement and Translation of the Fragments with Literary and Philosophical Commentary*, ed. Charles H. Kahn (Cambridge: Cambridge University Press, 1981), 168.

and be seen through, sometimes simultaneously. It is a microcosmic object which can mean anything, an object in which one might be able to see "an entire world reflected."[505]

Ultimately, all of Tarkovsky's Zones, like his films, mean what the audience find in them. At the beginning of *Stalker* the Writer remarks, "Give up your empiricism Professor, miracles are outside empiricism." Tarkovsky asks the same of spectators of his films. It is only then that the encounter can begin. Tarkovsky describes how then, experiences resonate "beyond the frame": "Everything will begin to reverberate in response to the dominant note: things, landscape, actors' intonation."[506] Tarkovsky remarked, "The Zone doesn't symbolize anything, any more than anything else does in my films: the zone is a zone, it's life, and as he makes his way across it a man may break down or he may come through."[507] The Zone and Tarkovsky's films do not symbolise anything, they symbolise *anything*.

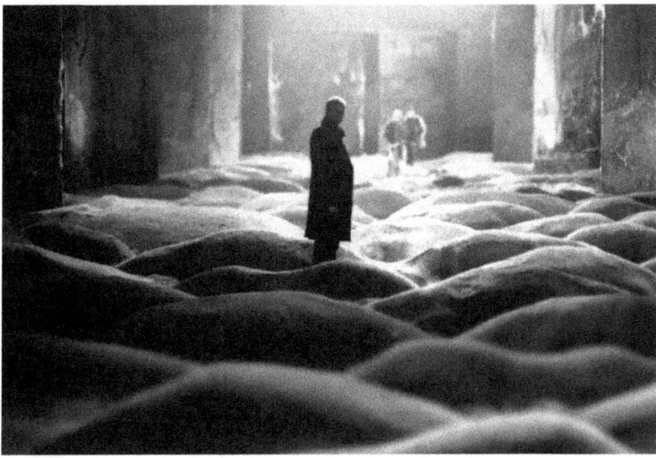

Figure 20 All of Tarkovsky's films resemble the Zones of *Stalker* in which one is able to see one's own life and experience reflected.

505. Tarkovsky, *Sculpting in Time*, 101.
506. Ibid., 194.
507. Ibid., 200.

Select Bibliography

Adair, Gilbert. "Notes from the Underground." *Sight and Sound* 50.1 (Winter 1980/1981): 63-64.

Altman, Rick, ed. *Sound Theory, Sound Practice*. New York: Routledge, 1992.

Andrew, Geoff. "Again, with 20 Percent More Existential Grief." *The Guardian* (February 13, 2003).

Andrew, Geoff. *Film Directors A-Z: A Concise Guide to the Art of 250 Great Film-makers*. London: Carlton Books, 1999.

Assayas, Olivier. "Tarkovsky: Seeing is Believing." *Sight & Sound* 7.1 (January 1997): 24-25.

Balázs, Béla. *Theory of the Film: Character and Growth of a New Art*. [1945] Translated by Edith Bone. London: Dennis Dobson, 1952.

Bandy, Mary, and Antonio Monda, eds. *The Hidden God: Film and Faith*. New York: Museum of Modern Art, 2003.

Barbash, Ilisa, and Lucien Taylor. *Cross Cultural Film-making*. Berkeley: University of California Press, 1997.

Bazin, André. *What is Cinema? Volume 1*. Translated by Hugh Gray. Berkeley: University of California Press, 1971.

—. *Orson Welles*. Paris: Les Editions du Cerf, 1972.

—. *What is Cinema? Volume 2*. Translated by Hugh Gray. Berkeley: University of California Press, 1972.

Bergan, Ronald. *Eisenstein: A Life in Conflict*. London: Little, Brown and Company, 1997.

Bergman, Ingmar. *The Magic Lantern*. Translated by Joan Tate. London: Penguin, 1988.

Bergson, Henri. *Creative Evolution*. [1910] Translated by Arthur Mitchell. New York: Dover Publications, 1998.

—. *Matter and Memory*. [1911] Translated by N.M Paul and W.S Palmer (New York: Zone Books, 1990)

Beumers, Birgit, ed. *Russia on Reels. The Russian Idea in Post-Soviet Cinema*. London: I.B Tauris, 1999.

—. *A History of Russian Cinema*. New York: Berg, 2008.

Bird, Robert. *Andrei Rublyov*. London: British Film Institute, 2004.

—. *Andrei Tarkovsky: Elements of Cinema*. London: Reaktion Books, 2008.

Bishop, S. R., Lau, M., Shapiro, S., Carlson, L., Anderson, N. D., Carmody, J., et al. "Mindfulness: A proposed operational definition." *Clinical Psychology: Science and Practice* 11/3 (2004): 230–241.

Bloom, Harold. *The Anxiety of Influence: A Theory of Poetry*. Oxford: Oxford University Press, 1997.

Bogdanovich, Peter. *This is Orson Welles*. London: Harper-Perennial, 1992.

Bogue, Ronald. *Deleuze on Cinema.* New York: Routledge, 2003.

Bordwell, David. *Narration in the Fiction Film.* Madison: University of Wisconsin Press, 1985.

——. "Art Cinema as a Mode of Film Practice." *Film Criticism* 4.1 (Fall 1979): 56–64.

Bordwell, David, and Kristin Thompson. *Film History: An* Introduction. Columbus: McGraw-Hill, 1994.

Botz-Bornstein, Thorsten. *Films and Dreams: Tarkovsky, Bergman, Sokurov, Kubrick and Wong Kar-Wai.* Lanham MD: Lexington Books, 2007.

Brakhage, Stan. "Telluride Gold: Brakhage meets Tarkovsky." *Rolling Stock* 6 (1983): 11-14.

Bryden, Mary. *Deleuze and Religion.* Edinburgh: Edinburgh University Press, 2004.

Burch, Noel. *Theory of Film Practice.* London: Secker and Warburg, 1973.

Chaudhuri, Shohini, and Howard Finn. "The Open Image: Poetic Realism and the New Iranian Cinema." *Screen* 44.1 (Spring 2003): 38-57.

Christie, Ian. "Returning to Zero." *Sight and Sound* 8.4 (April 1998): 14-17.

Coates, Paul. *Cinema, Religion and the Romantic Legacy.* London: Ashgate Publishing Ltd., 2003.

Cook, David. *A History of Narrative Film.* New York: W. W. Norton & Company, 1996.

Dalle Vacche, Angela. *Cinema and Painting.* Austin: University of Texas Press, 1996.

Deleuze, Gilles. *Cinema One: The Movement Image.* Translated by Hugh Tomlinson and Barbara Habberjam. Minneapolis: University of Minnesota Press, 2001.

——. *Cinema Two: The Time Image.* Translated by Hugh Tomlinson and Roberta Galeta. London: The Athlone Press, 1989.

Dempsey, Michael. "Lost Harmony: Tarkovsky's *The Stalker* and *The Mirror.*" *Film Quarterly* 35.1 (Autumn 1981): 12-17.

Dillon, Steven. *The Solaris Effect.* Austin: The University of Texas Press, 2006.

Dunne, Nathan, ed. *Tarkovsky.* London: Blackdog Publishing, 2008.

Eagle, Herbert, ed. *Russian Formalist Film Theory.* Ann Arbor: Michigan Slavic Publications, 1981.

Eisenstein, Sergei. *Essays in Film Theory*, New York: Meridian Books, 1957.

——. *S.M Eisenstein Selected Writings 1922-1934*, ed. Richard Taylor. Translated by Richard Taylor and William Powell. London: British Film Institute, 1998.

Eliade, Mircea. *The Myth of the Eternal Return: Cosmos and History.* Princeton: Princeton University Press, 1971.

Felperin, Leslie. "Divers of the Deep." *Sight and Sound* 14.7 (July 2004): 10-11.

Florensky, Pavel. *Beyond Vision: Essays on the Perception of Art.* Translated by Wendy Salmond. London: Reaktion Books, 2002.

Gillespie, David. *Russian Cinema.* Harlow, Essex: Pearson Education Limited, 2003.

Gianvitto, John, ed. *Andrei Tarkovsky Interviews.* Jackson: University of Mississippi, 2006.

Godard, Jean Luc. *Godard on Godard: Critical Writings by Jean Luc Godard.* Cambridge, MA: Da Capo Press: 1986.

Graffy, Julian. "Tarkovsky. The Weight of the World." *Sight and Sound* 7.1 (January 1997): 18-22.

—. "*The Return.*" *Sight and Sound* 14.7 (July 2004): 64.

Green, Peter. "Andrei Tarkovsky (1932-1986)." *Sight and Sound* 56.2 (Spring 1987): 108-09.

—. *Andrei Tarkovsky: The Winding Quest.* Basingstoke: Macmillan, 1993.

Hashaman, Yana. *Pride and Panic: Imagination of the West in Post-Soviet Film.* Bristol: Intellect, 2007.

Hillier, Jim, ed. *Cahiers du Cinéma: The 1950s-Neo-Realism, Hollywood, New Hollywood.* London: Routledge and Kegan Paul, 1985.

Horton, Andrew. *The Films of Theo Angelopoulos: A Cinema of Contemplation.* Princeton: Princeton University Press, 1997.

Husband, William. *"Godless Communists": Atheism and Society in Soviet Russia.* DeKalb: Northern Illinois Press, 2000.

Iordanova, Dina. *Emir Kusturica.* London: British Film Institute, 2002.

Jameson, Frederic. *The Geopolitical Aesthetic: Cinema and Space in the World System.* Bloomington and Indianapolis: Indiana University Press, 1992.

Johnson, Vida and Graham Petrie. *The Films of Andrei Tarkovsky: A Visual Fugue.* Bloomington and Indianapolis: Indiana University Press, 1994.

Jónsson, Gunnlauger and Thorkell Óttarsson, eds. *Through The Mirror: Reflections on Tarkovsky.* Newcastle: Cambridge Scholars Press, 2006.

Kennedy, Barbara. *Deleuze and Cinema. The Aesthetics of Sensation.* Edinburgh: Edinburgh University Press, 2002.

Kracauer, Siegfried. *Theory of Film: The Redemption of Physical Reality* [1965]. Princeton: Princeton University Press: 1997.

Le Fanu, Mark. *The Cinema of Andrei Tarkovsky.* London: British Film Institute, 1987.

Lejeune, Philip. *On Autobiography.* Minneapolis: The University of Minnesota Press, 1989.

Leyda, Jay. *Kino: A History of the Russian and Soviet Film.* Princeton: Princeton University Press, 1983.

Lumholdt, Jan, ed. *Lars Von Trier: Interviews.* Jackson, University Press Mississippi, 2003.

Macgillivray, James. "Andrei Tarkovsky's *Madonna del Parto.*" *Canadian Journal of Film Studies/Revue canadienne d'études cinématographiques* 11.2 (Fall 2002): 82-99.

Madden, John. *The Poetry of Cinema.* Kidderminster: Crescent Moon Publishing, 1994.

Marks, Laura. *The Skin of the Film: Intercultural Cinema, Embodiment, and the Senses.* Durham and London: Duke University Press, 1999.
Marshall, Herbert J. "Andrei Tarkovsky's *The Mirror.*" *Sight and Sound* 45.2 (Spring 1976): 92-95.
Martin, Sean. *Andrei Tarkovsky.* Manchester: Pocket Essentials, 2005.
Matusevich, Vladimir B. "Tarkovsky's Apocalypse." *Sight and Sound* 50.1 (Winter 1980/81): 8-9.
Mechior-Bonnet, Sabine. *The Mirror: A History.* Translated by Katherine Jewett. London: Routledge, 2002.
Menashe, Louis. "*The Return.*" *Cineaste* 29.2 (Spring 2004): 27.
Mitchell, Tony. "Tarkovsky in Italy." *Sight and Sound* 53.1 (Winter 1982/1983): 54-56.
Naficy, Hamid. *An Accented Cinema: Exilic and Diasporic Film-making.* Princeton: Princeton University Press, 2001.
Neale, Steve. "Art Cinema as Institution." *Screen* 22.1 (1981): 11-39.
Nichols, Bill, ed. *Movies and Methods.* Berkeley: The University of California Press, 1976.
Orr, John, and Olga Taxidou, eds. *Introduction to Post-war Cinema and Modernity.* Edinburgh: Edinburgh University Press, 2000.
Petric, Vlada. "Tarkovsky's Dream Imagery." *Film Quarterly* 43.2 (Winter 1989-1990): 28-34.
Pudovkin, Vsevolod. *Film Technique And Film Acting-The Cinema Writings Of V.I. Pudovkin* [1929]. Translated by Ivor Montagu. London: Unwin Brothers Limited, 1968.
Robinson, Jeremy Mark. *The Sacred Cinema of Andrei Tarkovsky.* Maidstone: Crescent Moon Publishing, 2008.
Rodowick, D. N. *Gilles Deleuze's Time Machine.* Durham, NC: Duke University Press, 1997.
Rushkoff, Douglas. *Present Shock: When Everything Happens Now.* New York: Penguin, 2012.
Schrader, Paul. *Transcendental Style in Film.* Berkeley: University of California Press, 1972.
Service, Robert. *A History of Modern Russia.* London: Penguin, 2003.
Sokurov, Aleksandr. "Death, the Banal Leveller (on Tarkovsky)." *Film Studies: An International Review* 1 (Spring 1999): 64-69.
Stok, Danusia, ed. *Kieślowski on Kieślowski.* London: Faber and Faber, 1995.
Strich, Christian, ed. *Fellini on Fellini.* Translated by Isabel Quigley. New York: Delacorte-Seymour Lawrence, 1976.
Synessios, Natasha. *Mirror: The Film Companion.* London: I. B. Tauris, 2001.
Tarkovsky, Andrei. *Sculpting in Time: Reflections on the Cinema.* Translated by Kitty Hunter-Blair. London: Faber and Faber, 1986.
—. *Andrei Tarkovsky: Collected Screenplays.* ed. Natasha Synessios. Translated by William Powell and Natasha Synessios. London: Faber and Faber, 2003.

—. *Time within Time: The Diaries, 1970-1986*. Translated by Kitty Hunter-Blair. London: Faber and Faber, 2002.

Turovskaya, Maya. *The Films of Andrei Tarkovsky: Cinema as Poetry*. Translated by Natasha Ward. London: Faber and Faber, 1989.

Wexman, Virginia Wright. *A History of Film*. Cambridge: Pearson Publishing, 2006.

Wise, Jennifer. *Dionysus Writes: The Invention of Theatre in Ancient Greece*. Ithaca and London: Cornell University Press, 1998.

Woll, Josephine. *Reel Images: Soviet Cinema and the Thaw*. London: I.B. Tauris 2000.

Youngblood, Denise. "Post Stalinist Cinema and the Myth of World War Two." *Historical Journal of Film, Radio and Television* 14.4 (1994): 413-19.

Žižek, Slavoj. *The Fright of Real Tears: Krzysztof Kieślowski Between Theory and Post-Theory*. London: British Film Institute, 2001.

Zorkaya, Neia. *The Illustrated History of Soviet Cinema*. New York: Hippocrene Books, 1989.

Zvyagintsev, Andrei. "Return to Nature." *Film Ireland* 99 (July/August 2004): 12-14.

Select Filmography

Alexander Nevsky (*Aleksandr Nevskiy*), dir. Sergei Eisenstein (Mosfilm, 1938).
Amarcord, dir. Federico Fellini (F.C Produzioni, 1973).
The Amphibian Man (*Chelovek-amfibiya*), dir. Vladimir Chebotaryov and Gennady Kazansky (Lenfilm, 1962).
Andrei Rublyov (*Andrei Rublyov*), dir. Andrei Tarkovsky (Mosfilm, 1966).
L'Argent, dir. Robert Bresson (France 3 Films, 1984).
L' arrivée d' un train en gare de La Ciotat, dir. Auguste Lumière & Louis Lumière (1895).
Ascent (*Voskhozhdeniye*), dir. Larissa Shepitko (Mosfilm, 1977).
Ashik Kerib, dir. Sergei Paradjanov (Qartuli Pilmi, 1988).
Au Hasard Balthazar, dir. Robert Bresson (Argos Films, 1966).
L'Avventura, dir. Michelangelo Antonioni (Cino del Duca, 1960).
Ballad of a Soldier (*Ballada o soldate*), dir. Grigori Chukhrai (Mosfilm, 1959).
The Banishment (*Izgnanie*), dir. Andrei Zvyagintsev (Ren-Tv, 2007).
Battleship Potemkin (*Bronenosets Potyomkin*), dir. Sergei Eisenstein (Goskino, 1925).
Bezhin Meadow (*Bezhin lug*), dir. Sergei Eisenstein (GUK, 1937).
Birth of a Nation, dir. D.W. Griffith (David W. Griffith Corp., 1915).
Blade Runner, dir. Ridley Scott (Warner Bros., 1982).
Blow-Up, dir. Michelangelo Antonioni (Bridge Films, 1966).
Boyhood, dir. Richard Linklater (IFC Productions, 2014).
Burnt by the Sun (*Utomlyonnye solntsem*), dir. Nikita Mikhalkov (Canal+, 1994).
Caché, dir. Michael Haneke (Wega Film, 2005).
Chapayev (*Chapayev*), dir. Georgi and Sergei Vasilyev (Lenfilm Studio, 1934).
Chronicle of a Love, dir. Michelangelo Antonioni (Villani Film, 1950).
Citizen Kane, dir. Orson Welles (RKO Pictures, 1941).
Clean, dir. Oliver Assayas (Canal+, 2004).
Clouds of Sils Maria, dir. Oliver Assayas (Palas Film, 2014).
The Colour of Pomegranates, dir. Sergei Paradzhanov (Armenfilm Studios, 1968).
Commissar (*Komissar*), dir. Aleksander Askoldov (Gorky Film Studios, 1967).
The Cranes are Flying (*Letyat zhuravli*), dir. Mikhail Kalatozov (Mosfilm, 1957).
Le Diable Probablement, dir. Robert Bresson (Gaumont International, 1977).
The Diary of a Country Priest, dir. Robert Bresson (Union Generale Cinematographique, 1951).
Earth (*Zemlya*), dir. Aleksander Dovzhenko (Wufku, 1930).
Eastern Promises, dir. David Cronenberg (Serendipity Point Films, 2007).
Fate of a Man (*Sudba cheloveka*), dir. Sergei Bondarchuk (Mosfilm, 1959).
Finis Terrae, dir. Jean Epstein (Societie Generale Films, 1929).
The Five Obstructions, dir. Jørgen Leth (Almaz Film Productions S.A, 2003).
Il Grido, dir. Michelangelo Antonioni (Robert Alexander Productions, 1957).

Hamlet (*Gamlet*), dir. Grigori Kozintsev (Lenfilm Studio, 1964).
Hiroshima Mon Amour, dir. Alain Resnais (Pathe Entertainment, 1959).
House of Fools (*Dom durakov*), dir. Andrei Konchelovsky (Bac Films, 2002).
Ivan Vasilevich Changes Profession (*Ivan Vasilevich menyaet professiyu*), dir. Leonid Gaidai (Mosfilm, 1973).
Ivan the Terrible: Part One and Two (*Ivan Groznyy*), dir. Sergei Eisenstein (Mosfilm, 1943 and 1958).
Ivan's Childhood (*Ivanovo detstvo*), dir. Andrei Tarkovsky (Mosfilm, 1962).
La Jetée, dir. Chris Marker (Argos Films, 1962).
Kasaba, dir. Nuri Bilge Ceylan (NBC Ajans, 1997).
King Lear (*Korol' lir*), dir. Grigori Kozintsev (Lenfilm studio, 1971).
Knife in the Water, dir. Roman Polanski (Zespol Filmowy, 1962).
Kutuzov, dir. Vladimir Petrov (Mosfilm, 1944).
Landscape in the Mist, dir. Theodore Angelopoulos (Greek Film Centre, 1988).
Last Year in Marienbad, dir. Alain Resnais (Argos Films, 1961).
Late August, Early September, dir. Oliver Assayas (Dacia Films, 1998).
Lenin Gate (*I Am Twenty*) (*Zastava Ilyicha, Mne dvadtsat let*) dir. Marlen Khutsiev (Goskino, 1964).
Leviathan, dir. Andrei Zvyagintsev (Non-Stop Productions, 2014).
Lighthouse (*Mayak*), dir. Mariya Saakyan (Andrevsky Flag Film Company, 2006).
Lundi Matin, dir. Otar Iosseliani (Canal+, 2002).
A Man Escaped, dir. Robert Bresson (Nouvelle Edition des Films, 1956).
Mirror (*Zerkalo*), dir. Andrei Tarkovsky (Mosfilm, 1975).
Moscow Cassiopea (*Moskva-Kassiopeya*), dir. Richard Viktorov (Mono, 1973).
Mother and Son (*Mat i syn*), dir. Alexander Sokurov (Lenfilm, 1997).
Mouchette, dir. Robert Bresson (Argos Films, 1967).
My 'ain Folk, dir. Bill Douglas (British Film Institute, 1973).
My Childhood, dir. Bill Douglas (British Film Institute, 1972).
My Friend Ivan Lapshin (*Moi drug Ivan Lapshin*), dir. Alexei German (Lenfilm Studio, 1984).
My Way Home, dir. Bill Douglas (British Film Institute, 1978).
Nostalghia, dir. Andrei Tarkovsky (Radiotelevisione, 1983).
The Nutcracker, dir. Andrei Konchalovsky (Vnesheconombank, 2010).
One Day in the Life of Andrei Arsenevitch, dir Chris Marker (La Sept, 2000).
Ordinary Fascism (*Obyknovenny fashizm*), dir. Mikhail Romm (Mosfilm, 1965).
The Other Sea, dir. Theo Angelopoulos (Theo Angelopoulos Films, 2014).
Persona, dir. Ingmar Bergman (Svensk Filmindustri, 1966).
The Postman's White Nights, dir. Andrei Konchalovsky (PCAT, 2014).
Que viva Mexico! (*Da zdravstvuyet Meksika!*), dir. Sergei Eisenstein (Mosfilm, 1932).
The Red Desert, dir. Michelangelo Antonioni (Film Duemila, 1964).
La Règle du jeu, dir. Jean Renoir (Nouvelle Edition Francias, 1939).
Repas de bébé, dir. Auguste Lumière & Louis Lumière (1895).
The Return (*Vozvrashcheniye*), dir. Andrei Zvyagintsev (Ren Film, 2003).

Russian Ark (*Ruskii Kovcheg*), dir. Alexander Sokurov (Egolli Tosell Film, 2002).
The Sacrifice, dir. Andrei Tarkovsky, feat. Erland Josephson, Susan Fleetwood, Tommy Kjellqvist (Svenska Filminstitutet, 1986).
Sans Soleil, dir. Chris Marker (Argos Films, 1983).
Shadows of Forgotten Ancestors, dir. Sergei Paradzhanov (Dovzhenko Film Studios, 1964).
Silence, dir. Ingmar Bergman (Svensk Filmindustri, 1963).
Solaris (*Solyaris*), dir. Andrei Tarkovsky (Mosfilm, 1972).
Solaris, dir. Steven Soderbergh (Twentieth Century- Fox Film Corporation, 2002).
Stalker (*Stalker*), dir. Andrei Tarkovsky (Mosfilm, 1979).
The Steamroller and the Violin (*Katok i skripka*), dir. Andrei Tarkovsky (VGIK, 1960).
Storm Over Asia (*Potomok Chingis-Khan*), dir. Vsevolod Pudovkin (Mezhrabpomfilm, 1928).
Strike (*Stachka*), dir. Sergei Eisenstein (Goskino, 1925).
Summer Hours, dir. Oliver Assayas (MK2 Productions, 2008).
That Obscure Object of Desire, dir. Luis Buñuel (Greenwich Film Productions, 1977).
There Will be No Leave Today (*Segodnya uvolneniya ne budet*), dir. Andrei Tarkovsky & Alexander Gordon (VGIK, 1959).
Through a Glass Darkly, dir. Ingmar Bergman (Svensk Filmindustri, 1961).
They Fought For the Motherland (*Oni srazhalis za rodinu*), dir. Sergei Bondarchuk Mosfilm, 1975).
Ulysses' Gaze, dir. Theo Angelopolous (Greek Film Centre, 1995).
Uzak, dir. Nuri Bilge Ceylan (NBC Ajans, 2002).
Voyage in Time, dir. Andrei Tarkovsky (Radiotelevisione Italiana, 1983).
Voyage to Cythera, dir. Theo Angelopoulos (Greek Film Centre, 1984).
War and Peace (*Voina i mir*), dir. Sergei Bondarchuk (Mosfilm, 1968).
The Weeping Meadow, dir. Theo Angelopolous (Hellenic Radio and Television, 2004).
Wild Strawberries, dir. Ingmar Bergman (Svensk Filmindustri, 1957).
Winter Light, dir. Ingmar Bergman (Svensk Filmindustri, 1962).

www.ingramcontent.com/pod-product-compliance
Lightning Source LLC
LaVergne TN
LVHW081300100826
845148LV00005B/927